Praise for *The Venture Mindset*

"*The Venture Mindset* distills how we—as corporations and individuals—can apply tenets from venture capital to our own lives, transforming traditional organizations into hubs for innovation. The book is full of powerful, practical lessons on changing how we think and act. The authors share many of the lessons I learned the hard way over decades in technology. I found this a digestible, propulsive, and insightful read for those within and beyond the walls of Silicon Valley."
Eric Schmidt, former CEO and Chairman of Google

"Many principles mentioned in the book helped us build Zoom and they will help you as well."
Eric S. Yuan, founder & CEO of Zoom

"Strebulaev and Dang really know their stuff—and they deliver their insights and advice with remarkable clarity."
Jerry Yang, founding Partner of AME Cloud Ventures, co-founder of Yahoo!

"A terrific insight into what business leaders can learn from the venture capital mindset. Strebulaev and Dang have deep knowledge of the way VCs and corporate innovators think and their impact on the modern economy. Their book is an invaluable guide."
Lionel Barber, former Editor of the Financial Times

"The authors show how the VC playbook can bring new ideas, deeper clarity and increased momentum to every leader's decision making. A must read for anyone facing a fast-changing business world."
Lynda Gratton, Professor of Management Practice, London Business School

"Reserve a spot for this book next to *Built to Last*. Together they provide a powerful guide for a new generation of leaders."
Jerry Porras, co-author of bestseller Built to Last

"THE book of the year if not the decade. My team is already brainstorming how to improve our processes from the 9 Key Principles."
Nicolas Sauvage, President of TDK Ventures

THE VENTURE MINDSET

How to Make Smarter Bets and Achieve Extraordinary Growth

• • • •

ILYA STREBULAEV

ALEX DANG

NICHOLAS BREALEY
PUBLISHING

London • Boston

First published in the United States by Portfolio/Penguin, an imprint of
Penguin Random House LLC.

First published in Great Britain by Nicholas Brealey Publishing in 2024
An imprint of John Murray Press

2

Copyright © The VC Mindset LLC 2024

The right of Ilya Strebulaev and Alex Dang to be identified as the Author of the Work has been asserted by them in accordance with the Copyright, Designs and Patents Act 1988.

Graphics by the authors. Photo on page 91 from the authors' collection.
Book design by Alissa Rose Theodor

All rights reserved. No part of this publication may be reproduced, stored in a retrieval system, or transmitted, in any form or by any means without the prior written permission of the publisher, nor be otherwise circulated in any form of binding or cover other than that in which it is published and without a similar condition being imposed on the subsequent purchaser.

A CIP catalogue record for this title is available from the British Library

Hardback ISBN 978-1-39980-9-979
Trade Paperback ISBN 978-1-39980-9-986
ebook ISBN 978-1-39981-0-005

Typeset in Bulmer MT Std

Printed and bound in Great Britain by Clays Ltd, Elcograf S.p.A.

John Murray Press policy is to use papers that are natural, renewable and recyclable products and made from wood grown in sustainable forests. The logging and manufacturing processes are expected to conform to the environmental regulations of the country of origin.

John Murray Press
Carmelite House
50 Victoria Embankment
London EC4Y 0DZ

www.nbuspublishing.com

John Murray Press, part of Hodder & Stoughton Limited
An Hachette UK company

to Anya, Daniel, and Elizabeth
I.A.S.

to Masha and Tim
A.D.

CONTENTS

PREFACE — ix

INTRODUCTION
What is Saasbee and why does it matter? — xi

ONE
Home Runs Matter, Strikeouts Don't
Why VCs are failure champions and you've got to be too — 1

TWO
Get Outside the Four Walls
How not to miss the next big thing — 31

THREE
Prepare Your Mind
What is the one question VCs ask that will change the way you evaluate opportunities — 69

FOUR
Say No 100 Times
Why you need to be selective, but not in the way you may think — 91

FIVE
Bet on the Jockey
Why VCs spend more time evaluating teams than you may — 115

SIX
Agree to Disagree
Why you should encourage dissent and be wary of consensus   147

SEVEN
Double Down or Quit
Why you should pull the plug faster and more often   175

EIGHT
Make the Pie Bigger
What's wrong about incentives that VCs get right   207

NINE
Great Things Take Time
What's the main killer of innovation   233

CONCLUSION   261

ACKNOWLEDGMENTS   267

APPENDIX: VENTURE MINDSET PLAYBOOK   273

NOTES   275

INDEX   329

PREFACE

What is the next big thing that will transform industries, make established companies redundant, and change the world? This book is about the people who answer these questions for a living. They are venture capitalists (VCs), the masterminds behind the most innovative organizations surrounding us. Every day, VCs seek and find innovative ideas. And they do so with extraordinary success. They identify big ideas and amazing teams and help to turn them into Amazon, Apple, Google, Tesla, Netflix, Moderna, or SpaceX. VCs find and fund the future.

But this book is *not* about how to be a successful venture investor. It's about how *every* decision maker—in *any* sector—can up their game and help their company reach new heights by learning from venture investors, those masters of innovation. This book teaches you to spot new opportunities, nurture the right talent, foster a culture of innovation, and take calculated risks in order to achieve extraordinary growth. How? By developing and using the Venture Mindset.

The Venture Mindset is a new mental model where failure is a must, due diligence is put on its head, dissent is encouraged, ideas are rejected in their myriads in search of a single winner, plugs are pulled, and time horizons are extended.

We, a Stanford professor and a technology executive, have studied the Venture Mindset for many years and have identified ways to apply it in organizations that want to leap forward and outrun the competition. Over the last decade we have developed the Nine Principles of the Venture Mindset and created a Playbook to introduce these principles to any organization.

We wrote this book in Silicon Valley, where the heartbeat of innovation is heard loud and clear, but it is intended for people far beyond this innovation epicenter. Disruptive innovation knows no borders and should not be limited to VC funds and VC-backed companies.

Now is the time for *you* to use the Venture Mindset to find and fund the next breakout success, no matter your industry or geography. In a small factory or an office tower. In marketing or in supply chain. What matters the most is the right mindset. The Venture Mindset.

INTRODUCTION

What is Saasbee and why does it matter?

It was November 2012, and three venture capitalists, Sachin Deshpande, Patrick Eggen, and Nagraj Kashyap, were facing a decision: Should they invest $500K in a small startup called Saasbee?

Earlier in the year, through the prolific Silicon Valley angel investor Bill Tai, Kashyap was introduced to the founder of Saasbee, who was promising to revolutionize the way people did videoconferencing in the post-PC era. The name Saasbee came from SaaS, which stands for "software as a service," plus the hardworking insect. Kashyap led Qualcomm Ventures, the investment arm of a large semiconductor manufacturer, charged with putting money into promising startups. At Qualcomm's headquarters in San Diego, Kashyap and his team invested in more than 300 startups all over the world. One day the team would evaluate nanotechnology in Korea; the next, they might be trying to make sense of a Brazilian software startup. Kashyap was accustomed to hearing extraordinary claims of guaranteed success from every single entrepreneur he met. Was this time different?

In 2012, the competition in video communications was already tough. WebEx, a unit of Cisco, a telecommunications giant, was a mighty incumbent with millions of registered users. Skype had been purchased by Microsoft the previous year. Google was working to improve the Hangout feature of Google Plus. The web-hosted service GoToMeeting had recently expanded to accommodate larger audiences. And there were recent startups such as the well-funded BlueJeans Network and Fuzebox to contend with.

Saasbee's founder argued that his small startup would successfully outdo them all, even WebEx. But as of November 2012, Saasbee did not have a single paying customer. Besides, it was 2012 and people preferred in-person meetings or simply picking up a phone.

The founder of Saasbee, a Chinese-born engineer with imperfect English, had moved to Silicon Valley a dozen years earlier. After his arrival in the United States, WebEx recruited him, and he stayed on when Cisco acquired the company in 2007. But he left Cisco after management turned down his pitch to develop a smartphone-friendly videoconferencing tool.

Was Saasbee as good as the founder claimed it was? To learn more, Kashyap turned to his colleague Sachin Deshpande. "Could you look into this?" he said. "You're our video guy. Have a good look." Deshpande had cofounded a TikTok-style video startup that Qualcomm acquired in 2010, and he had devoted a lot of time and energy to understanding the burgeoning video space, which he was very passionate about.

"I was in love after the first call with the founder," Deshpande told us in an interview. He flew to the San Francisco Bay Area to meet the founder two days after the call. With his experience in the video space, Deshpande could see how Saasbee differed from the competition. Video was the single hardest application to get working over a mobile interface, and yet as he clicked the button, the video stream was clear and without any interruption or delays. Deshpande then switched to his phone and voilà—the picture was smaller but it was of the same quality as the one on his laptop. The product worked wonderfully. Awed by the founder's inside-out knowledge of the videoconferencing market, Deshpande flew back to

San Diego. "This is beyond special," he told Kashyap. "We have to put $5 million into Saasbee."

Deshpande was joined in this meeting by his colleague Patrick Eggen. A liberal arts major with no knowledge of finance, Eggen underwent a baptism by fire working 100 hours a week in a large investment bank in London. Afterward, he went back to school for an MBA. Most of his job interviews were with hedge funds and classic investment management companies. Then he was invited to become a junior team member at Qualcomm Ventures, where he became, as Deshpande called him to us, "a creative seed financing whiz."

Qualcomm was based in San Diego, but in 2010 Eggen moved to Silicon Valley, where he quickly became a deal junkie, sourcing startups for his colleagues' due diligence. Eggen was impressed by the Saasbee founder's obsession with building a superior product. After their second meeting at a Philz Coffee shop in downtown San Francisco's SoMa district, Eggen thought the Saasbee founder was a pretty good salesman too. "What a technical virtuoso with natural sales chops," Eggen exclaimed to us years later.

In early October 2012, Kashyap and the team flew in from San Diego to Qualcomm's Silicon Valley office to meet with six startups in one day, Saasbee among them. According to some participants, as the demo was about to begin, the connectivity failed. The founder said, "Hey, I'm just down the road." So they all went to Saasbee's small office, where a seamless demo across many devices made Kashyap realize immediately that the total addressable market could be huge.

Now all three were pushing for Qualcomm Ventures to become the lead investor in Saasbee, with a sizable commitment of at least $3 million. Within a week, Deshpande and Kashyap presented the opportunity to the rest of the ventures team, its investment committee. There were no other takers. Every other team member felt uncomfortable investing in Saasbee. Kashyap, Deshpande, and Eggen were disappointed but not entirely surprised by their colleagues' doubts. They saw too much uncertainty and too many red flags. Not only was the videoconferencing space already crowded, but Saasbee was trying to target small businesses, a tough market to break into. The technical differentiation from other players was not clear-cut. The founder's imperfect command of English was a distraction. And the proposed valuation of $20 million seemed very high for a startup with one founder, a team of China-based engineers, and not one single customer. The skepticism was buttressed by the uncomfortable fact that at least eight other VC firms had passed on funding Saasbee. Why? They all had expensive Cisco TelePresence rooms with high-speed internet in their offices. If you have a private driver, it's easy to underestimate the potential of Uber.

The rejection would have been the end of the story—if not for one distinctive feature of Qualcomm Ventures' operation: there was a side pathway for unconventional deals of this kind. In 2010, an early-stage fund was created for smaller and often riskier investments. "Of course, it was not legally a real fund per se," Kashyap recollected to us years later, "but conceptually it was." The underlying idea was to invest small amounts of money at high velocity without much bureaucracy. Eggen was leading this early-stage fund and was therefore authorized to make investments of up to $500,000 from the preapproved capital pool, all by himself. Of course, this freedom came with greater responsibility should his selected investment fail.

Thus, the three of them had a backdoor way to pursue an unorthodox deal. They could put $500K of Qualcomm's money into Saasbee despite the opposition from the rest of the team. But was the risk worth it?

Kashyap and Eggen ended up making the bet, supported by Deshpande. It has turned out to be by far the best investment, dollar for dollar, in the history of Qualcomm Ventures, and it helped to transform the daily routines of hundreds of millions of people worldwide. You're probably one of those people.

Here's Why You Haven't Heard of Saasbee

You know this videoconferencing company, but by a different name. It was initially founded as Saasbee in 2011, but by the time Qualcomm got involved in late 2012, the company's founder, Eric Yuan, had changed the name to Zoom Video Communications.

Yes, that Zoom. The Zoom that got millions of us through the gray days of COVID-19 lockdowns. The Zoom that—thanks to the trio of perceptive investors—Qualcomm owned 2 percent of when it went public in 2019 at a valuation of more than $9 billion, reaching a market capitalization of more than $150 billion at one point in 2020.

Zoom has since been touted as one of the greatest innovations of the modern era. Founder Eric Yuan has been glorified as an amazingly ambitious, forward-thinking, and visionary entrepreneur. How could Zoom, a young entrant with a very modest budget and workforce, achieve a series of revolutionary advances in video communications? How could it outcompete giants such as Cisco, Microsoft, and Google, with their huge budgets and hundreds and hundreds of talented engineers? How unique is Zoom's story relative to other successful innovative companies? What makes them different? Did the Qualcomm VCs just get lucky?

Zoom was indeed a smashing success, but it hasn't been the only one. Rather, it's one of a slew of revolutionary young companies that have reached stratospheric heights and substantially transformed the world over the past fifty years. Think of Apple, Cisco, Facebook, Google, Netflix, Amazon, Uber, Tesla, SpaceX—or think of three of Qualcomm's other investments, Noom, Cruise, and Ring. What Zoom has done to the way people interact and communicate online, these and many other companies have done in other fields, disrupting and revolutionizing industries and traditions around the globe. Many more remarkable companies are no doubt on the way—companies that nobody has heard of yet, but that have already been started in someone's garage or bedroom.

All these now famous success stories have something in common. All are private entities created by small entrepreneurial teams. All are quite recent. Apple, the oldest of the companies mentioned thus far, was founded in 1976. And many of them were located in or connected to California's Silicon Valley during the most sensitive part of their early growth cycle.

The most important feature of these companies' trajectories, however, is how they were funded. Generally, entrepreneurs have great ideas and nowhere near enough money to implement them. Eric Yuan is a good illustration. When Yuan founded what would become Zoom, he was by no means a poor man. But to build a product that would have any chance of surviving in a crowded marketplace, much less one that could outcompete the likes of Cisco's WebEx, he needed to raise far more funding than his personal wealth. That's easier said than done.

The financial system offers many options for companies seeking capital. Some companies raise equity in public markets, but the stock market prefers more mature companies with existing cash flows and reasonable expectations of future profit. Zoom had none of this when Deshpande and Eggen first met Eric Yuan. In fact, Zoom didn't get its first paying customer, Stanford Continuing Studies, a department within Stanford University, until December 2012—and that contract was worth just $2,000. With that kind of revenue (or lack thereof), it's hard to pass the smell test of many investors. Companies do routinely raise debt from banks and debt markets, of course—and if you, as a bank loan officer, had been ready to sign off on a loan to Zoom, your supervisor would have fired you on the spot. And your supervisor would have been making a wise move. Not only did Zoom have no revenues at the time, but it also had no collateral should it go bankrupt. Banks just can't lend to such companies without tangible physical assets, revenues, or guarantees. Other companies get grants, and many access initial capital from family, friends, and individual investors (they're known as "angel investors" for a good reason), as

Zoom did in 2011. That capital, though, is insufficient to fund companies through their scaling-up phase.

In short, very few people would have had both the available capital and the guts to bet on Zoom in 2012. But one type of investor did.

Enter Venture Capital

After Eggen negotiated a deal to put in $500,000 on behalf of Qualcomm Ventures, in 2014 another Silicon Valley–based firm, Emergence Capital, invested $20 million in Zoom. Two years later, when Zoom was prominent but not yet profitable, Sequoia Capital and others invested another $115 million.

Qualcomm Ventures, Emergence Capital, and Sequoia Capital are venture capital, or VC, funds. Until recently, VCs operated largely under the radar. Relatively small in dollar value compared to the gigantic size of the overall financial system, they are overwhelmingly located in California, primarily Silicon Valley. They specialize in investing in small, young, entrepreneurial companies. They are not household names.

To provide some perspective, in 2014, the year when it invested in Zoom, Emergence managed less than $600 million of capital. Sequoia, one of the largest VCs out there, invested in Zoom from a fund of around $2 billion. By comparison, Vanguard, a mutual fund family, managed more than $2 *trillion* in assets in 2012, or about 800 times as much as the value of the Emergence and Sequoia funds combined. Until a decade or so ago, many professionals and investors had barely even heard of VC funds, a niche sector hidden far away from the world's financial centers.

Yet VC investors make companies such as Zoom, Uber, and SpaceX possible. They invest early money in seemingly crazy ideas, and sometimes these ideas succeed spectacularly, as did the VCs who backed Google, Cisco, Facebook, Netflix, Amazon, Tesla, and most of the other splashiest new American success stories of the past several decades. Moreover, VC is now a global phenomenon. It has made possible companies such as Canva and Atlassian from Australia, Alibaba and Tencent from China, Shopee from Singapore, Mercado Libre from Argentina, and Gojek from Indonesia. VCs find and fund startup companies that are completely unknown and often consist of just a small management team and a business plan scribbled on a paper napkin.

And yet even as awareness of VC and its importance, particularly in the tech industry, has grown, most people outside Silicon Valley—and many inside it as well—do not understand how VC firms actually function. Selecting what they consider the most promising startups out of the hundreds or even thousands vying for their money is only the first step. When VCs invest in a company, unlike Fidelity and many other investment firms, they become actively engaged in their investments and work to help the fledgling companies succeed. When Qualcomm Ventures invested in Zoom, Sachin Deshpande joined the Zoom board. In December 2014, Santi Subotovsky of Emergence Capital followed Deshpande onto the board after Emergence invested. In fact, the VCs making the largest investments in a company almost always demand a board seat as a condition of investing. They proceed to play a very active role in the life of those companies. Many attract other investors with even more capital to fuel growth.

Despite a few idiosyncrasies, Zoom's story is not unique. In fact, it's typical of startups that succeed. Think of Airbnb, Uber, Salesforce, or Tesla, all of which took on big, successful incumbents even though they initially had less funding, fewer resources, less support, and less experience than their mature, successful, cash-rich competitors.

So how important has VC been since it first emerged a little more than fifty years ago? Back in 2015, Ilya and one of his PhD students at Stanford, Will Gornall, explored the funding history of every single company that had been founded since the mid-1970s and was publicly traded in the United States at the time of their research. They wanted to find out where each company got its money before its initial public offering (IPO) on the stock market.

As it turned out, out of every 100 publicly traded firms founded since the 1970s, 50 were backed by VC funds. And using the market capitalization of each firm as our measuring stick, we found that VC-backed companies accounted for three-quarters of the total market value of all these businesses. In this regard, on July 29, 2016, a seismic (though relatively unnoticed) event took place in the business world. On that date, as Facebook surpassed Berkshire Hathaway in total market value, the top five US companies by market capitalization were all VC-backed: Apple, Microsoft, Alphabet/Google, Amazon, and Facebook. Amid all the market gyrations in the years since 2016, these companies (more recently joined by two more VC-backed businesses, Nvidia and Tesla) were always close to the top.

Ilya and Will also made cross-national comparisons. Have you ever wondered why there are so many new, huge technology companies in the United States? Have you ever heard of a German Google, French Tesla, Japanese Amazon, Italian Facebook, British Apple, or Canadian Microsoft? No. The reason why not: venture capital. Even as the US VC industry has rapidly expanded since the late 1970s, other G7 countries did not have viable VC sectors until recently (and some arguably still don't have them). After the rise of the US VC sector in the 1970s, the US produced twice as many new companies as all the other G7 countries combined. Ilya and Will's research indicates that venture capitalists are causally responsible for the launch of one-fifth of the 300 largest US public companies in existence today. Moreover, they estimate that three-quarters of the largest US VC-backed companies would not have existed or achieved their current scale without VC support. This is one reason why the recent rise of global VC is so important to the future of global economies.

To us, the data suggest persuasively that the VC industry is the leading business growth engine in the United States (and we wish more people in Washington, DC, and Sacramento would take notice!). But this book is not about patting venture capitalists on the back. This book is about how today's decision makers—including you—can understand and apply the skills that VCs have honed and applied with such world-changing results.

The world is changing. Before now, the protagonists at the heart of familiar stories—stories about the development of the personal computer, the commercial internet, the smartphone, social networks, plant-based meat, or privately built space rockets—have always been founders. Although we are fascinated by those unique individuals whose entrepreneurial spirit drove them to make their vision of the future a reality, they couldn't have done it without the investors who funded their vision. VCs did more than fuel the rise of these world-changing companies with their money; they brought with them a unique approach to success and failure that has been baked into the DNA of every company they back. We call this unique way of thinking and working the Venture Mindset.

The Venture Mindset

Our experience has taught us how different this way of thinking is from the thinking found at large corporations all over the world. The differences run the gamut of almost every decision a business faces, from hiring processes and selection of investment projects to attitudes toward incubating ideas and decision making. The Venture Mindset approaches decision making in a distinct way from traditional business managers, government leaders, regulators, and nonprofits.

The Venture Mindset didn't originate overnight; it evolved over several decades through trial and error by generations of decision makers, many of whom were based in Silicon Valley. VCs developed this mindset because they needed a different approach to adapt, survive, and thrive in an environment that requires extreme selectivity combined with extreme flexibility. In this book, we demonstrate the many subtle yet effective ways that VCs' unique behaviors have flourished in an ecosystem of thousands of startups, some of which went on to disrupt or create entirely new industries. We observe the companies who have successfully adopted the Venture Mindset to find astronomical success and show you how your company can achieve extraordinary results by following in their path. We explain why the traditional mindset does not, and cannot, work in environments with the high levels of uncertainty we are now facing.

Historically, all around the world, from New York to London to Mumbai to Sydney, success has been built on continuity, conservatism, and tradition. Stable growth has been a corporate and political mantra for decades. In the world of small, incremental, step-by-step innovation, stability and continuity are great things. If that describes your business, you don't need the Venture Mindset—or at least you don't need it for those *parts* of your business where stability and continuity are the goals. But these can no longer be a business's *only* goals. The rapid progress of technology (in large part coming from VC-backed companies) means that no industry can truly be stable any longer. No one is immune from the possibility of disruption.

Corporate leaders know this, of course. In fact, they now overwhelmingly *expect* disruption to occur in their industries. Their responses have, for the most part, been driven equally by fear and opportunity. Fear because the onslaught of disruption will make many business models and companies redundant; opportunity because people see an excellent chance to get ahead of the competition and cement their industry leadership. However, too often we encounter innovative ideas that have been pursued and built in the same way as any other business unit of a company. That is a recipe for failure. What today's leaders too often fail to understand is that disruptive innovation must start with a different mindset.

Nine Principles of the Venture Mindset

In this book, we show modern decision makers how to apply the Venture Mindset effectively in any organization. In nine chapters, we present nine distinct ways in which the Venture Mindset succeeds where most people fail—or don't even try (see Figure 1). In each chapter, we identify specific takeaways and practical actions that you can implement in a traditional environment with immediate impact (see the Appendix for the list of thirty mechanisms in the Venture Mindset Playbook). We also identify more fundamental approaches that may require rethinking how your organization's pathways are structured. We'll even point out ways in which the Venture Mindset is applicable to many of our individual life decisions.

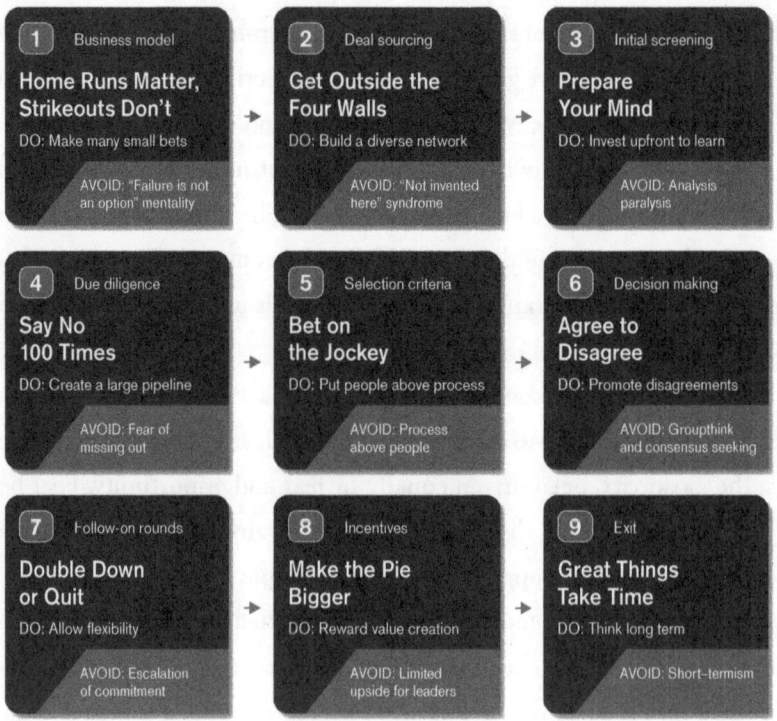

Figure 1.
Nine Principles of the Venture Mindset

Looking back at Zoom's story, we can see these principles at work. For Zoom investors, the main concern was how big the company would become. The people betting on Eric Yuan's company envisioned—and eventually enjoyed—enormous returns. VC investors know that, in their world, **(1) home runs matter, strikeouts don't.** Most VC investments fail. It is the wildly successful ones you found (or missed!) that determine whether you are a successful venture investor. In many corporate settings, one failure can ruin a career. In direct contrast, venture investors insist forcefully that failure *is* an option. In fact, many VCs tell us they are worried if they don't fail often enough. For them, failure is not just an option—it's a must. We will discover how VCs put this striking principle into practice, and how you too can fail successfully so that you might innovate more.

Eggen and his fellow VC investors don't spend much time in their offices. Eggen met Zoom's cofounder in a coffee shop and then visited Yuan's office half an hour away. Indeed, you are more likely to find a VC in a coffee shop than in their fancy offices. This illustrates another key principle, as powerful as it is simple, yet not easy to implement in a traditional corporate environment: VCs **(2) get outside the four walls.** We will see how the VC approach to sourcing ideas and meeting founders can be profitably transplanted into your environment.

Equally disturbing to many non-VC executives is the critical principle of **(3) preparing your mind.** Deshpande decided to push for investment in Zoom immediately after meeting Yuan in his shabby office due to his background in the video space. Another early investor in Zoom wrote a check even before Yuan had a chance to show the pitch deck.

Eggen got excited about Zoom early on, but he met dozens of founders of other promising startups (he was a deal junkie, after all) without getting excited. And as we saw, some of his colleagues also showed no excitement about Zoom! The VC business is all about saying no again and again. Venture investors walk away from seemingly good opportunities more often than one may expect and they **(4) say no 100 times** before they finally say yes to someone. Of course, they can become successful at saying no only because they have a particular method by which they decide to say yes. We will uncover that method for you.

From Zoom to SpaceX to Facebook, VC investors prefer to **(5) bet on the jockey** rather than the horse. Deshpande was taken by Yuan's obsessive client focus and his knowledge of the videoconferencing space. As one legendary VC investor puts it, he would rather invest in an A team pursuing a B idea than back a B team pursuing an A idea. We will see how this approach can work in many other environments and how to implement it successfully.

In organizations driven by consensus, Zooms don't happen. Qualcomm Ventures' investment committee turned down Zoom's investment. VC investors instead use many tricky mechanisms to help them **(6) agree to disagree**. You too can apply this principle in most of your decision-making group meetings.

Zoom prospered and its investors eagerly piled on more money. Similar to gardeners thinning the plants so that only the best and strongest ones are left, investors have to kill many of their darlings to reserve capital for promising ones like Zoom. This decision **(7) to double down or quit** is central to the Venture Mindset, and we will also see the successful application of this principle in a traditional setting.

One of the first decisions Eric Yuan made after Zoom became a large, successful company was to launch Zoom's very own $100 million VC fund to invest in startups. In this way, Yuan began applying venture principles just as his own investors had done when deciding to invest in Zoom, and as he himself had applied them as Zoom's leader. One might find Yuan, now a multibillionaire, pulling up a temporary desk and sitting right next to his team of engineers as they dive into a new project. Each one of them is not just an employee but a shareholder determined to make

Zoom an even bigger and more valuable company. After all, **(8) making the pie bigger** is another invaluable part of the Venture Mindset.

As Eggen made the $500,000 investment in Zoom, he could not know how successful the company would eventually be, but he did know that any success would not be waiting just around the corner. The Venture Mindset understands that **(9) great things take time.** To force long-term thinking, VCs have developed various innovative mechanisms that you too can put to good use.

Some of the lessons offered by the Venture Mindset are easy to implement, with immediate results; others are less so. But each lesson offers a powerful opportunity to change how you think and act within your own organization.

Our Path to the Venture Mindset

The idea for this book originated with our common hobby and passion: not VCs, but wine. Ilya's wine cellar holds quite a few bottles of precious wine and one day he called upon Alex, his former student and friend, to help him organize and categorize his wine in his chilly cellar. Discussions about different terroirs, famous winemakers, and excellent vintage years gave way to discussions about venture capital decision making and stories of launching innovation businesses from corporate trenches.

What started as a discussion about VCs soon expanded to other decision makers: angel investors, entrepreneurs, corporate innovators, executives in large technology companies, and even regulators. We both saw clear patterns. What particularly struck us was the many commonalties between successful venture investors and successful corporate innovators. Many of these corporate innovators came from companies that were themselves VC-backed. All of them broadly followed a very similar playbook. We also realized that in many other cases we could perceive which decisions deviated from that playbook—the disastrous outcomes often made it obvious. Successful VCs, we realized, follow a specific mindset. We call this mindset the Venture Mindset (or VC mindset). Successful corporate innovators use it too. Less successful ones generally don't.

As a Stanford academic, founder of the Venture Capital Initiative at the Stanford Graduate School of Business, and adviser to many companies, Ilya speaks to executives around the world on a regular basis. Alex is an innovation practitioner. He's been there and done that as an Amazon product leader, a partner at McKinsey & Company, and a CEO of a technology startup.

We have been presenting the Venture Mindset Playbook to our clients and students in lectures, workshops, meetings, and corporate off-site events. Our message immediately resonated with these audiences. Corporate executives' faces would light up when we spoke about this idea. The more we talked with global executives, the more we found that they were surprised by the idiosyncratic and often counterintuitive nature of the way VCs think and make decisions. As one of our workshop participants summed it up well, "VCs do it differently. Whatever you have learned before, do not look back!"

We knew we were onto something and wanted to help more leaders step up their innovation game by applying the Venture Mindset. That's what led us to writing this book, which we hope will become a movement within business. However, as Sherlock Holmes famously noted, theorizing without data is meaningless. Getting data is where many researchers and practitioners alike bump into an insurmountable challenge. The VC world is extremely secretive, with very little data available publicly. Venture investors prefer not to disclose the investment contracts they sign. They rarely discuss how they find and evaluate innovative ideas, some of which end up worth billions. The same holds true for corporate innovation initiatives within large companies, hidden behind closed company doors.

Despite this secretive VC culture, Ilya and his Stanford research team have pried these doors open after more than a decade of studying all aspects of the venture world—from startups to VC funds, from corporate venture capital investors to the impact of VC-backed companies on the economy. Combine this with Alex's firsthand experience of designing and launching ideas in a corporate setting and you get a super collaboration that leads to unexpected insights and novel practical takeaways.

This book also draws from Ilya's research about "unicorns"—successful VC-backed innovative companies with at least one private round of funding with a post-money valuation of $1 billion and above. Companies like Zoom, SpaceX, Instacart, Canva, OpenAI, DoorDash, and Moderna.

Since 2015, Ilya and a team of research assistants, PhD students, lawyers, and others have been keeping up with the herculean task of collecting information about every such US startup. The team left no stone unturned. For each unicorn, they investigated the founders' background and age, as well as the time frame from birth to becoming a unicorn or a publicly traded company, and much more. We soon realized that recognizing characteristics of unicorns makes it easier to identify early on revolutionary ideas and companies destined for spectacular success.

Our research on unicorns attracted lots of attention not only from VCs and founders interested in reaching the Mount Olympus of the venture world, but also from leaders of traditional businesses and regulators who were intrigued at how innovative ideas worth of billions of dollars could be hatched and cultivated in just a few years.

Among corporations, the hunt for internal corporate unicorns also took off. It's not easy to put a value tag on the unicorns that companies breed internally, but many new large-scale projects could easily have been on the list of unicorns if they were stand-alone businesses. Think of Zelle, an instant payment service founded by a consortium of large banks. Or the new South American business founded by the Asian e-commerce player Shopee. Or Azure, the cloud computing platform of Microsoft.

Alphabet, Amazon, and Apple are more than a search engine, an online bookseller, and a manufacturer of a PC alternative. They're innovation factories. One does not need to start the company's name with A to achieve this. Take Z. Zoom envisions itself not just as a videoconferencing tool but also as an innovative platform experimenting with hardware, AI-powered translation, and even call centers. And don't forget Zoom Ventures, which has invested in a few dozen startups from chatbots to virtual working space solutions. It was clear to us that companies looking for big growth needed to harness the Venture Mindset.

To demystify the internal workings of VCs, Ilya and his colleagues surveyed more than a thousand of them and interviewed hundreds of them, looking under the hood to understand what happens in their offices (or, more often, outside their offices) and how they make decisions. As a result, we learned that there is a method to their seeming madness.

In this book, we share what we have learned, and we offer advice that is practical, accessible, and relevant. The farther you are away from the world of VC and Silicon Valley, and the less you think your industry is vulnerable to being affected by what is happening in the VC realm, the more you need this book. Because you're probably wrong. Knowledge is power, and that has never been truer than today.

THE VENTURE MINDSET

ONE

Home Runs Matter, Strikeouts Don't

*Why VCs are failure champions
and you've got to be too*

1.1
Against All Odds

Let's play a game called Would You Invest?

In early 2013, one of the most promising e-commerce startups knocked on the doors of top VC investors. Its founder was seeking to raise another round of funding. By this point, he had built a business he could brag about. One million members had joined the platform within just five months after its launch in 2011. To put that in perspective, it took Facebook ten months and Twitter two years to reach the same number. The startup didn't stop there; it hit 10 million members a year later, in December 2012. It was also generating quite a bit of revenue: within the first eighteen months, sales exceeded $100 million. The founder was now raising money to scale that already astounding growth to even greater heights. Would you invest?

As a savvy investor, you might want to know who else was interested in the deal. Less than two years earlier, famous Silicon Valley VC firms including Andreessen Horowitz (also known as a16z) and Menlo Ventures had poured $40 million into the startup. By the time the company raised another funding round in July 2012, its reported valuation had reached $600 million.

What about the founder? He was a Stanford graduate and a serial entrepreneur who had started his first company in the early 2000s. The e-commerce company we are talking about was founded in 2010, focusing on unique designer products.

The startup's mission was simple and ambitious: "to become the world's #1 design store." The company made its own line of products and partnered with designers to manufacture and sell exclusively through its own platform. The founder even coined the term "emotional commerce" to separate his company from the comparatively dry customer experiences offered by Alibaba, eBay, Amazon, and Rakuten. And customers all over the world loved the concept. By 2013, orders had come in from twenty-seven countries.

Investing in this company seems a no-brainer, right? That's certainly what investors thought. In early 2013, they pumped another $150 million into the startup's bank account.

Before you get upset about missing this great opportunity, there is one fact we left out. The startup's name was Fab.com. In October 2013, just three months after founder and CEO Jason Goldberg raised $150 million, the company laid off most of its staff and went into a death spiral. A series of unsuccessful acquisitions in Europe and an extremely high cash burn rate proved to be Fab.com's undoing. The company failed spectacularly and those famed VC investors lost their money. Fab.com is an example of a billion-dollar business going bust in just three years and burning up plenty of cash. It's hard to find a more obvious failure.

What were these investors thinking? To solve the mystery, we take you to New York, the scene of the "crime." Not to the abandoned Gramercy Park headquarters of Fab.com, but a museum. After a transcontinental flight, we were immersed in a world of clues and exhibits, fancying ourselves a modern-day Sherlock Holmes and Dr. Watson.

New York is famous for its museums. But you may never have heard of this one. Buried in a former industrial district of Brooklyn, its rich collection proudly displays more than 150 innovative products. Right next to the entrance, a red MoviePass card sits on the glass-protected shelf. The card, owned by someone named Joanna, is valid until October 2024 and allows its owner to watch one movie per day at a local cinema for only $9.95 a month. A few rooms further on, there is an all-in-one electronic card called Coin, designed to replace all other debit and credit cards. Nearby is a device combining a powerful game console with a phone, Nokia with its N-Gage. Next you see a device called Juicero that can produce a cup of freshly squeezed juice at the touch of a button. The museum also has a detergent named Persil Power with a special "accelerator" ingredient and a synthetic leather substitute known as Corfam from DuPont.

What do all these items have in common? They're all failures. What else would you expect at the aptly named Museum of Failure? The Coin card was too bulky and buggy. Juicero lost its appeal when customers realized they could squeeze the juice from branded packets with their own hands. The detergent was so powerful that it destroyed not only dirt but also clothes. MoviePass turned out to be too popular as people watched far more movies than the company ever expected.

Many of the featured exhibits were funded by well-known VCs. Coin was backed by Y Combinator, Spark Capital, and Redpoint. MoviePass received capital from True Ventures and AOL Ventures. Juicero was backed by Google Ventures and Kleiner Perkins. As the museum's guide app asks, "What were they thinking?"

We can guess that the investors were thinking about successful ideas that also could have failed. They thought about Fever (the app that led us to the museum), PayPal (which we used to pay for our tickets), and Uber (which got us there). Each of these inventions was created by a VC-backed company. Each became an extraordinary hit. And each could have ended up in the Museum of Failure. Failure is not an unusual outcome. In fact, it's exactly what VCs expect. The failures are a feature of VC work, not a bug. Simply put, VCs don't know in advance which ideas will fail.

The expectation of frequent failure defines the VC industry. Despite the Fab.com collapse, both major VC firms involved in the project, Menlo Ventures and a16z, attracted more funds from investors. And the founder, Jason Goldberg, successfully raised capital for his next startup, which might end up in the Museum of Failure—but it also might find its place in the VC hall of fame.

1.2
Swinging for the Fences

What makes VCs so resilient to failures and why don't they sweat writing off investments? Your smartphone can help answer that question. Open your phone. Which ride-sharing app do you use? If you live in the US, it will likely be Uber or perhaps Lyft. If you are from other regions, the answer could be DiDi, Ola, or Careem. In our workshops for executives, we ask them to name the third most popular ride-sharing app in their region. Nobody can come up with an answer. The same holds for other categories. In each new vertical funded by VCs, one clear winner emerges, with a second player trailing, and nobody else in the running. This is not for want of trying. Dozens and dozens of ride-sharing startups were backed by VCs. Almost all failed. But a couple became home runs. Welcome to the land of the best and the rest.

In one industry after another, disruptive innovation and new business models separate home runs from afterthoughts. This holds true for more than technological industries. Starbucks has around 40 percent of all coffee shops in the US. Player number three? Twenty times fewer. VCs have always felt the pressure of the "best and the rest" principle, which is affecting larger and larger swaths of industries today. Including yours.

VCs have had more time to come up with mechanisms to survive and succeed in relentlessly competitive environments in which the winner takes everything (or almost everything). In Silicon Valley, the best startup is more successful than all the others in the same space combined, and the second best is more successful than all the rest combined. Since the fourth-ranked startup may not survive at all, the third could be infinitely better than all the remaining ones combined. Just look again at your smartphone apps.

Or look at the game of baseball, which gave us the concepts of home runs and strikeouts. Baseball fans expect home runs from their favorites, but the greatest home run hitters of all time, such as Alex Rodriguez and Reggie Jackson, were notorious for striking out. Since the live-ball era started in 1920, the ratio of strikeouts to home runs has remained stable at around 6.4. Interestingly, it took time for baseball pros to appreciate the importance of strikeouts. A generation ago, Eric Davis—viewed as one of baseball's most talented players—had an initially tough time in the major leagues, all due to a strikeout rate of 24 percent, considered by experts as absurd. But in the 2019 season, when Pete Alonso broke a Mets rookie home run record, his strikeout rate of 26 percent, though higher than that of Davis, was not a concern. Strikeouts and home runs hit together.

VCs have adopted a home run approach. They expect to fail most of the time, but when they win, they win big. VC investors have come up with distinctive ways to manage failure, disruption, and uncertainty—the tricks that are becoming more useful to each of us with every passing day. In the unpredictable VC world, you simply can't know who will win the race and who will lose. But you do know that only a select few will win. The rest will lose, sometimes spectacularly.

To truly appreciate the success-to-failure ratio VCs face, consider twenty typical early VC-backed startups, chosen at random. Of those twenty, most will fail, wiping out all investments. Investors often lose every penny in such hard landings, because startups tend to have very few if any tangible assets. Not much can be realized from selling office chairs and desks. Occasionally, something of value is left over, such as patents, but more often, when the investment goes south, a very real possibility is losing one's entire investment.

Some of those twenty startups will do well, though they won't make the front page of the *Wall Street Journal*. On average, three or four of every twenty will return the original investment and perhaps produce a modest cherry on top. For example, Apple acquired Shazam, an application that can identify music, for about $400 million. The payoff provided a decent but not spectacular return to Shazam's backers, who had infused $150 million prior to the acquisition.

Of every twenty startups, usually only *one* will become a runaway success story, providing a 10X or even a 100X return to VC investors (see Figure 2). This one 100X success will more than cover all the failures.

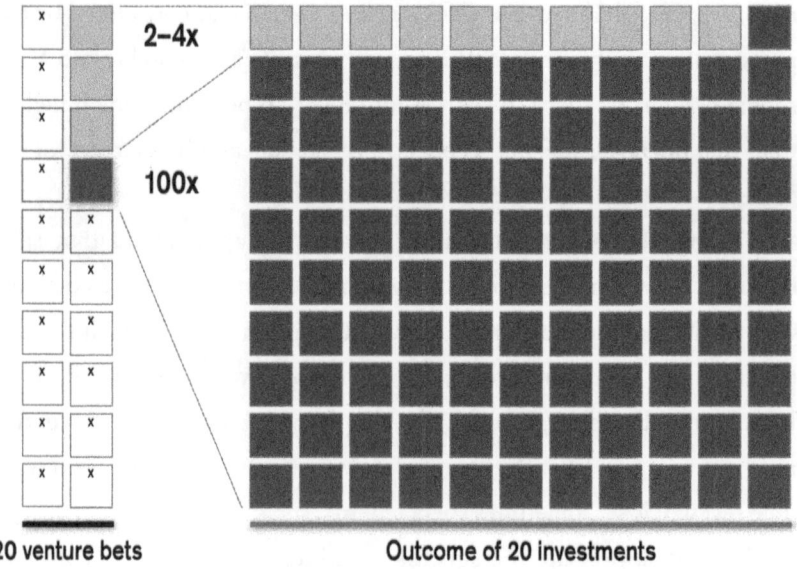

Figure 2.
The impact of a 100X "home run" on the
venture capital portfolio performance

VCs live and breathe for these home runs. This is why home runs matter for VCs and strikeouts don't.

The clearest way to see the "best and the rest" principle at work is to look at the most successful early-stage VC funds—those in the top 10 percent of all such funds. Suppose we remove from their portfolio the most successful investment each fund made. If you take out just one extremely successful startup, many of the funds that were outperforming nine out of every ten comparable VC funds suddenly become only a little better than the median. If we now go one step further and remove the second most successful startup in the portfolio, some of those top-performing VC funds start losing money for their investors.

To acquire the Venture Mindset, you first need to appreciate that VC success does not come from pure luck, as you might have thought. Successful VCs perform successfully again and again. Disruptive innovation is about outliers. It's about outsized gains and asymmetric returns. In our everyday lives we are surrounded by averages: average returns, average performance, average ratings. But innovative ideas break the pattern. One day there is no Uber, WhatsApp, or Spotify, and just a few years later you can't imagine your life without them. VCs systematically identify such breakthrough ideas and ignore the failed attempts. They care about the portfolio of ideas rather than individual bets. Corporations should do as well. How can one be persistently successful in a world full of failure? The first principle VCs employ is "home runs matter, strikeouts don't." Of course, VCs, like the rest of us, have sleepless nights. But their nightmares are different.

1.3
The Worst Nightmare of a Venture Capitalist

When we lead sessions on VC investments for people outside Silicon Valley, we often ask our audience this question: What do you think the biggest fear of VCs is? What is their most excruciating pain point? What gives them sleepless nights? Participants usually respond with an intuitive answer driven by their own experience: VCs fear making a bad decision by backing losers and losing their money. The traditional mindset prioritizes avoidance of failure.

For Silicon Valley VCs, it's exactly the opposite. "If you invest in something that doesn't work, you lose 1X your money. If you miss Google, you lose 10,000X your money," said famed VC investor Bill Gurley, a partner at Benchmark Capital. As Alex Rampell, another highly successful VC at a16z, told us, "In the VC world, the errors of omission are much more damaging than errors of commission."

If you back a lame horse, you lose your investment. As unfortunate as that is, the most you can lose is your investment. That's the error of commission. However, if you walk away from a deal that could have landed you the best investment in your entire fund, or even your entire career, that is truly painful. Such a deal would have covered all your slowly accumulating losses in one brushstroke. "In the VC business model," the founder of Floodgate VC firm Mike Maples tells us, "you have to think of risk not as chance of failure, but as a chance of an upside success."

This asymmetric dynamic gives rise to a unique culture and mindset in the VC ecosystem that differs from most people's approach to risk and failure. Many VC investors can recount with sadness an instance when they walked away from what turned out to be a once-in-a-decade success story. Many VCs even keep records of what they call their antiportfolio, or those companies they passed on that later became very successful. Bessemer Venture Partners, one of the oldest VC firms, even created a dedicated page on their website listing companies they decided not to invest in. Among their most notable misses are Apple, Airbnb, Google, FedEx, PayPal, and Zoom. But such a celebration of failures hasn't prevented them from catching other big fish, such as Shopify, Twitch, LinkedIn, Pinterest, Yelp, and Skype.

David Cowan of Bessemer, who initiated the antiportfolio list, told us he was not proud of Bessemer's failure to identify such great startups. But he is proud of being transparent about them. "If we can't confess our mistakes," Cowan told us, "how will we get better?" Of course, you have to have big enough hits to make up for such mistakes (or soon you won't have a website on which to announce your failures!).

Mistakes are unavoidable and VCs admit they don't know everything. "The blunders we profile in the antiportfolio," Cowan explained, "help us not to repeat those same mistakes." After a pause, he added, "Instead, we make new ones."

So how do VCs hit the home runs? VCs do this by making relatively small bets and acknowledging up front that most of them will fail. Smart VCs know they cannot reliably pick winners. Instead, they spread their bets by diversifying. Diversification, of course, is nothing new; it's a mantra for many investment advisers. But the diversification VCs pursue is of a different variety. VCs are betting on individual companies, not on the market as a whole. The VC strategy, then, is something we might call "meaningful diversification." The bets are relatively small, but each bet, if successful, can meaningfully impact the return of the entire portfolio. But remember: to succeed with this strategy, you must accept many strikeouts before hitting a home run.

Most of us are trained to think that failure is not an option, and this mindset naturally restricts our willingness to take risks. VC investors think the opposite. They do more than diversify; they swing for the fences. They search for the deal with the 10X or 100X results that will compensate for the failures. When one is seeking incremental gains in a typical market—whether in the world of finance or a large corporation—this VC mindset is generally not useful and could even be dangerous. But when a company is seeking to achieve extraordinary growth and to leave its competition behind, when an industry is going through a disruption and new markets suddenly capture the old ones, the VC mindset is the only one that works.

In this context, risk taking helps the early investor achieve a smashing success.

1.4
Innovate to Fail, or Fail to Innovate

The Venture Mindset has always been present in some corners of the corporate world, although its very existence can be fragile. In 2001, Dr. Geoff Nicholson, after thirty-eight years with the 3M company, decided to retire. You have almost certainly used one of his team's inventions in your office or at home, even though it didn't generate as much media buzz initially as the newly introduced iPhone did. We are referring to Post-it notes—those small, colorful pieces of paper that effortlessly stick to any surface but can be peeled off in a second. Today, the Post-it is a giant business for 3M, generating annual sales of more than $1 billion. To put that figure in perspective, it's more than the monthly sales of Office Depot, the largest US brick-and-mortar seller of office supplies. It's hard to believe that the success of the Post-it note could have been an accident. But it was.

It all started in 1968, when 3M was developing new ultrastrong adhesive at its central research laboratories for use in aircraft construction. A senior scientist accidentally created a weak, pressure-sensitive adhesive. To their chagrin, the scientists could find no practical use for their invention, so they filed it away in the "solutions without a problem" drawer.

Six years later, one of Nicholson's colleagues, Art Fry, discovered a problem that this invention could resolve. When Fry was singing in his church's choir, he bookmarked his hymnal with small pieces of paper, but they kept falling out. "Everybody else started singing and I'm still trying to find what page we're on," Fry explained. "So I'm looking over the guy's shoulder next to me, trying to find the page." Here was a situation where a sticky but removable piece of paper could solve a real problem. Fry decided to test sticky notes with some of his coworkers. To his surprise, everyone liked the product. His supervisor responded to Fry's report about the invention by attaching a sticky note with comments on it! As Fry recalled, "It was a eureka, head-flapping moment!"

This story may lead you to conclude that the Post-it note represents invention-by-coincidence. And so it does, taken in isolation. But the Post-it was far from 3M's only instance of developing innovative, out-of-the-box products. 3M started as a small mining venture (hence the name, Minnesota Mining and Manufacturing Company) and through success and failures became a global manufacturing giant. Its systemic management-level support and its culture of tolerance of failure certainly didn't happen by pure luck. 3M director Richard Carlton even documented this corporate trait in an internal company manual in 1925: "Every idea evolved should have a chance to prove its worth," he wrote. "If it is good, we want it. If it is not good, we will have purchased our insurance and peace of mind when we have proved it impractical."

In this regard, Carlton (way back in 1925!) clearly had a Venture Mindset, and the company developed internal processes that applied it long before the modern VC era began. 3M explicitly encouraged risk and failure. This strategy paid great dividends—literally. The company has paid dividends to its investors for more than 100 years and has never reduced its dividends for more than 50 years. Wall Street calls such companies "dividend kings," and only a few dozen companies qualify. Analysts have even called 3M an "invention machine." 3M's employees have come up with Scotch tape, Dobie cleaning pads, ACE bandages, and much more (3M has been granted more than 100,000 patents, in fact). Just as remarkably—perhaps even more so—the company has been enormously successful in commercializing these inventions. It used a revolutionary metric to measure "innovativeness" by setting a goal of earning 25 to 30 percent of all sales from products released in the preceding five years. Post-it notes themselves became widely used in brainstorming and design sessions, thereby becoming associated with the idea of innovation.

But eventually that tradition of innovation was abandoned. In December 2000, James McNerney, a General Electric veteran and a part of legendary GE CEO Jack Welch's team, was appointed as 3M's CEO, breaking the century-old company's tradition of promoting from within. In his first days, he immediately focused on financial performance issues, bringing to 3M the cherished GE playbook, which mandates streamlining operations, trimming costs, and establishing financial discipline with an iron hand. McNerney immediately tightened controls, intensified the performance review process, and introduced the well-known Six Sigma program.

Six Sigma, which is lauded around the world for improving manufacturing processes and applied in a wide variety of industries, seeks to remove variability from a process. For example, if the number of defects or malfunctions in a manufacturing process is increasing, Six Sigma calls for addressing the problem immediately. It thereby achieves more predictable outcomes, because avoiding defects—which we might think of as failures—radically improves efficiency and thereby saves time and money. It's not surprising that General Electric applied Six Sigma with great success in its manufacturing processes.

When 3M announced McNerney's appointment, shareholders cheered the decision, believing that cost reduction should be an important goal for a new CEO. But does Six Sigma, squarely focused on reducing uncertainty and cost minimization, work in a creative, innovative environment? Some had doubts.

As Charles O'Reilly, Ilya's colleague at Stanford, once noted, "If you take over a company that's been living on innovation, clearly you can squeeze costs out." In his first years as CEO at 3M, McNerney did exactly that. He cut capital expenses and started to control R&D expenses tightly. But that's where the second part of Professor O'Reilly's statement kicks in: "The question is, what's the long-term damage to the company?"

Many stakeholders inside and outside 3M think the company lost its creative juices under McNerney's leadership. Researchers Mary Benner and Michael Tushman concluded that 3M has not been the only casualty of such an approach. Their analysis of patents confirmed that programs such as Six Sigma, while leading to significant performance improvement, also create a radical shift from blue-sky work to incremental innovation.

This brings us to our critical observation: both the Venture Mindset and the Six Sigma approach have merits, but their usefulness in a particular setting depends on the goals. The cultural atmosphere and the organizational processes created by the VC mindset are productive when you need to encourage employees to come up with radically new products and ideas. Six Sigma, in contrast, works best in an environment of "known unknowns." As Art Fry, who first came up with the idea of using the adhesive as a sticky bookmark, commented, "Innovation is a numbers game. You have to go through 5,000 raw ideas to find one successful business. Six Sigma would ask, why not eliminate all that waste and just come up with the right idea the first time?"

Perhaps tragically for the corporate world, the same word, "innovation," is used to describe two types of processes: one that leads to the creation and smashing market success of the Post-it sticky note, and the other, like Six Sigma, that can achieve cost reductions in the manufacturing of existing products. Most of the time, the latter form of innovation works just fine. But there are times when this form of innovation can be detrimental.

The 3M story shows that the Venture Mindset in a large organization is not only fragile—it's also exceedingly rare. When we look at a wide range of companies across an extended period of time, it's obvious that 3M managed to survive for more than 100 years while pursuing a strategy starkly different from almost any other company. If we compare the list of Fortune 500 companies in 2022 and 1955 (the year when this famous list was published for the first time), we find that only about 10 percent of the original companies have been on the list every year, with 3M among the lucky ones. Today, companies are disappearing from this list faster than ever, usually replaced by much younger technology newbies. In 1958, the companies in the S&P index had been there for an average of 61 years; in 2012, the average was just 20 years. BlackBerry, Nokia, Sears—the list of recent disappearances is long.

There are plenty of reasons why well-established and successful companies tend to innovate less and launch fewer products as they grow older. One reason is that their processes and their culture become more similar to Six Sigma—designed to avoid failures, which are seen as defects to be eliminated. To reiterate, in many cases Six Sigma can be an exceptional management technique for driving costs down and efficiencies up, which often makes shareholders happy along the way. But in times of disruption and uncertainty, a company needs an openness to experimentation, which goes hand in hand with accepting failure.

One danger inherent in corporate life is that managers are incentivized to play it safe and avoid bold ideas. In the corporate environment, errors of commission loom much larger in the minds of decision makers than errors of omission. Executives are rarely fired for not pursuing promising initiatives, but they easily become scapegoats for failed projects. Failures are feared and remembered. Uninitiated projects that would have achieved a huge, asymmetric gain never show up on the balance sheet and are rarely retained in corporate memory. Therefore, managers would rather miss an opportunity by sticking with the status quo than take a risk and fail.

Here's the lesson: set your organization goals thoughtfully. If the organization celebrates and pays bonuses only for successfully achieved targets, don't be surprised by endless sandbagging and employees setting low-risk, easily achievable targets in the first place.

Let your people fail. Keep announcements of your successful and unsuccessful launches on the wall in your office. Set aside the budget for innovative bets like 3M sticky notes. Expect most of them to fail, but one or two may bring you a jackpot. Push your team members to come up with big ideas rather than business-as-usual ones. You can't win big without placing bold bets.

The goal is not to win each time. The goal is not to miss the opportunity to win big at least once.

Once when Ilya was explaining the Venture Mindset to the CEO of a large company and some of his lieutenants, the CEO was suitably impressed by the VC failure statistics. Turning to the head of his corporate innovation unit, he asked, "And how many failures do we have?" He received this proud, somewhat patronizing reply: "Almost none. We are doing a really good job." If the corporate innovation unit does not register or own up to a lot of failures, most likely its innovations are not very innovative. The sad truth is that many companies are intolerant of failure. To understand why, let's become a fly on the wall and observe a typical corporate investment budgeting process.

1.5
For Everything Is a Season

Traditional companies are typically well-oiled machines with planning processes that run as smoothly as a Swiss watch. This is especially true for approving new investments. The budgeting process normally requires submission of a detailed set of forward-looking financial metrics such as ROI (return on investment). Small projects are filtered out early on, as they are not considered large enough to merit discussion. Projects are then compared with one another, and the ones with the highest impact and the most impressive metrics are allocated a budget. The budgeting cycle typically occurs once a year, with quarterly updates. Once the budget is approved, it is rarely reshuffled during the year unless there are major external reasons to do so. Quarterly updates are often quiet meetings, with only minor deviations from the plan.

But aren't the most experimental projects small fish at the time of their creation? Do the most innovative ideas even have metrics at the start? They tend to be rejected early on due to insufficient information, or they are easily criticized as not fully vetted. And they drive planning departments nuts with their unpredictable nature. A corporate budget allocation process is designed to protect companies from investing in projects that are too small or too unpredictable and that could become a complete flop in just a few months. Of course, for the VC mindset, these are exactly the opportunities to explore. This is why thinking like a VC is so unnatural for executives and managers at traditional companies. The projects are too small and risky, and they may require immediate and abrupt interventions to pivot quickly. Traditional corporate organizations are just not set up to do that.

Being risk-averse while carefully husbanding company assets is not a sin. And being diligent with capital and resources is a responsibility of senior management. Corporate mechanisms are designed to protect shareholders, and often protecting shareholders means avoiding failures, particularly costly ones. Consider, for example, how Procter & Gamble (P&G) persuades customers to buy its blades or detergent each year. Launching a new variation of a blade or detergent is a very systematic, organized process with laser-focused testing, pricing models, and focus groups. Or take Intel, a large chip manufacturer. Intel's new $20 billion chip factory can't be treated as a gamble; rather, it goes through a robust budgeting and investment process, as it should. What these examples have in common is that they face known unknowns: the market environment is predictable, the company knows its consumers, and each modification of a product is an incremental variation, even if it costs $20 billion.

This process presages serious trouble, however, during more turbulent times when tectonic industry shifts are happening. In this context, masterfully avoiding failures and minutely careful planning can become a curse, not an advantage. It's difficult for traditional companies to shift gears. While they are playing it safe, smaller, more risk-tolerant players—often backed by venture capital, and not accountable to public shareholders—are developing new ways to seize emerging market opportunities. Many of their attempts fail—indeed, some of the companies themselves may fail—but some will succeed. The ones that do will begin to diminish the market power of an incumbent and disrupt its business model.

This is exactly the story of brick-and-mortar bookstore chains such as Borders, which was crushed by Amazon's entry into online bookselling. Borders was the second-largest US bookstore chain around the turn of the millennium, and it didn't expect such a dramatic punch from a small technology startup in Seattle. But that initially insignificant startup ultimately forced Borders to close all its stores and file for bankruptcy. The same story has been repeated again and again, in one industry after another. Google and Netflix disrupted traditional media and advertising titans. Skype and later Zoom challenged telecommunication incumbents. One reason corporate leaders should continue reading this book is that, sooner or later, there will be an Amazon in their industry. Maybe it's already lurking in a Silicon Valley garage, or somewhere on the West Coast, or in a small office in Berlin or Shanghai.

1.6
Every Unhappy Firm Is Unhappy in Its Own Way

What does it take for a company to be set up for home runs and countless unavoidable failures? Often, when we speak to corporate leaders, we start with a few simple questions. Does your organization regularly make aspirational and bold bets to deliver an outsized impact? Does it have a portfolio of ideas to diversify risks? And does the company have mechanisms to regularly defund and close initiatives that don't work? Each of these elements is crucial; leaving out any one of them may prevent a company from harnessing the power of failure. Here are three pitfalls to avoid:

Don't play it too safe

What if you make bets, but only within your comfort zone? They are not risky and bold enough. Playing it too safe is one of the major flaws we observe. Many executives, on hearing the words "bets" or "experiments," immediately point to A/B tests or to a few test locations where they are introducing new technology or devices. To be sure, A/B tests can be useful. When the *New York Times* A/B tests its headlines and discovers that one attracts three times as many readers for the same article as another, that's a significant result editors can use going forward to optimize the delivery of the company's product to its customers. But although A/B tests do qualify as experiments, they're nonetheless examples of incremental innovation, analogous to P&G focus-grouping a new blade or 3M testing a new color of Post-it notes in a handful of select markets. You need to be making bolder, riskier plays than you think.

Don't bet the farm

What if you make a bold bet, but it's the only one the company is making? A second flaw we regularly observe is all-or-nothing behavior among large companies, in striking contrast to the VC principle of diversification with many small bets. In a typical scenario, a senior corporate leader searches for one big idea and finally, after long consideration, decides to go "all in," placing all the chips on that idea and rolling the dice. But winning big does not always require betting big.

Business schools are full of case studies in which companies pursue a single, big, bold bet that makes it hard for them to pivot later. When Airbus committed itself to designing and building the world's largest passenger airplane, the A380 superjumbo, its executives probably expected to win the jackpot. The A380 was supposed to become the eighth wonder of the world. Unfortunately, it instead became a textbook case of a company putting all its eggs in one basket, as well as a dramatic fiasco that cost the European consortium more than €25 billion (compared to the initial budget of less than €10 billion!). The aircraft faced multiple delays and significant cost overruns, and by the time it was finally ready, nearly twenty years later, almost no airline wanted to buy it. In the years since the project was undertaken, air travel had undergone a fundamental paradigm shift, as passengers preferred direct flights rather than going through large airport hubs. The airlines that Airbus had expected to become the A380's customers instead turned to Boeing's much smaller, more fuel-efficient, and budget-friendly 787 Dreamliner. Like at Airbus, quarter after quarter, executives often continue to throw good money after bad, driven by a "failure is not an option" mindset combined with an all-or-nothing mood.

In our daily lives, we subconsciously understand that making many small bets is a safer strategy than making a single big one. We can wait, see the results, then pick a potential winner and shift our chips toward a promising alternative. However, applying the same approach in a corporate setting is challenging, for many reasons. It is easier to focus on one initiative than to juggle multiple ones. It's much easier to secure a budget for a single, shiny project than to allocate funding for a portfolio of smaller ideas. As a result, executives often bet their careers on a single idea. Companies do too, sometimes beyond the point of no return. Compare this to the VC mindset, where you are not pretending that you know the future winner, but you always remain in a "see and learn" mode.

Weed your garden of ideas regularly

What if you built a stream of ideas and had myriads of them floating around? Sadly, this won't work either. A common flaw is to "let a thousand flowers bloom," or simply to keep too many bets in the portfolio without killing unsuccessful ones and therefore not committing sufficiently to any one of them. This is almost the opposite of the all-or-nothing flaw, in which a single "Manhattan Project" sucks up all of a company's resources and attention. In this case, innovative ideas get just enough funding to entertain their creators within a corporate environment, but not enough to have any impact.

Too many ideas may distract and disorient the management. Lego is now a well-studied example of a company that at some point had *too much* innovation going on. Ideas were launched one after another, from theme parks to digitalizing every single Lego element and a McDonald's Happy Meals partnership, to TV shows and new characters and even a buildable action figure, Galidor. One thing was missing, though: the focus. By 2003 the company was in trouble, and the new leaders were brought in. Their first action was to establish a disciplined approach to innovation. Discipline was the first step that revitalized almost a century-old Lego that became known as "the Apple of toys."

It's easy for a startup founder with a bunch of recent grads in a garage to say, "Fail fast, fail often." It's not so easy if you lead a large, established organization. This is why avoiding these three pitfalls is critical. It's important to know how to fail without wrecking yourself.

To become an innovation champion, you may have to become a failure champion first.

1.7
Failure Champions, Home Run Hunters

Fifty adults in their forties and fifties stand up and raise their hands. All are successful. Many are senior executives of large global companies.

Then, one by one, with smiles on their faces, they shout, "I failed!" The whole room is filled with repeated exclamations of "I failed!" This is not a meeting of a religious sect or a self-blaming exercise. Rather, it's the beginning of a famous Stanford improvisation class taught by Dan Klein. The exercise allows our bodies and minds to accept the notion of failure, even if in a childish way. Each human being is afraid of failure, as we are trained by our nature and society to avoid mistakes and danger. Additional effort is needed to unwind this logic and acknowledge that high risk (including failure) is a natural side effect of high rewards.

Changing the organization is much harder than making people raise hands in class. By now, you may have concluded that there are too many systemic hurdles preventing large, established organizations from being as flexible and innovative as smaller companies and VCs. However, with appropriately designed processes, companies should in fact have a much higher chance of success than startups. Startups are like small stand-alone experiments that may or may not succeed. Each startup team has limited resources, and there are many ways for a startup to fail. If it runs out of money before finding a fit between its product and the market, the startup will fail. If the product doesn't make it to market, the startup will fail. If the founders can't attract talented employees, the startup will fail. Startups bet everything on an often slim chance of success. Larger organizations, on the other hand, have enough resources to play the innovation game. They can run many startup experiments. They have the resources, talent, and customers to experiment, and they can survive many failures. As we've seen, most companies don't use this paradigm, because it runs afoul of their corporate nature. But some do.

What are the most innovative companies today? There are plenty of innovation beauty contests, and we could dispute the various rankings and methodologies ceaselessly. However, technology companies funded by Silicon Valley VCs are indisputably among the top examples.

What are the common features among these technology innovators that drive their success, common features that your company can learn from and apply? It's not their technology itself, but other factors that create their technological dominance. They all share the same approach, which they have naturally adopted, both consciously and subconsciously, from the VCs who funded them. These companies have continually applied the Venture Mindset to up their game. They constantly seek the next growth engine or "flywheel" that will determine their future success. They take many risks and make many bets. They are prepared for failure; in fact, they expect many of their bets to fail. They are driven by the expectation that at least one of these often seemingly wild bets will become bigger than their current business, and when it starts to appear that one of them might, they double down on that one and abandon the projects that clearly won't. In short, they have effectively internalized and replicated within themselves the model that gave birth to them in the first place.

Apple started out in the PC industry; today, the iPhone provides more than 40 percent of Apple's revenue. Everybody knows about the iPhone's success, but Apple also experienced a lot of failures. Remember Newton, an earlier Apple tablet? You may not. Released in 1993 with expectations to sell one million in the first year, it sold only 50,000 in the first three months and was officially killed in 1997. And for every Newton you may or may not remember, many others never reached the public eye. Similarly, profits from AWS, Amazon's cloud arm, and its advertising businesses constitute well over half of Amazon's operating profits today. Yet both AWS and Amazon's advertising side were small, controversial ideas at the time of their launch. And of course, many other products launched by Amazon failed dramatically.

One such dramatic example is the Fire Phone, released with great fanfare in 2014. Amazon founder and CEO Jeff Bezos personally introduced the product at the company's studio in Seattle's Fremont art district. It was a mountaintop moment after four years of hard work by hundreds of employees. But once the phone was released, at a price of $650, customer feedback was brutal. The Fire Phone sold barely 35,000 units in its first two weeks. In the same year, Apple's iPhone sold 4 million units—at the same price as the Fire Phone—in its first twenty-four hours on sale, a humiliation for Amazon. The $650 Fire Phone device was too expensive for what it could do, and critics complained about its unnecessary features and clunky user interface. A few months later, Amazon wrote off the project.

The story of the Fire Phone's failure is nothing unusual in itself. The unusual aspect of this story is Amazon leadership's attitude toward that failure. In a traditional organization, the vice president in charge of the product would have been demoted or fired, and the CEO, after making human sacrifices, would have swept the story under the rug and dismissed it as a nightmare to be forgotten. At Amazon, however, the opposite happened. Jeff Bezos still refers to the Fire Phone more often than almost anything else Amazon does. He goes as far as boasting to journalists that they are currently engaged in much larger failures, some of which will make the Fire Phone seem insignificant in comparison.

Of course, failures like the Fire Phone need to be balanced by successes like the Echo, Amazon's smart speaker. To say the least, it was a big hit. Tens of millions of households now use Echo in their homes. Well, guess what? Both product launches were led by the *same* person, Ian Freed. "You can't, for one minute, feel bad about the Fire Phone. Promise me you won't lose a minute of sleep," Jeff Bezos assured Freed after the product's demise. Amazon's meteoric rise and continued success owe a great deal to how Bezos and his lieutenants apply the VC mindset in their approach to failure. Traditional organizations can learn from Amazon.

1.8
Build Your Pyramid

Do these home run hunters make only risky, venture-like bets? Of course not. Amazon continues to expand its warehouse footprint, Google scales its server capacity, and Apple improves its products by gradually introducing new features and services. All these are relatively low-risk investments, representing incremental innovation in the companies' profitable core businesses. None of these investments are even close to high-risk venture deals. These companies understand how to blend risky investments with more traditional investments.

We believe that corporate leaders should view their portfolio of investments as containing three types of projects, which can be visualized as a pyramid (see Figure 3). The widest part, at the bottom, is a collection of core businesses. In core products, incremental innovation happens all the time, but no radical changes happen to existing products (think of a product color change, adding an insignificant feature, or tweaking a product to launch it in a new country). Typically, such programs have a well-defined, manual-like blueprint. They represent a low-risk part of a portfolio, and usually the cost and time frame are very predictable.

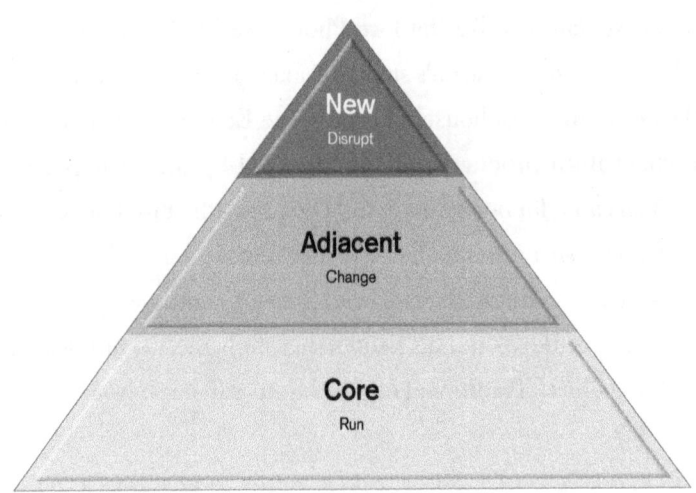

Figure 3.
Three types of initiatives, projects, or bets in a well-balanced corporate portfolio

If you dial up the risk level a bit, you encounter new programs and services—for instance, personalization engines that change how customers shop, or new oil drilling technologies—that build on existing technology and business models or introduce a change to an existing product or service. We call this middle part of the pyramid "adjacent innovation." Google leadership jokingly calls such incremental and adjacent innovation "roofshots," as opposed to "moonshots."

Finally, at the top of this pyramid is disruptive innovation. These are the bets that could fundamentally transform the company and its business if they pay off, such as the AWS cloud business, Alipay by Alibaba, or Netflix's streaming service (back when its primary business was DVD by mail). They are inherently risky and uncertain at the time of their launch. They could be expensive failures—or they could disrupt the industry, usher an entirely new business model into the world, or create a new set of customers for the company. In this top part of the pyramid, applying the Venture Mindset is critical.

Google, under Eric Schmidt's leadership, even set up a rule of thumb: the split among these three types of projects should be 70/20/10, with at least 10 percent of the time and effort being deployed to truly moonshot initiatives. Google houses its collection of such moonshot bets within Google X, its secretive innovation arm. Google X operates almost like an innovation factory. Its mission is to create new companies that could eventually become the next Google—and that's no exaggeration. When Alphabet, Google's parent company, was created, Larry Page and Sergey Brin even reminded stakeholders that "you could expect us to make smaller bets in areas that might seem very speculative or even strange when compared to our current business." Google X evaluates hundreds of ideas each year, ranging from clean energy to artificial intelligence. Only a few ever become staffed and funded. Some of those seeds have become big trees by now, such as Waymo, a self-driving car company that may change the whole transportation industry as we know it. In some ways, Google X sounds pretty much like an internally run VC fund.

Google X has its own scars, of course. Google Glass is an obvious one; the first version was roundly ridiculed and quickly discontinued. However, in striking contrast to other companies, Google X employees are *rewarded* for their failures. Similarly, Ratan Tata, founder of Tata, created a prize for the best failed idea. Intuit not only gives a special Best Failure award to its employees, but also holds celebratory "failure parties." These companies know that among their many small bets, one smashing success may outweigh all the failures combined.

The Venture Mindset has been successfully employed in many industries. Hollywood is a perfect example. The movie industry, with its hits and flops, is surprisingly similar to the VC world. Movies also have a high failure rate. It is believed that of every ten movie scripts purchased by a top Hollywood studio, only one is actually filmed and released. And only half of all the movies released manage to recoup their production budget. Like the VC world, the film industry is a blockbuster game. Hits like *Game of Thrones* or *House of Cards* are overwhelmingly successful; the top 20 percent of all movies bag 80 percent of the revenue. And they take a long time to produce: for *Spider-Man*, the time from rights acquisition to becoming a box-office hit reached seventeen years. That is an extraordinarily long time frame—but it's the same amount of time it took for Palantir, the data analytics software company, to go public and become a $20 billion win for its founders and investors.

Smart film executives, in their search for big hits, leverage the Venture Mindset. They tolerate failures and encourage experimentation. The then CEO of Netflix went so far as criticizing his team for too high a hit ratio: "I'm always pushing the content team," Reed Hastings said, "'We have to take more risk, you have to try more crazy things,' because we should have a higher cancel rate overall." Netflix, of course, was a VC-backed startup. The then-president of Pixar, Ed Catmull, echoed this approach, noting that "at the outset of making these movies, we simply didn't know if they would work," and then adding, "We as executives have to resist our natural tendency to avoid or minimize risks."

Another industry that employs the Venture Mindset is the pharmaceutical industry. Successful companies in this sector make wild bets to win big. A technology startup may be able to start testing its idea within months, but it takes years for a biotech team to learn if their idea—which is really just a specific molecule to be used in a particular health intervention—will succeed or fail. Many well-known drugs, such as penicillin, Valium, and Viagra, were discovered by accident. With a high entry cost, extremely long timelines before reaching the market, and low chances of success, pharmaceutical companies have had to establish a culture of high risk and failure tolerance to survive.

You should consider applying the Venture Mindset toward home runs and strikeouts across your organization. If anyone asks you where to start, start with a failure.

There is a wonderful joke about a man named Jacob who enters his synagogue and prays, "God, you see how poor and unhappy I am. Please, let me win the lottery." The day of the draw comes, but Jacob doesn't win. The following week he returns to the synagogue: "God, please, I'm desperate. If I don't win, I'm ruined. Let me win the lottery." Again he wins nothing. The story repeats itself for several weeks, and Jacob never wins. Finally, after yet another prayer, God shows up with lightning and thunder and exclaims, "Jacob, I really want to help you, but please, buy a ticket!" Many modern corporate leaders are like Jacob, not buying their ticket to the innovation lottery.

MINDSET CHECKS

○ Does your organization make bold bets with outsized 10X to 100X impact in case of success?

○ Is your organization positioned for making many small bets with the understanding that many of those will fail?

○ Does your organization avoid failure at all costs, or does it view failure as a normal outcome?

TWO

Get Outside the Four Walls

How not to miss the next big thing

2.1
Are You Here to Buy a Carpet or to Get Funding?

Would you write a $1,200,000 check for dinner at Pane e Vino, a onetime traditional Italian restaurant on Union Street in San Francisco? That's a lot even for a really nice meal. But what if the check also included a relatively small seed-stage investment in a company called Evenflow Inc.? Some venture capitalists thought it sounded like a good deal. They managed to turn a small early investment in a then unknown technology startup into a jaw-dropping $2 *billion* return in about ten years.

The check for $1.2 million, written at Pane e Vino one evening in September 2007, was on behalf of Sequoia Capital, one of the most storied venture capital investors in Silicon Valley. The company in which they purchased a stake later became known as Dropbox, a popular service to share files with clients, colleagues, and classmates. The investment deal was agreed on over dinner between Sameer Gandhi, then a partner at Sequoia, and Dropbox's founders, young MIT graduates Arash Ferdowsi and Drew Houston.

That dinner at Pane e Vino might not have been possible without one of the most unlikely venture capitalists in Silicon Valley, Pejman Nozad. In 1992, Nozad dropped out of college in Iran and emigrated to the United States. In fifteen years, he went from working in a yogurt store and living in the attic directly above it to becoming one of the most praised investors in Silicon Valley, a man whose calls are always highly anticipated and answered by partners at prestigious venture capital firms.

Just days before the Pane e Vino dinner, Nozad greeted Arash Ferdowsi and his buddy Drew in Farsi at a rug store in downtown Palo Alto, a small Bay Area town that is home to Stanford University and regularly ranks among the most expensive communities in the US. Arash and Drew were not in the rug store to buy beautiful décor for their newly rented apartment, which was too small for most of the rugs sold there anyway. Nozad had met them a few days earlier at one of the demo days hosted by Y Combinator (YC), which arranges opportunities for promising founders to make pitches to potential angel and venture capital investors.

Nozad traveled a circuitous route to becoming a participant in YC pitch events. Some years earlier, he had seen a TV ad for the Medallion Rug Gallery in Palo Alto. It said they were looking for a salesperson. Nozad got the job. While working at this high-end rug store, he realized that the way to sell an expensive rug, often costing more than $20,000, was to establish trust relationships with his customers. Over years of building these relationships, going into his customers' homes and learning about their lives and work, Nozad became deeply familiar with the incredible technologies being developed around him in Silicon Valley. One day he went to his boss, the rug store owner, and convinced him to start—of all things—a tech venture fund at the back of the rug store. This is how Nozad ended up at the YC event and became excited about the idea pitched by these two MIT graduates.

The world in 2007 was quite different from what we know today. The first iPhone had just been released. People still had to rely heavily on USB flash drives (and even floppy disks) and carry them from one computer to another. But the day when USB flash drives would no longer be needed was quickly approaching. It was clear to many in Silicon Valley that file sharing and file synchronization would be a huge market.

The idea of file sharing infected many budding entrepreneurs. In July 2007, the technology blog *Mashable* published a list of companies active in the data storage and virtual sharing space. The list contained eighty competing solutions! Many of them had been funded by angel and venture capital investors. More than half of them failed, and only a few still operate today. Two of them became household names: Box and Google Drive. Neither Dropbox nor Evenflow (the company's original name) showed up on the *Mashable* list, because this startup was still flying under the radar.

Over a cup of strong black tea, Pejman Nozad got excited about the opportunity presented to him by Houston and Ferdowsi (who was also of Iranian descent). He immediately sent a note to his friend Doug Leone, a partner at Sequoia Capital. Two days later, Sequoia's Mike Moritz, one of the most legendary VC investors (he was in on Google, YouTube, and Zappos, to name just a few), dropped in on Drew and Arash in their tiny apartment full of empty pizza boxes. The now famous Pane e Vino dinner happened soon afterward, and the deal was closed shortly. This set of seemingly random events led to outstanding success that many of us enjoy whenever we share files with one another via Dropbox.

To make investments, venture capitalists first need to find them. In a long chain of actions, this is the first one that makes the Venture Mindset so vastly different from that of corporate decision makers and almost everybody else.

The story of how Sequoia ended up investing in Dropbox is neither exceptional nor random. Instead, it's a natural consequence of the Venture Mindset, which contrasts significantly with the predominant mindset in the corporate world. Corporate decision makers have lots of people and resources at their disposal within their four walls. As a result, project ideas arise from what is available *within* the organization. In fact, researchers found that, in over 300 large companies, more than six of every seven innovation leaders considered internal innovation sources the most important ones. That would be impossible for VCs. Their offices are small and the only place to look for new ideas is outside their four walls. They know that deals like Dropbox are happening outside their offices—in garages and flats, coffee shops and demo days, meetups and university labs. This is why the story of Nozad, Leone, Moritz, and Gandhi is common rather than unique, instructive rather than just cool.

Mark Siegel, a VC at Menlo Ventures, checked all the consumer startups he could find that had a net promoter score (a metric that calculates how likely people are to recommend a company favorably) higher than Apple's. In this way, he identified and became the first investor in recently founded eyeglass startup Warby Parker.

Steve Anderson, a VC at Baseline Ventures, met Kevin Systrom serendipitously at a bar, where Systrom pulled out his iPhone and started showing him the app he was building, called Burbn (after his preferred drink). Within days, Anderson wired a small check and became the first investor in what we now know as Instagram.

Jeremy Liew of Lightspeed, another VC firm, found his VC partner's daughter and her friends huddled around the kitchen table looking intently at their phones. Jeremy asked to look at the app that had riveted their attention. He found out who was behind it, sent a Facebook message to its cofounder Evan Spiegel, and soon was the lead investor in Snapchat.

Examples like these abound. Seek and you shall find.

Being able to recognize a raw diamond among stones is critical. VCs call it their "picking" skill. Or think of a mushroom picker trying to separate edible chanterelles from poisonous webcaps. But ask any mushroom hunter and you'll be told that, before you can find the right mushroom, you need to know how to locate a forest full of mushrooms. In the VC world this is called "sourcing."

"Success in VC is probably only 10% about picking and 90% about sourcing the right deals," Chris Dixon, a partner at the prominent VC firm a16z, once said. Dixon leads the ranks of VCs who perceive deal sourcing as the most important contributor to their value creation and success. Although all the early investors in Dropbox recognized the market opportunity in file sharing, it took them some time to source many entrepreneurial teams to look at. Gandhi probably met with dozens of file-sharing startups. To decide on which one to invest in, you need to find a way to meet as many startups as possible and then select the one you consider most promising. And remember: these startups might be found in unusual places.

Are people in traditional companies great or even good at sourcing ideas and deals? Well, let's think about that question. Can you imagine a corporate executive sitting next to two recent MIT grads in a rug store? What are the chances that a top manager would spend her Saturday in a small apartment with two entrepreneurs, imbibing their ideas when they have no ready-made product to display—not even a prototype, or even a phantom of a prototype? How feasible is it for corporations such as GM or AT&T to go from meeting with idea creators for the first time to committing resources to the idea in a matter of weeks (even if the size of the investment check is negligible compared to their turnover)? Many corporate decision makers we have worked with wave their hands in disbelief and say, "We just can't do that."

Sourcing is a huge challenge for most managers and leaders we meet. This inability to source deals from outside the four walls, and to do so quickly, is one of the main reasons why innovation in so many companies is stifled. The pipeline of ideas inside your four walls is simply not big enough. The challenge is often not lack of resources or smart people, but lack of a critical mass of ideas or too great a similarity between those ideas. Too often, organizations select initiatives from a small number of internally available options. This works if your goal is to achieve a small improvement in something the organization already does very well. But it doesn't bring in entirely fresh ideas that could grow your company in dramatic ways. VCs review hundreds, if not thousands, of startups annually to make perhaps a dozen investments. What corporate decision maker can review that many internal projects each year? In our experience, very few.

Where do VCs source their potential deals? After all, there aren't many Iranian rug stores in Palo Alto.

2.2
Cast Your Networks Wide

Zynga, the developer of popular social games such as *FarmVille*, might not have prospered without a connection between cofounder Mark Pincus and Reid Hoffman. They got to know each other in 2002, when Reid was still a senior executive at PayPal (before he cofounded LinkedIn) and Mark was seeking advice about his (non-Zynga) startup ideas. Five years later, in 2007, when Pincus got the idea of launching a social poker game on Facebook's platform, he called Hoffman to talk about his project. Hoffman swiftly came on board as a Zynga investor. Similarly, when Hoffman was raising money to build LinkedIn, one of his own friends from PayPal, Peter Thiel, gave him a hand.

Even before meeting Hoffman, Pincus was a founder of a company called Freeloader, and in 1995 he hired Sean Parker as an intern there, while Parker was still in high school. Parker went on to become the founder of Napster (a precursor to iTunes). In 2004, Parker learned about Facebook by looking at the laptop of a roommate's girlfriend while she was a student at Stanford. Facebook was then in its very early stages, but Parker became curious and, as a fanatical networker, immediately shot an email to the generic address, seeking to connect with twenty-year-old Mark Zuckerberg. Soon they had dinner together in a Chinese restaurant in New York. As you can guess, Parker pulled strings in his network and

Thiel, Hoffman, and Pincus all became investors in Zuckerberg's now famous startup.

Exclude any link from this network of connections, and we may never have ended up with the ability to connect with people through social networks like Facebook and LinkedIn, or to play games created by Zynga with them.

As obvious as it may sound, networking still matters. Ilya and his colleagues conducted several studies to look under the hood of VCs' decision-making processes. In one study, more than a thousand VC investors (almost one-sixth of the total VC population!) were asked to identify key sources for startups they invested in. About half of all deals come either from other investors in the company or from an investor's professional network (see Figure 4). Unlike many corporate executives, VCs work tirelessly on expanding and maintaining their professional networks.

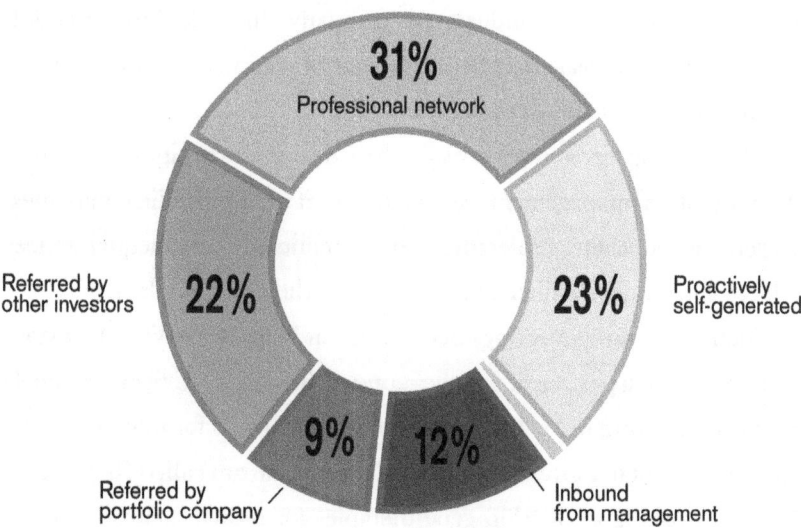

NOTE: Source of the data is "How Do Venture Capitalists Make Decisions?" by Paul Gompers, Will Gornall, Steven N. Kaplan, and Ilya A. Strebulaev (2020). The percentage of deals closed in the past twelve months originating from each source; values don't add to 100 percent because of rounding; 1 percent represents "quantitative sourcing."

Figure 4.
Sources of investments for early-stage venture capital deals

Another one of Ilya's studies compared the LinkedIn contacts and followers of institutional VCs (such as partners at Sequoia and Benchmark) with those of VCs who work for large corporations. Even though corporate VCs are supposed to look outward, since they are investing corporate money in independent startups, their LinkedIn network is on average only about half the size of that of institutional VCs! We bet the situation is even worse for other internal teams within corporations. Of course, it's natural that people working inside large companies won't be as active externally as VC investors, but this might be one reason why these companies' business plans are so often disrupted by small VC-backed teams from Silicon Valley and elsewhere. Connections and networks take time to materialize into exceptional deals and ideas, and you never know where the next one could be coming from.

But networking is more than sheer numbers of contacts. You may know a thousand people, but if they are all from the same background, or in a similar job function, industry, or company, this lack of diversity will limit your flow of ideas. It's not just the size of your network that matters. It is also its quality and diversity.

VCs develop diverse networks. Their deal opportunities come from other investors, management team members at their portfolio companies, lawyers, accountants, professors and academic advisers, acquaintances in large companies, bankers, or friends from their student days.

Such networking meetings become second nature for VCs. Consider Cami Samuels, a partner at Venrock, one of the oldest VC firms. Samuels has been investing in healthcare and biotech startups for more than two decades. One of her investments was in a small startup called RegenXBio that was working to develop gene therapies for retinal, neurodegenerative, and metabolic diseases. You might think that she spends all her time conducting unemotional scientific analyses of clinical trials. Nothing could be further from reality. Although Samuels eagerly dives into scientific details about new and promising drugs, her week is full of meetings with experts, academics, senior executives, employees, and founders of companies she has backed in the past. Over meals, she learns about emerging trends and opportunities and about companies on the cusp of developing them. In this way, she builds a complex chain of connections that may lead to breakthrough ideas or investments.

As she confided to us, Samuels pays considerable attention to building relationships and long-lasting partnerships within her diverse professional network. This strategy has paid off nicely. As a junior VC and board observer, she established and nurtured a relationship with a young founder, Ned David. Samuels often called him while driving home from Venrock's Palo Alto office so that they could discuss new ideas. She backed five of David's companies. Had Samuels not partnered with Ned David, these biomedical companies may never have gotten off the ground.

Some connections may surprise even extraordinary networkers. Can an executive coach be instrumental in building the largest e-commerce company in the world? Apparently, this is exactly what happened in 1996 when coach Bill Campbell connected Kleiner Perkins's John Doerr to Leslie Koch, the marketing director at a then fledgling startup called Amazon. This connection resulted in one of Doerr's best-ever investments. Or take David Cheriton, a computer science professor at Stanford. He once introduced two unknown Stanford graduate students to Andy Bechtolsheim, a cofounder of Sun Microsystems, and Bechtolsheim ended up writing them a $100,000 check. Who could have known that these two ambitious young men would become the founders of Google? Cheriton's decision to invest would make him one of the richest professors in the world, with a net worth of almost $10 billion.

It's hard to think of a more unusual place to find startup funding than a locker room. But it was at a gym in Palo Alto that Philip Winter met Tim Cook, the CEO of Apple. Winter had just invented an environmentally friendly showerhead called Nebia and had convinced his gym to try it out. He was standing outside a shower room, asking patrons what they thought of the new showerhead, when, lo and behold, Tim Cook came out of the shower. Cook, who generally does not invest in companies other than Apple, became a Nebia investor.

What would you do if you were introduced to somebody with an unusual idea? Often, even if people have a chance to meet a disruptor-to-be, they dismiss the idea. That problem applies to everyone—Fortune 500 bosses, experts in various domains, and the average investor. "Can this nerd in a messy black T-shirt and a navy hoodie really be important enough for me to spend fifteen minutes with him?!" you might say. "Nah, ignore him. My day is super busy." It's such a common thought. But successful VCs are different. As part of their tireless efforts to diversify their network and interact with interesting people and their ideas, they are open to unusual encounters. When Don Valentine, an investor at Sequoia, came to meet Steve Jobs for the first time and inspect the new Apple computer, he found Jobs wearing cutoff jeans and sandals while sporting shoulder-length hair and a Ho Chi Minh beard. Valentine later asked the person who made the introduction, "Why did you send me this renegade from the human race?" Yet Valentine continued his due diligence and ultimately became an investor.

In the fast-changing world of uncertainty and disruption, you never know where your best opportunity might come from. Connections you formed a long time ago have the advantage of familiarity, but they may all be too similar and similarly outdated. If your professional network consists of people who share the same background and experience, you are less likely to meet an unusual, innovative idea—and even if you encounter one, the people in your network might uniformly reject it.

In one of our workshops, we asked a group of senior executives at a large European bank to assess their own leadership team. As they turned their heads, they realized how similar their backgrounds were. Most of them had grown professionally within the same four walls and had been with the company for many years. There were no outsiders. Even newly recruited people were from direct competitors. Is it surprising they struggled to source new ideas?

To generate fresh ideas, you need to diversify where your employees come from. Different backgrounds mean different ideas, different cultures, and different perspectives. The leaders of that bank had the courage to make a change. One of their new senior hires was an experienced executive from an innovative firm in the consumer products industry, the first such outside hire in the bank's long history.

The more unusual and blue-sky the opportunity, the more likely it is to come from unexpected sources. Consider your own organization and your own network. Look at your rolodex, full of perhaps hundreds of people with whom you interact professionally. Maybe it is time to give a call and have a coffee chat with someone outside your industry and your organization.

To discover new lands, you need to leave yours.

2.3
Don't Wait for Opportunities; Create Your Own

Can you find a new opportunity at a construction site? If you are curious about things, pay attention, and expect the unexpected, then the answer is definitely yes. Ask Brian Jacobs, a cofounder at Emergence Capital, a venture firm that invested in Salesforce as well as many other innovative software-as-a-service startups. When Salesforce was building its famous 1,070-foot-tall tower in San Francisco, one of the products the company used came from a small startup called Building Robotics. The software that Salesforce purchased helped to optimize heating and cooling in large commercial buildings. Brian and an associate at Emergence, Jake Saper, had been looking for cloud "internet of things" opportunities. While visiting the Salesforce Tower construction, Brian and Jake immediately saw the potential of advanced temperature control. They asked for an introduction to the founders, and soon Building Robotics became one of Emergence's investments. Later, it was acquired by the German company Siemens. Rather than waiting for an opportunity to come to his net, Brian created his own.

Good VCs are good fishermen. Great VCs, like Brian Jacobs, are also great hunters. They take the lead, they venture beyond their comfy offices, and they are constantly on the lookout for new ideas.

Consider the case of Paul Madera, a former US Air Force pilot who cofounded the VC firm Meritech back in 1999. One of Meritech's first investments was a bet on the potential of customer resource management (CRM) systems, when they invested in Salesforce, the startup just mentioned. The investment was more than a success. It was a resounding success. Salesforce, with its first cloud-based, easy-to-deploy and -use solution, immediately conquered the hearts and minds of salespeople. Which space, they asked themselves, would become the next CRM market and the next Salesforce?

The answer was social media. Back in 2005, Madera perceived that social media would transform the whole media ecosystem and make it difficult for existing giants like CNN or the *New York Times* to keep up with online communities. Only 7 percent of all US adults were using a social networking website as of 2005, but Madera knew that figure would soon explode. The firm started proactively exploring all social media startups (it may be hard to imagine now, but there were only a few at the time). One undisputed leader they concentrated on was MySpace, a two-year-old company headquartered in Santa Monica with more than 20 million users as of June 2005. Madera and his partners did a preliminary assessment, tracked down the founders, and traveled to Beverly Hills to meet with them.

They negotiated the investment and were very close to finalizing the deal. But just days later, Madera was staring with envy at the newspaper headlines announcing that MySpace had been sold to Rupert Murdoch's News Corporation for more than half a billion dollars. Obviously Meritech's partners were not the only people who had noticed this new social media phenomenon! Madera's hunch was a good one: one year later MySpace surpassed Google and Yahoo as the most-visited website in the United States. Soon it became the first social network to reach a global audience and by 2008 hit 100 million users.

Madera, however, didn't waste time licking his wounds. He reviewed all the startups they had identified in the social network space. One small startup blipped on their radar. It was called TheFacebook. It was open only to students at several top colleges and was much smaller than MySpace. But Madera quickly realized it had better features and a superior user interface. He was particularly impressed by a *Stanford Daily* news article that reported students were living in "that Facebook thing." According to the article, "Classes are being skipped. Work is being ignored. Thefacebook.com craze has swept through campus." One headline was particularly intriguing: "All the Cool Kids Are Doing It." An accompanying chart depicted the craze. From when it first appeared on campus, TheFacebook grew to 2,815 Stanford student participants—in just seven days.

Madera sat down with TheFacebook CEO Mark Zuckerberg and decided to invest $10 million to own about 2 percent of the company. Some other investors thought the price "very bubblesque," as Madera told us years later, but you don't need to be a professor of finance to guess that Meritech ended up with a pretty decent payoff.

Some VCs practice what for thousands of years all humans did. They hunt and gather. Today, many use data science to help them identify the target. Paul Arnold founded Switch Ventures to apply a data-driven approach to finding startups. His algorithmic approach makes him an unusual prospector in how he separates less valuable quartz from diamonds. His data science team explores hundreds of founders of newly formed startups every week. Using a model that relies on a dataset of more than 100,000 founders, Arnold assigns scores to each founding team based on their likelihood to build a unicorn startup. Then he tries to find a mutual connection to those who score in the top 1 to 5 percent, or he makes a cold call to get founders' attention. Recently, the model guided Arnold to reach out to the founding team of Ribbn, a Swedish-based startup that Arnold describes as Shopify for the resale economy. Without his approach, Arnold would never have heard of the startup. One factor that helped place Ribbn at the top of the model's rating system was its team composition. "Diversity in experience is really important for scoring," Arnold said. Then he smiled and added, "I can't tell you all the factors, can I?"

VCs go to great lengths to get noticed by startup founders they are interested in. Sequoia and its partner Jim Goetz built a system they called "Early Bird" to track the activity of app stores and spot the up-and-coming leaders early on. One day in 2010, the bird started to chirp especially powerfully as a single app began topping the charts in dozens of countries based on its number of downloads. Today, WhatsApp is a dominant messenger known to every fourth person on earth, but back then it could easily have been missed, with its low ranking on the app list in the United States. The "Early Bird" system may have helped Jim Goetz see the target, but catching the worm still required a lot of legwork. Literally.

Sequoia decided to invest in WhatsApp. But how? The founders weren't looking for capital and instead relied on bootstrapping (or self-funding). They ignored emails and had no office address for prospective investors to visit. Even when word got out that their "office" was somewhere in Mountain View, an 80,000-person suburb in the San Francisco Bay Area and headquarters of Google, the exact location was unknown. So, Sequoia partners took a chance and walked the streets of Mountain View. You've read it right. Sequoia VCs were walking around the twelve-square-mile town, with the sole purpose of locating and mingling with the WhatsApp founders. A few months later, Sequoia managed to invest $8 million in the startup, acquiring about an 11 percent stake. Not long after, in 2014, Facebook acquired WhatsApp for $19 billion.

Sequoia's partners perfectly personify the VC mindset. Ilya and his colleagues found that in around one-quarter of all their deals, VCs are the pursuers. They form a thesis regarding a good idea and go looking for any glimmer of startups developing that idea. They participate in all sorts of events, from demo days to trade fairs, where they can meet promising startups they hope nobody else has paid much attention to. They use fancy AI algorithms to identify founders they want to meet and then they draw on their network to make introductions.

You might be surprised by how many ideas are dreamed up or meet capital in unusual places. In Finland, innovation and promising technology disruptions are discussed at 200 degrees Fahrenheit. This isn't happening in Dante's Inferno, but at "sauna parties" in a country often described as the world's happiest. Slush is a major conference for entrepreneurs, investors, and technology professionals that takes place when the tough northern winter descends on Finland. To stimulate unusual networking, in 2017 the conference organizers built Slush Sauna Village as an attractive venue. Similarly, the Burning Man festival held in August near Reno, Nevada, attracts a surprising number of VCs and technology innovators looking for opportunities to network. As described by the San Francisco newspaper *SFGate*, Burning Man is a "hot spot for technology titans."

To think like VCs, you need to be willing to brave the cold and the heat. You need to be open to unusual sources of new ideas. But you don't have to make a pilgrimage to Finnish saunas or don a nifty costume for a Nevada desert festival. There are plenty of standard events to explore. After all, it was at a demo day that Pejman Nozad met Dropbox's founders.

Often when speaking with leaders of large and successful companies, we offer examples of recently founded startups attempting to disrupt those companies' industry. And we often find that neither the leaders nor their colleagues, including those nominally in charge of innovation and development, have even heard of those startups. If that is your style, beware.

Don't expect ideas to come knocking on your doors. Ideas are the door; you're the one who knocks.

2.4
Every Response Counts

"Professor, are you sure that our accounts won't be immediately blocked by Google?" one research assistant wondered when asked to send a few fictitious emails to investors at leading VC funds in Silicon Valley. Well, yes, that was possible. But nothing ventured, nothing gained. And besides, most of the emails would probably end up in spam folders. Nevertheless, this became one of Ilya's most successful research experiments on how VCs make decisions.

In 2018, more than 30,000 active angel investors and VCs in our investor database received a short introductory email from a startup founder. The message briefly introduced the founder and the (very early-stage) startup with a one-paragraph pitch, concluding with a request for a meeting to discuss a potential investment. There is nothing unusual in such cold pitches. VCs receive them by the dozens each day.

Well, one thing was different.

The entrepreneurs and the startups were fictitious, dreamed up for the glory of science. Ilya and his collaborator Will Gornall created fifty fake startups, complete with websites, logos, founders, email addresses, and pitches. As you can imagine, the researchers and Stanford MBA students taking Ilya's VC class got a kick out of coming up with fifty different fictitious but very plausible-sounding startup pitches! Here is one example.

TO: John Smith
FROM: Erica Snyder
DATE: August 28, 2018
SUBJECT: Investment in MysticGame Inc.

Hi John,

My name is Erica Snyder, I am an engineering student at Stanford and a cofounder of a startup called "MysticGame." I am reaching out as we are looking for investors in our seed funding round.

At MysticGame, we want to help people reengage with each other in the real world, instead of just on social media. We provide on-demand "game master" service at social gatherings. Our game masters are trained to guide groups of various ages and sizes through a series of games that are not only entertaining, but also intellectually challenging. Our services are perfect for company offsite events for team building, as well as for families and friends who want to have fun together.

Our team has worked with behavioral scientists, game developers, and storytellers to develop our games, and we have successfully tested our games in several communities.

Are you available for a quick call in the next week or two? Thank you for your time.

Best regards,
Erica Snyder
CEO & FOUNDER, MYSTICGAME
[website link followed]

As often happens in research, interesting results pop up unexpectedly. Our intent was to explore how investors respond to founders of different genders and races. But if you send information on real startups founded by real women and men of various races, the response rate won't tell you much, because the pitches themselves are so different. We needed an apples-to-apples comparison. So, for every fake startup, we associated the identical pitch with four different founder names. The MysticGame founder was either Erica Snyder, Gregory Stone, James Wu, or Grace Wong. In this way, we could study investors' responses based on whether the founder was perceived as a white male, Asian male, white female, or Asian female.

We found that angels and VCs were a bit more likely to respond to female and to Asian founders. But we also got an unexpected bonus finding: the cold emails were more effective than we thought. Cold calls have a bad reputation and people tend to ignore them, hanging up the phone, tossing the mail in the trash, or clicking the delete button instantly. When we planned the experiment (in great secrecy, because we didn't want recipients to hear about it in advance), our big worry was that investors just wouldn't respond at all and that all our efforts would be in vain. Even though VCs, in our prior research, had reported that 10 percent of their deals result from founders contacting them, a few VC friends we used as advisers (sworn to secrecy) predicted that our fictitious entrepreneurs would get no replies. One prominent investor opined, "A bunch of losers may reply, but not a single reasonable VC will."

After months of preparation and planning, we sent out the first batch of emails and waited patiently by our inbox folders. Literally minutes later, the email counter showed the first few responses. The experiment started to look a bit less hopeless. Ten responses. Then twenty. Then more than a hundred. Hours later we could not believe our eyes. Positive, meaningful responses continued to roll in. Overall, one of every twelve emails got a nontrivial response, and two-thirds of the responses contained a request for a meeting or a phone or video call, for more information such as a presentation deck, or for a referral to an investor's partner to conduct due diligence.

One response to every twelve emails is amazing, especially since undoubtedly a large fraction of the emails went to the spam folder. Even more impressively, the five pitches with the most responses attained an overall positive response rate of 15 percent from VCs. That is, every sixth venture capitalist responded to a cold pitch by these startups! One out of ten investors contacted in the study responded with interest to at least one pitch (most investors received one to three pitches, and nobody received more than four). Successful VCs with a proven track record and high-quality investments replied at an equally high rate. Our skeptical VC friend was proven wrong.

Why would investors do this? Although the overall quality of cold pitches is lower than that of referrals or proactive self-generation, these cold pitches may *still* uncover a unicorn. Missing even one great opportunity is a big loss. As a result, VCs—even those who publicly downplay the value of cold pitches—have their antennas up for these unsolicited approaches. They then apply the red flag approach (see the next chapter) to filter through these opportunities quickly and efficiently.

Whereas people at traditional organizations are tired of random emails hitting their mailboxes and tend to open emails from someone within the company first, the Venture Mindset starts from the opposite premise. When we ask VCs about their biggest regrets, almost no one mentions failed investments in which they lost all their money. Inevitably, they cite some ultimately successful startup on which they passed. Often they were the first investors to see that startup. Many such opportunities came in the form of cold calls.

David Cowan of Bessemer Ventures once visited his friend Susan Wojcicki at her home, where she tried to introduce him to "these two really smart Stanford students writing a search engine." She had rented space in her garage to Sergey Brin and Larry Page. Cowan's reaction: "Students?" He literally ran off and made a point of not going anywhere near the garage. As a result, he missed the chance to be the first VC investor in Google. Decades after the miss, Cowan still remembers it with a smile. A sad one. Yes, even VCs miss—in fact, they miss quite often. And this is also probably why many VCs now think that every email could lead to the next Google.

Has any investor ever won a jackpot in such a wild cold email game? Ask Garry Tan, who responded to a cold email from the address contact@bitbank.is in March 2012. It contained 0.05 BTC, where "BTC" is an acronym for "bitcoin," a now famous digital currency. It looked as suspicious as a spam email from the infamous "Prince of Nigeria" (and you know better than to pay attention to those messages). Tan did read on. Not long after that, Tan invested $300K in Bitbank, which later became Coinbase, the largest platform for digital currencies. In just a couple of years, his $300K became more than half a billion!

Now, imagine what could have happened to the head of corporate marketing at some traditional company if she pursued a similar opportunity in marketing technology touted by an unknown vendor. Would anyone praise her for taking a chance? Doesn't our more traditional and commonsense mindset tell us not to take these chances? We all underestimate the likelihood of finding a diamond in the rough. But when faced with disruption, organizations should encourage their members not to protect themselves from the outside world, but to be more curious.

Mark Cuban, an investor in many unicorns and a frequent shark on the TV show *Shark Tank*, responded to a cold email from first-time founder Aaron Levie, a twenty-one-year-old dropout from the University of Southern California. Cuban soon led the seed round of investment in Levie's company, Box, which would become one of the major competitors to our chapter's opening example, Dropbox. Cuban is especially systematic in carving time out of his busy schedule to read random emails. Adam Lyons, a twenty-five-year-old founder of The Zebra, guessed Cuban's email address and sent him a short email with the subject line, "Wanna disrupt the insurance industry?" Twenty minutes later, Lyons got an email back. Cuban invested in The Zebra—which now lets customers get real-time access to 1,800 car insurance products from more than 200 national insurers—and serves as an adviser to its founder. The startup was valued at $1.1 billion in April 2021.

Serendipity is all around us. Just consider one of the more touching stories in the history of science. At the beginning of the twentieth century, an impoverished office clerk from rural South India named Srinivasa Ramanujan taught himself mathematics. He sent world-leading mathematicians heavy packages of proofs he had discovered—the equivalent of cold pitches from startup founders. All were returned unopened. He was getting no traction until G. H. Hardy, a famous Cambridge mathematician, opened a package and peeked inside. Later that day, Hardy could not stop thinking about the strange formulas, proofs, and unfamiliar mathematical notation contained in the box. It turned out that Ramanujan had rediscovered, on his own, many important mathematical results. In the course of doing so, he also made startling discoveries. Why? Because he did not know what was or was not already known. Hardy recognized his genius and invited Ramanujan to England. Several years later, Ramanujan was inducted into the British Royal Society, becoming one of the most important mathematicians who ever lived.

To his dying day, Hardy believed that his discovery of Ramanujan was his most important service to mathematics. Because VCs don't want to miss their Ramanujans, they respond to cold-pitch entrepreneurs who might become the next unicorn.

Whatever you do, don't miss your Ramanujan.

2.5
Who Needs a Copy Machine?!

You can tell a truly disruptive technology has conquered the world when the company's name enters the English lexicon as a verb. Today we Google for information, PayPal our bills, Venmo cash to friends after shared dinners, and Photoshop our pictures. Xerox was also the name of a revolutionary company prior to becoming a synonym for making copies.

The Xerox technology followed an unlikely path to success. Today it's hard to imagine a world without copy machines, yet there was a time when this technology could have been laid aside and not seen the light of day. Chester Carlson, who was born in Seattle and grew up in California, had the misfortune of embarking on his career during the Great Depression of the 1930s. A graduate of both the California Institute of Technology and law school, he landed a job as a research engineer at Bell Telephone Laboratories in New York City. Finding the job too dull and routine, he transferred to the patent department, only to be laid off. When he finally became a manager of the patent department at an electrical equipment company, P. R. Mallory in New York, he noticed there were not enough copies of important documents around the office. This casual observation soon led to his eureka moment. Carlson invented xerography, a scientific term for a dry photocopying technique.

The resulting company, Xerox, became a darling for investors, delivering nearly 1,500 percent stock growth in the first four years after its 1961 debut on the New York Stock Exchange. From 1961 to 1971, the company was the fifth fastest-growing corporation in the United States. Its copy machine 914 became "the most successful single product of all time." But the company had a circuitous and tortured path to success. For five years, between 1939 and 1944, Carlson's invention was roundly rejected by one super-successful company after another: RCA, GE, Kodak, IBM. Carlson himself described their response as "an enthusiastic lack of interest," meaning, "We're too busy with other things." Decision makers at all of these then mighty companies might have been skeptical about Carlson's unimpressive background, considering him a soft-spoken patent attorney and a not very successful engineer. They no doubt later wished they had invested in xerography.

Is the Xerox story an exception? Not at all! Steve Jobs, cofounder of Apple, started his career at Atari as its employee number forty and helped to build arcade games. As he was raising capital for a new company in 1976, he reached out to his former employer, Atari founder Nolan Bushnell. Bushnell rejected the offer to invest $50,000 in return for one-third (!) of Apple Computers. "It's kind of fun to think about that, when I'm not crying," Bushnell said later. Meanwhile, Apple cofounder Steve Wozniak, or Woz, was a loyal Hewlett-Packard (HP) employee and presented to his leadership the idea of what would soon become Apple I, an eight-bit desktop computer. They turned him down five times. The company could not see why anyone would use a personal computer, and "nobody in HP was interested" in the idea. Instead, Woz got a green light from HP's legal department to continue with his invention outside the company, and soon Apple was on its path to success, becoming the first company ever to hit a trillion-dollar valuation. As Apple was continuing its growth trajectory in 1984, the new owner of Atari Corporation ordered major layoffs across the organization after acquiring it for $240 million. What a tale of two companies.

The story repeats itself again and again: internal inventors reach out unsuccessfully to their leaders with an idea that turns out to be so revolutionary it changes the market landscape. These leaders didn't even need to reach out proactively to the outside world or take a cold call; their own entrepreneurs-to-be were knocking on their door. But their bosses ignored them or even pushed them out the door. And for each Chester Carlson, Steve Wozniak, and Eric Yuan, there surely have been dozens and dozens more innovators who didn't leave. Their ideas simply died, and so we have nothing to write about. Compare all this to those VCs who are sweating with entrepreneurs in the Nevada desert or in a Finnish sauna to be the first to get their hands on a novel idea.

Corporate executives who are rarely seen outside their offices have locked themselves inside both their physical and mental "four walls." As a result, they tend to reject ideas coming from outside. This common mindset has even been given a name: the Not Invented Here (NIH) syndrome. NIH can take many forms, from "we don't think the company can do these things" to "that's not how we do it here" and "we can do it much better here," resulting in a "we just won't do it" mentality. If this were a disease, wouldn't you want to find a cure?

We know NIH is widespread. In a study of almost one million patents, Ajay Agrawal from the University of Toronto and coauthors Iain Cockburn and Carlos Rosell found that inventors employed by large firms tend to draw disproportionately from their firm's own prior inventions. This "creative myopia" (as the researchers termed it) implies that inventors in large companies pay less attention to (or simply ignore) what their colleagues at peer companies are doing. This evidence from many companies is well supported by on-the-ground experience. Ilya worked closely with Claudia Fan Munce, founder and for many years the managing director of the IBM Venture Capital Group (IBM was among the firms studied by Agrawal and his colleagues). The single biggest challenge that Fan Munce faced in twenty years was NIH. She would present an amazing startup and the technologists inside the company would say, "We can do it much better." And perhaps they could, but that idea wasn't among their top hundred priorities, and so it never got done.

In another revealing study, Markus Reitzig from the University of Vienna and Olav Sorenson from Yale analyzed nearly 12,000 innovation proposals submitted inside a large, multinational consumer goods firm. The proposals were evaluated by the firm's middle managers. The study found that these evaluators were biased in favor of ideas submitted by employees who worked in the same corporate division as the managers did. Birds of a feather flock together, indeed.

Thus, the NIH syndrome holds not only for new ideas coming from outside the organization, but even for ones coming from elsewhere within the same organization. The "Here" in the Not Invented Here syndrome is very picky.

It is hard to blame corporate leaders and technologists for such attitudes. Not Invented Here syndrome may indeed seem to be a rational though shortsighted response, at least for some in an organization. Internal technologists are often more knowledgeable and technically adept than their counterparts in struggling startups. They just have different priorities and a different mindset. Many senior executives have told us that, as leaders of multibillion-dollar corporations, they often have to add $1 billion to $3 billion in new revenues annually to justify working on a product. If this is the strategy, the typical initial payout of tens of millions of dollars from a successful spinoff wouldn't make a dent economically.

New products may also have to compete with a currently profitable internal product, as when the Zoom idea had to compete with Cisco's WebEx. Kodak's digital effort competed with its own analog film. Yet another common reason for the NIH syndrome is that the more time internal people spend with one another, the more they start listening to their own words, in what is often called the "echo chamber" effect. An echo chamber is an environment in which people encounter only information or opinions that reflect and reinforce their own. For example, consider a belief that the earth is flat. Now, this belief would strike you as bizarre—unless your network consists only of other flat-earth believers. If your close friends all believe the earth is flat, maybe soon you will too. The effect of "flat earth" thinking is no less dangerous in the business world.

Nortel was another company studied by the "creative myopia" researchers. It was a Canadian multinational telecommunications and data networking equipment manufacturer, once an industry leader. Back in its heyday in 2000, Nortel employed more than 94,000 people, accounted for more than one-third of the Toronto Stock Exchange's main market index, and was among the fifteen most valuable companies in the world. Yet when we hear this name today, we are likely to ask, "Who?"

Nortel is a case study of how a market leader can miss multiple trends and become overly specialized and focused on what they do well. As early as 1982, its management was presented with cellular technology by their own innovation staff. They turned it down. One senior executive remarked, "Who would ever want to walk around with a phone in their hand?" The same story was repeated in 1997, when internal innovators presented a smartphone concept. Rather than looking and thinking beyond their four walls, Nortel's executives increasingly focused their R&D resources on enhancing their existing products, thereby starving long-term initiatives. Remarkably, between 2000 and 2008, Nortel didn't release one single major new product. By the time Nortel started to invest heavily in cellular technology and smartphones, it was too late.

The NIH and echo chamber culture, punctuated by arrogance and hubris, led to the eventual demise of Nortel. Theirs is a clear example of the anti–VC mindset, which becomes particularly heartbreaking with the realization that commercially viable and disruptive ideas existed, evolved, and were developed internally, often earlier than elsewhere in the marketplace, yet these ideas could not surmount their organization's virtual (and sometimes physical) walls.

As an even more heartbreaking example, consider Alto, developed in 1973. Alto was a computer with many "firsts." It was the first system to have graphical user interface, or GUI, meaning that it was operated with a mouse and screen where you could click on things. It was the first computer to use object-oriented programming. And it was the first computer from which an email was sent. Some even argue that without the Alto the internet would have taken much longer to develop, or that it would not have been possible at all.

Alto was not a common "garage" story; it was a corporate invention. This revolutionary minicomputer was designed and developed within an R&D lab in Palo Alto, near the Stanford University campus. One such innovation would be enough to justify the lab's existence. Yet dozens and dozens of projects originated from the same lab. At least ten went public, including Adobe (the maker of Adobe Acrobat) and 3Com (a force behind hugely successful computer network products in the 1980s).

The company management created excellent conditions for corporate inventors, attracted superb talent, and thus had access to dozens of disruptive ideas. Ironically, they then studiously avoided implementing them. The ten successful projects that came out of the lab were spun off or commercialized outside the company. The company did not invest in these spinoff companies and did not benefit from them. The reasons: they were too different from the company's core technology and the initial revenue was too negligible compared to that of the main business units. NIH syndrome strikes again.

And what about Alto? Did that breakthrough succeed? Well, only about 2,000 units were ever built and they never became generally available for sale. Owners of the R&D lab didn't see the potential and were too slow to commercialize the product. By the time the next generation of Alto (called Star) was launched, the IBM personal computer had hit the market, with a price ten times lower. IBM triumphed.

Once, in an interview, Steve Jobs said that the company behind Alto "could have owned the entire computer industry today. [It] could have been IBM . . . [and] Microsoft." The combined valuation of IBM, Microsoft, and Apple is in the trillions of dollars. Their valuation is more than a thousand times that of the market capitalization of the company that created that lab in Palo Alto. That company still exists today. Can you guess its name?

Xerox.

Yes, Xerox invented but failed to benefit from so many inventions, in spite of its own history. It was Xerox that set up an R&D lab near the Stanford campus in 1970. Palo Alto Research Center, PARC, as the lab became known, was located 3,000 miles away from Xerox headquarters in Rochester, New York. PARC generated a remarkable stream of inventions. In fact, PARC was so revolutionary in its day that a technology magazine described it as one of the "Top 12 Holy Sites in IT." Sadly, no company is resistant to the drama caused by hubris. Like a colossus with feet of clay, Xerox committed the same error as the companies that had turned down Chester Carlson and ignored xerography.

Not Invented Here syndrome is like an immune system response that protects against invaders. Organizations, like organisms, protect themselves from external forces, whether these take the form of competition, regulators, or activists. When the defenses work, they preserve the culture and support internal talent. People proudly believe that their teams or companies are superior to those of other organizations. However, the immune system can break down, and the NIH syndrome is a case in point. What used to be a protective force now creates allergic reactions. The NIH syndrome is especially dangerous whenever an organization faces potentially disruptive changes. Like mold, it spreads across the organization, especially as the organization grows older, more profitable, and more risk-averse. Beware of this pattern and uproot NIH early on. Formalities don't matter. The mindset has to be changed.

2.6
Always on the Lookout

To put these words into action, here are some specific mechanisms an organization can implement.

Are you surprised to learn that many coffee chains were initially backed by VCs? Although Starbucks, Blue Bottle, and Philz coffee shops are commonplace today, each was originally a novel and risky idea. Indeed, many great things start with a cup of coffee, and this idea-stimulating beverage points to a few specific mechanisms you can use to source ideas. Here is one of them.

Have faith in your Favres

If you ever find yourself in Rome, take a chance and visit a small coffee bar known as Caffè Sant'Eustachio, located a short walk away from the Pantheon. Alex visited the bar in summer 2022 and ordered what Italians call the *specialit della casa*, or house specialty, the "Gran Caffè." He was expecting a regular if delightful tiny espresso, but it turned out to be quite a unique drink. Its thick, slightly bubbled aromatic foam on top of espresso, or crema, was nothing short of magical. You will find it challenging to match this experience at other coffee bars, even in Italy.

Alex was not alone in his appreciation; this very coffee also captured the attention of one visitor from Switzerland. In summer 1975, almost fifty years before Alex enjoyed his magical Gran Caffè, Eric Favre, an aerodynamics engineer, spent his vacation exploring the espresso culture of Italy. He was hunting for the best espresso in the world. Eric's wife, Anna-Maria, Italian by origin, once told her Swiss husband that Swiss coffee was pretty bland and way below Italian standards. This claim initiated the chase that eventually brought him to Caffè Sant'Eustachio in Rome. When Eric tried to tease out secrets of making Gran Caffè from the barista, he heard back only "I just press a button," which was not satisfying for a demanding engineering mind. Finally, Eric discovered that the key to Sant'Eustachio's superior crema was repeated aeration while the water is pumped through the coffee. Instead of pumping the piston of the machine just once, the barista pulled the lever quickly several times. Favre explained the simple rule in an interview: "It's chemistry: oxidation brings out all the flavors and aromas."

The story might have ended here, but for one small detail. Eric Favre was not just an engineer. He had just started working in Nestlé's packaging department. Nestlé, a food and drink company founded in the nineteenth century, was well known for its instant coffee, baby milk, and frozen food products. At the time, Nestlé was thinking about developing a pod for its instant coffee, Nescafé. When Eric returned to his Nestlé office in Vevey, Switzerland, he developed a prototype espresso machine. In doing so, he invented a sealed capsule in which air is trapped before water is forced through, filling the cup with frothy espresso. This product would encapsulate the coffee taste and smell into a small pod. Legendary Nespresso, the favorite brand of millions around the world, was born.

Nestlé's Nespresso reimagined the whole coffee-drinking culture. Its proprietary machines and a long list of coffee pods can now be bought via an app in a few clicks. Today the Nespresso pod is a multibillion-dollar global business for Nestlé. Though its path to success was long and thorny, it started as an invention proposed by an internal innovator from outside the corporate headquarters.

But if you imagined that Nestlé's bosses were initially overjoyed by the invention, you would be mistaken. After all, Nestlé was already making Nescafé, and its sales were rising. For years after the invention, Nestlé's management was unconvinced. It took ten years for Favre's perseverance to pay off. After many more challenges and twists and turns, Nespresso became a world-famous brand.

The next time you see a Nespresso pod, recall that it was an innovation created by an employee, from outside corporate headquarters. If you are a corporate decision maker, think about supporting your Eric Favres, the people who dare to venture outside, expose themselves to risky ideas, and create new growth engines.

Use innovation scouts and balance your internal and external innovation

Like the Nespresso pod, another famous invention and huge commercial success started miles away from a corporate headquarters with coffee—specifically, a spilled cup of coffee. When a salesman working for the German chemical company BASF spilled coffee during a phone call at a Japanese construction company, the first thing he grabbed was a foam insulating material, Basotect. This melamine resin foam, manufactured by BASF, is used in recording studios, cinemas, and exhibition facilities. To the salesman's surprise, the material worked exceptionally well. It not only soaked up the liquid, but it also gently scrubbed the surface. What had been developed as a reliable soundproof material appeared to have a surprising new application.

Soon Japanese customers could find a stain-removing sponge for sale in their local retail stores. This surprising discovery, however, could have remained a closely hidden secret among happy Japanese parents, had there not been another twist to this story. Enter Procter & Gamble (P&G). A Japan-based technology entrepreneur working for P&G discovered the sponge in an Osaka grocery store and immediately realized its global potential. What was once just an insulation material is now known to millions of customers as Mr. Clean Magic Eraser, a P&G blockbuster product and a lifesaver for countless parents trying to clean crayon-decorated walls.

Was the Magic Eraser serendipitous? Was it nothing more than the outcome of one random action? No. It is one of many inventions that P&G deliberately searched for outside its corporate walls. Olay Regenerist, Swiffer Dusters, and Glad ForceFlex are other breakthrough product innovations that resulted from a "Connect and Develop," or C&D, strategy initiated by P&G's former CEO Alan George "A. G." Lafley. After his appointment in 2000, he challenged his R&D teams to reinvent the whole innovation business model to look outside itself for new innovations.

P&G has one of the largest armies of talented in-house scientists. But Lafley pointed out that for every engineer inside the company, there were 200 engineers not employed by P&G "who were just as good." Lafley defined an ambitious goal of acquiring half of all product innovations outside the company. Former P&G executives later admitted that the major challenge was to move the company's attitude from NIH to PFE—"Not Invented Here" to "Proudly Found Elsewhere."

To make this shift, P&G designated dozens of employees as technology scouts to create external connections with researchers from universities, suppliers, and other potential industry collaborators and to immediately share what they learned with headquarters. The overall number of ideas identified by this team of technology scouts has exceeded 10,000, reportedly leading to more than 100 new products introduced by P&G from outside the company. The results speak for themselves. A few years after Connect and Develop was launched, the company's senior executives proudly declared that "more than 35% of our new products in the market have elements that originated from outside P&G. . . . And 45% of the initiatives in our product development portfolio have key elements that were discovered externally." P&G paired the C&D model with the R&D one, appreciating that sourcing ideas should not be constrained by corporate borders or departmental silos.

Is Procter & Gamble alone? Certainly not. Paul Stoffels, formerly chief scientific officer at the pharmaceutical giant Johnson & Johnson (J&J), attributed its innovation success to giving "equal weight to internal and external innovations." This comment highlights the simple yet powerful fact that the best science and technology are just as likely to emerge from within as from outside. One tool that J&J uses effectively is JLABS, the company incubator where, after a robust screening process, hundreds of external innovators gain access to many of J&J's resources, experts, and services, with a chance to ultimately deepen the partnership and have their products commercialized by J&J. Their innovative products vary from maternal health solutions and precision skin care platforms to cancer surgery tools and oral mRNA vaccines.

JLABS leaders created a model that mimics the manufacturing engine of early-stage companies. Although it is easy in theory to argue that external and internal innovation have equal chances of success, the reality is more challenging. When the idea originates from the outside, there are many more hurdles in the way of becoming a viable commercial entity and getting all the way to patients. Outsiders need help. It won't happen without support.

J&J came up with an idea to solve that problem. It invites its employees around the world to lend a helping hand, serving as sherpas for innovative outsiders. Such sherpas are called JPALs. They are J&J experts and mentors, primarily within the R&D function—an insider to assist and empower outsiders.

The bet has paid off handsomely. Outsiders have unlocked an impressive pipeline of ideas that led to the creation of 800 new companies, 47 IPOs, 40 acquisitions, and $69 billion in deals and partnerships for J&J. Behind these remarkable statistics are numerous lifesaving products, the consequence of a very successful company's willingness to venture outside to source ideas. Not surprisingly, in 2023 J&J was in the top twenty on *Fortune*'s list of America's Most Innovative Companies.

Rely on the wisdom of crowds

To improve its Cinematch algorithm, which was designed to predict people's movie ratings, Netflix started a competition. The now famous Netflix Prize crowdsourced ideas in an attempt to answer a nontrivial question: Would you appreciate *Gladiators* if you liked *A Beautiful Mind*, or would you prefer *Amélie*? More than 30,000 data geeks and computer science fans worked on the problem, and tens of thousands of solutions were received. Improving the customer experience for millions of users resulted in a $1 million award to the team that managed to achieve substantially more precise recommendation results than the original Netflix algorithm. Amateurs (albeit enthusiastic, well-informed ones) won against professionals. Even more remarkably, just six days after the start of the competition, one external geek team had already beaten Cinematch. After two weeks, three teams had outperformed Cinematch, including the one that qualified for the prize. Moreover, the competition attracted an increase in job applications to Netflix, along with many newly formed connections and friendships. Asking the general public or a more specialized community for their feedback and input on a problem can be an effective way of sourcing new ideas.

These three mechanisms are part and parcel of the Venture Mindset. Get outside your company, build networks of informants and scouts, bring the public into your largest projects—and expect serendipity, which may occur in a grocery store in Osaka or a coffee bar in Rome.

2.7
The Power of Unpredictable

If you are in a relationship, where did you meet your partner? What about your friends? Researchers from Stanford and the University of New Mexico explored this question. They asked thousands of participants to write the story of how they met and came to know their partners. As in the VC world, matches came through various networks: work, school, church. There are both "inbound" and "outbound" ways to find a spouse. And of course, there is always a place for serendipity. Many cupids (nearly 40 percent) shot their arrows online, whether through dating websites, social media apps, discussion forums, and even gaming.

The beauty of unpredictable but potentially life-changing meetings is that it is hard to predict exactly when and where they will happen. We eagerly accept the idea that one may find a spouse simply by chance, but we often reject the same concept when we discuss business decisions.

The same thing applies to job searching. Eighty-five percent of all jobs are believed to be filled through networking. Two-thirds of people are hired at companies where they had a networking connection. In contrast, just one of every ten jobs is secured through direct approaches (i.e., cold calls) to the company. The same goes for innovative ideas. We can't point you to the exact place to dig them—and this in itself is an important piece of actionable information. We know that ideas come from networking, often in unpredictable ways.

You don't know who from your network will bring you the next killer idea, but your best sources are more likely to come not from the inside but from the outside. New marketing ideas, new supply chain solutions, and new financial partners may all hit your mailbox not through your corporate intranet but from your diverse networks, or even from a village in southern India.

VCs work hard to diversify their networks, and you should as well. They don't lock themselves to one sector and don't rely on a single source of ideas. Brian Jacobs, whom we met earlier in this chapter, is also Ilya's co-teacher in the Stanford course on VC. Brian likes telling the class that the best time to work on expanding your professional network was yesterday. But of course it is never too late. Today could be the right time to write a few emails to long-ago contacts, or to think proactively about what value you can offer to people in your network.

The Dropbox story is an example of how great things may start with a random connection. Without Pejman Nozad, many entrepreneurs may not have received funding from Sequoia. But how did Pejman know Leone, Sequoia's partner, in the first place?

Well, Doug Leone of Sequoia Capital was a rug customer of Pejman Nozad. One day, as Nozad was leaving Leone's home after looking at rugs for two hours, he suggested to Leone that he could help Sequoia, given his access to many Iranian PhDs. In the purest display of the Venture Mindset, Leone replied, "Be at your office Monday morning, 7 a.m." And he was.

You never know, maybe your best idea may come from a random email or as you are shopping for a nice rug.

MINDSET CHECKS

● ● ● ●

- ○ Does your organization source ideas exclusively from the inside, or does it have a flow of ideas coming from external networks?

- ○ Does your team spend time with startups, research labs, and experts from your sector?

- ○ How open are your culture and organization to unexpected ideas coming from outsiders?

THREE

Prepare Your Mind

What is the one question VCs ask that will change the way you evaluate opportunities

3.1
Why Don't I Want to Invest?

"Aye" or "nay": that is the question! One day each year, a Stanford Graduate School of Business auditorium becomes a trade fair of ideas, with startups invited to make pitches to students. We invite you to come join the class!

You are one of six members in a group of Stanford MBA students playing the role of partners at a VC fund. Your task: to approve or decline startup investment opportunities. The room is crowded and you can feel the tension as the competition among 144 students to identify and invest in the most promising startup heats up. Five founders, one after another, pitch their startups to VC partnerships.

What's special about the startup pitch case in Ilya's class is that, although the twenty-four VC firms that the student groups represent are fictitious, the startups are real. They are carefully selected so that at the very time of the class, these promising companies are actually raising capital from real VC investors. This is what we call a *live* case, meaning that nobody—not the students, Ilya, Ilya's co-teacher Brian Jacobs, or the startup founders—knows which of these companies will be successful. To add a realistic twist, we give the student VC partnerships limited budgets, so they can invest in only one startup of the five.

Let the pitches begin. Pick your favorite!

First, imagine a stress-alleviating therapy device the size of a small phone that can calm you down and address mental health issues when placed on your chest. Its name is Sensate, and it can already be bought online. As cofounder Anna Gudmundson explains, Sensate generates sound waves that, when paired with your headphones, create a soothing effect on your body.

Next, students listen to Christof Wittig, an impassioned founder of Queer Spaces, which is creating a safe place online for the LGBTQ+ community. Described by *Forbes* as a "booming start-up," Queer Spaces enables users to build safer communities centered on shared interests and authentic connections.

Then students' attention switches to Mandar Shinde of Blotout, promising to help small businesses with their online advertising, but without compromising online privacy.

Next, Thomas Kunjappu, cofounder and CEO of Cleary, energetically discusses how his young startup simplifies companies' experience of digital onboarding of their employees.

Finally, we hear from Fran Maier, a Stanford alumna herself and a cofounder of Match.com. Maier asks how many of the students already have kids. A few do. She then asks them: Wouldn't it be wonderful to travel without any heavy baby equipment? Her company, BabyQuip, promises to make traveling with children easier for parents by letting them rent strollers, car seats, cribs, and other baby gear in over 1,000 cities. Will this become the Airbnb of baby gear?

These are just a few of the dozens of startups that have made pitches to the Stanford class in recent years.

So what was your favorite? Which one would you have picked?

The students need to say a relatively quick no to all but one opportunity based only on reading the teaser deck, a quick team discussion, and team members' observation of the founders during their pitch. Students look puzzled. How could you ever make a decision with so few facts about the company and founders? Each startup looks amazing. But you have to pick one.

Before attending twenty-minute pitches from the founder of every startup, student teams review startups' blurbs and investor decks, hold preliminary discussions in their groups, and come up with a multitude of questions that could easily overwhelm even an experienced presenter. The students then decide which startup they wish to perform more careful due diligence on. Many decisions need to be made on the fly, without much information. You just don't have enough time to perform in-depth due diligence on all the pitching startups, so you need to select one initial favorite while being fully cognizant that you still don't know everything about the candidates. After selecting a startup to explore in more detail, students pore over the materials (financial projections, customer reviews, detailed investor decks), meet again with the founders, try the product out, and write investment memos summarizing their work.

It might surprise you that these students have *more* information than many real-life VCs, who often have to decide on a startup idea without meeting the founders or seeing the teaser deck. In addition, real-life VCs are deluged with thousands of opportunities, not just five in a day. As a result, VCs face a harsh trade-off. They work tirelessly to increase the flow of great ideas coming to them. Then, with no time to investigate all of them thoroughly, they have to increase their processing speed without unduly sacrificing quality. With only a few questions as their headlamp, they must decide quickly whether each idea is a gold mine or a trap.

Students are always surprised to discover that VC investors never inspect each data point about every potential opportunity, even if the information is right there in front of them. Rather, they search for one signal that would lead them to *reject* the opportunity. This is one of the Venture Mindset shortcuts, which we call the "critical flaw approach" or "red flag approach." When making initial screening decisions, investors are looking for red flags and asking themselves one question: "Why *don't* I want to invest?"

3.2
Sharks, Dragons, and Fatal Flaws

This fast-rejection mindset may feel alien to you, and indeed it feels different from how we normally make decisions. But is it? Imagine that your travels bring you to a new city and you have to pick a restaurant for a family dinner. You open Yelp or Google and see a hundred options to choose from. If you examine every option with the same level of scrutiny, you risk going hungry all night, perhaps with a screaming baby sitting next to you. Rather than thoroughly scrutinize, you may discard options by applying the red flag approach. For example, you may remove all the restaurants that are too expensive, have reviews below four stars, or are not baby-friendly. You don't need *all* the facts to reduce the list to a small handful; to reject most options, a single red flag is enough. Soon you are fastening your seat belts as you head for your favorite pick.

You often have to make decisions on the fly when dealing with an overwhelming number of options, as you do when booking a hotel, choosing a book as a present for a friend, or purchasing kitchenware on Amazon. You probably apply the critical flaw approach quite effectively and often without realizing it. But when it comes to business and professional decisions, we somehow stop trusting the red flag approach. Instead, we try checking all the boxes, when a single one is enough.

This is exactly what we find in a traditional business environment. You start with a very limited list of ideas and analyze each one in detail. But what is fine for routine situations may not work in times of disruption.

So how can you survive this exhaustive process? Simply by not considering all the options. VCs start instead with an extensive, seemingly unwieldy deal funnel and then nimbly and effectively shrink the funnel to concentrate on the most promising prospective deals. Adopting this mindset enables you to expand the initial set of opportunities—an essential ingredient of success for VCs.

VCs reduce the seemingly inordinate complexity of deal selection by searching for a decisive reason to reject an opportunity rather than advancing it to the next stage of consideration. "Reject" is a keyword and a distinct feature of the VC mindset, for VCs start by looking not for a compelling reason to invest, but for a way out. Rejection rates at this stage of the VC deal funnel are sky-high. Most startups that come to investors' attention never progress to the next stage of consideration. Rather, investors discard the investment promptly after a quick review. A few minutes are often enough to reach a rejection decision. If you don't believe us, then let's go together to LA.

Lights, camera, action! Here we are in the Sony Pictures Studio, where the famous, wildly popular *Shark Tank* show is filmed. Entrepreneurs pitch their startups to angel investors (called the "sharks") in the hope of raising capital. The entrepreneurs briefly introduce themselves and the nature of their idea. The sharks then quiz the entrepreneurs on their experience and details of the business. This interaction continues until either all the sharks withdraw (that is, decline to invest) or one or more sharks propose investing. Before pitching to Stanford students, Fran Maier of BabyQuip (the startup for renting baby gear) pitched to the sharks. Let's eavesdrop and see if BabyQuip managed to raise funds. Maier was seeking to raise $500,000 in exchange for 5 percent equity in BabyQuip.

Among the sharks are experienced entrepreneurs and investors such as Mark Cuban and Katrina Lake, who from the very beginning pepper Fran and cofounder Joe Maier with questions. "What is the cost of a double stroller?" "What do you take from the transaction?" "Tell us about your background." "How much are you paying to acquire on each side [of a marketplace]?" It sounds like a random set of questions. The TV viewers see the sharks pull out, one after another. If you analyze their responses carefully, you realize that when each one identifies a factor that they believe to be a "critical flaw," they immediately lose interest. The last remaining shark, Kevin O'Leary—whose company was once acquired by Mattel, the maker of Barbie dolls—offers to acquire 20 percent of the company (the founders declined).

Is this a representative episode? We checked it out for ourselves. We randomly picked dozens of pitches from different seasons of *Shark Tank* and wrote down all the questions on each pitch and the sharks' reactions. Here's what we learned. On average, sharks ask a dozen or so questions before making a decision. The same pattern happens again and again. Investors drill down and ask questions until they identify a weak spot they consider a red flag. They often start with general questions, and if founders survive that initial set of queries, the sharks progress to more company-specific questions. Once a critical flaw is identified, sharks reject the pitch almost immediately. It is the VC "red flag" mindset approach in action.

Is there a specific "make it or break it" factor? Canadian researchers looked at interactions between angel investors and entrepreneurs on the Canadian reality TV show *Dragons' Den*, which is similar to *Shark Tank*. Researchers recorded and carefully analyzed interactions between founders and investors. They used both verbal and nonverbal clues to code investors' rationale and carefully examined the investors' decision-making process.

Again, the researchers found that investors use the critical flaw approach. They identified eight "fatal flaw" factors. One such factor was adoption, or whether customers in a target market will easily adopt the product that the entrepreneur is proposing. If the Dragons could not see clear benefits for customers or if they unearthed major adoption issues that could not be explained right away, they were likely to pull the plug on the deal instantaneously, without feeling any need to spend time on other factors. If that critical factor was passed, the Dragons would consider many others, such as the go-to-market strategy, relevant experience of entrepreneurs, and the size of the target market. For the most part, if the business idea or the entrepreneur failed on any one of these critical factors, the Dragons withdrew immediately.

This decision-making shortcut diverges sharply from a traditional process in which each factor is considered carefully and subsequently synthesized into a balanced conclusion. A traditional business school class emphasizes this approach: evaluate benefits and costs (pros and cons), collect all the facts, and inspect all the consequences. This could be a viable approach when there is infinite time—but who has limitless time these days? This could also be a sound approach if the number of opportunities is small. You can see now why the traditional mindset isn't interested in going outside the four walls to source opportunities—why attract more options than we can properly evaluate? But if you are in the world of innovation, disruption, uncertainty, and turmoil, that approach doesn't work. This is why VCs use the red flag approach to say no quickly and move on to the next opportunity (even if they know they will occasionally kick themselves years down the road).

Whenever a large degree of uncertainty is present, the trade-off between speed and accuracy is fundamental. High speed ensures that a decision maker can screen many potential opportunities quickly. Higher accuracy enables an investor to make a better decision by collecting and processing as much information as possible. And there's a natural tension between speed and accuracy. Accuracy requires acquiring and then processing more information, which takes more time and reduces speed. If you can devote a thousand hours each year to processing new opportunities, you can evaluate twenty deals a year carefully and slowly at fifty hours per deal, or you can consider thousands of deals very quickly. That's why, at this stage, those with the Venture Mindset err on the side of speed. Critically, VCs do not yet make a final decision to invest; they make a final decision *not* to invest.

The next time you have to make a decision, ask yourself: Are you prioritizing speed or accuracy? Are you missing opportunities because you spend too much time on accuracy? Sometimes it's better to speed up the decision process and find efficient ways to say no early so that you can evaluate more ideas rapidly.

What enables VCs to serendipitously select promising startups? This story takes us from nineteenth-century French labs to innovation labs sitting right next to Stanford.

3.3
You Know It When You See It

Do you recall how Sameer Gandhi, a Silicon Valley venture capitalist, met the two founders of Dropbox who were dreaming up the future of file sharing in 2007? It might seem that when Gandhi and his partners decided to invest almost on the spot, it was a lucky choice. But actually, he was fully equipped for that meeting. He knew about file sharing and was certain that it would become a reality sooner or later.

In his pursuit of deeper knowledge, Gandhi met with dozens of entrepreneurial teams working on file sharing, so he'd been diving into the topic in great detail before he even heard about Dropbox. Gandhi described his quest, noting, "The failure of all of the prior online storage products is that they didn't understand how to make it incredibly simple for users to adopt that product." Until he met Drew Houston and Arash Ferdowsi, he was passing up one investment after another: "Nobody prior to [the Dropbox founders] had solved both the technical and the design challenges," he said. "And at that point, they hadn't solved them either, but they understood them all." Was Gandhi lucky? Of course he was! But recognizing that Houston and Ferdowsi "understood it all" took a lot of sweat. As Thomas Jefferson is reputed to have once famously said, "I find that the harder I work, the more luck I seem to have." This dictum applies equally to Gandhi and the VC mindset.

Gandhi knew the solution to the file-sharing problem existed. It had just not been invented yet. It is like when Dmitri Mendeleev proposed his elegant periodic table of chemical elements, he had to leave some gaps with then unknown elements. For innovation, David Singer from Maverick Ventures calls such promising areas "white spaces." To fill in the gap, he meets with myriads of startups in that "white space" area until he discovers the one that perfectly fits "the table." Gandhi and Singer both had developed what we call the "prepared mind."

The prepared mind of successful VCs is most at work when they strike out ideas one after another or "serendipitously" decide to inspect the most promising ones more deeply. VCs rely on their pattern recognition skills, developed through numerous meetings with entrepreneurs and hundreds of hours spent flipping through pitch decks and industry studies and connecting the dots in the vague universe of startup facts and outcomes. This is their method of frontloading. As a result, when the time comes to make a call, VCs are soundly equipped and can reach a decision in minutes. It may seem, even to them, like a gut decision, but it has been foreshadowed over a long period of tireless effort.

Such preparedness helped Sequoia secure one of the best venture deals of all time. Its total stake in Airbnb reached $12 billion by the time Airbnb went public. Airbnb's exponential growth might not have been possible without Greg McAdoo, an investor with Sequoia, who led a seed round of $600,000 in the fledgling startup. David Rosenthal, an angel investor, notes that Greg "had looked at HomeAway, Vrbo, and the vacation rental space before. He's like, 'No, I think these guys [Airbnb] are doing something different.'" According to Paul Graham, a peer investor,

Greg "may have been the only VC anywhere who understood Airbnb's promise." And then Graham adds, "He'd spent much of the previous year studying related businesses." This is the prepared mind in action.

Of course, venture investors are not the only ones who benefit from prepared minds. The history of science is replete with prepared minds. One of many remarkable examples we can cite is Alexander Fleming's miraculous discovery of penicillin. Fleming left the plates teeming with bacteria on his bench when he left on summer holiday. Upon returning, he saw that certain plates—the ones that had been contaminated by a mold—were clear of bacteria. In the usual retelling, the rest is history. In reality, years earlier Fleming had discovered, only after tireless experimenting, a naturally occurring antiseptic substance called lysozyme. He published many papers on the topic, which were met with indifference by his colleagues. Undaunted, Fleming prepared thousands of samples to observe the minute changes in bacteria colonies. When serendipity intervened, Fleming was prepared for it. He later commented that if it weren't for his previous experience, he might have thrown the plate away, as many bacteriologists had likely done before. He also suggested that some bacteriologists might have observed similar occurrences. However, due to a lack of interest in naturally occurring antibacterial substances, those cultures were likely discarded. Whereas many scientists had likely noticed but ignored what Fleming had seen, his mind was prepared. Sound like the Venture Mindset?

Scientific discoveries and startup investing have deep similarities: for both, decision making takes place in circumstances of high uncertainty. Even if researchers call such breakthroughs "accidents," they are not. X-rays, microwaves, and pacemakers are all the results of seemingly magical coincidences that would have been highly unlikely without months and years of hard work. Louis Pasteur, a giant of nineteenth-century science, summarized the prepared mind of scientists when he said during an

1854 lecture at the University of Lille, "In the fields of observation, chance favors only the prepared mind."

Just as the prepared mind can give birth to a scientific breakthrough, equally often a commercial vein unlocks its potential. In 1979, shortly before Apple's successful IPO, Steve Jobs and a bunch of his engineers visited PARC, the division of Xerox Corporation that we met earlier. To negotiate the visit, Jobs made this offer: "I will let you invest a million dollars in Apple if you will open the kimono at PARC." Xerox accepted. Its executives agreed to show Apple its new technology. In return, Xerox was able to buy 100,000 of Apple's shares at about $10 each.

There are multiple versions of what exactly happened in the lab that day, with some claiming that many future products (which later made Apple such a successful company) originated in or at least were inspired by what Apple's engineers observed in the PARC lab. Jobs and his team were glued to different devices under development in the lab, from laser printers to the commercial version of a mouse, and they were blown away by many pieces of software. Jobs himself immediately recognized the potential of many inventions, jumping around and shouting, "This is the greatest thing! This is revolutionary!" As he later said, "It was one of those sorts of apocalyptic moments. I remember thinking within ten minutes . . . that every computer would work this way some day." And then he added:

"It was so obvious once you saw it."

But it was obvious to Jobs only after years of preparing his mind by building his own personal computer business, thinking through scenarios of how computers might work in the future and discussing his conjectures with colleagues. With that background, it took Jobs just ten minutes—less time than we spend putting together a to-do list for the day—to recognize the revolutionary potential of PARC's inventions.

But why Jobs and not PARC? Why wasn't it PARC's owner, Xerox, that hit the trillion-dollar valuation mark with this gold mine located in its lab? Although PARC's employees were surely highly knowledgeable and sophisticated, they did not have prepared minds tuned to the same wave. Worse yet, all the senior executives of Xerox were beset with engineering ignorance, according to the fascinating book *Fumbling the Future* by Douglas Smith and Robert Alexander, provocatively subtitled *How Xerox Invented, Then Ignored, the First Personal Computer*. Xerox was an established, highly profitable company with most of its revenue coming from printers and copy machines. According to one senior executive, while Xerox was spending hundreds of millions of dollars a year on research, development, and engineering, there was no one in top management who could explain to the engineers that such-and-such product should cost less or should work faster.

Most observers believe Xerox executives failed to see the light because they had no computer skills, because Xerox's main business line was not computers. Yet Elon Musk lacked space skills or auto manufacturing skills and look what he has done with SpaceX and Tesla. Xerox's main problem was that its executives didn't have the Venture Mindset. They had no interest whatsoever in what was going on at PARC. Although PARC generated lots of breakthrough inventions, none was "life and death" for the survival of Xerox.

Consider the computer mouse. PARC's version cost more than $350 to make, had three buttons, and due to a design flaw didn't roll smoothly. PARC's engineers and their bosses at Xerox weren't on the lookout for an opportunity to commercialize their inventions. Jobs, on the other hand, immediately commissioned a design team to come up with a $15 single-button mouse. And yes, he wanted it to move smoothly on any surface—even on "my blue jeans," as he specifically insisted. Jobs could see in a split second the promising signal amid the white noise. As a result, he was able to turn a small spark into a big innovation, thanks to his prepared mind.

You know it when you see it, they say. Or maybe it should be: you know it because you've seen it before.

It might at first appear that VCs and others equipped with the Venture Mindset make decisions too quickly, too spontaneously. But this precipitous speed is driven by a well-prepared brain that is tuned to recognize patterns and positioned to quickly identify critical flaws and unexpected twists. Without careful study of the sector, investors like Gandhi or McAdoo wouldn't have recognized future champions like Dropbox and Airbnb. Jobs could "see" and "feel" the connections others missed because he had spent countless days and nights thinking about these issues. Marc Andreessen, a cofounder of both Netscape and of the well-known VC firm Andreessen Horowitz (a16z), once told Stanford students regarding startup selection, "This has been a surprise: after you have been in it for a while, the thing that's actually fairly easy to tell is, Will this team and company be fundable by a top VC." It is easy for Andreessen to spot these companies due to the prepared mind he's cultivated through many years of investing.

So how do you train your mind? Well, we know what does *not* work. The common statement that you need 10,000 hours of practice to become an expert may not help you much when operating in a world of unknown unknowns. In fact, it might confine you to a cage where you know too much about too little. To recognize patterns, what you need is not necessarily 10,000 hours, but a 10,000-foot view. To get that view, let's take off into the sky and learn not from birds, but from a former pilot who became a VC.

3.4
Expertise Is a Fuel to Take Off

When new ideas knock, traditional companies use numerous traditional tools to evaluate them. Analysts collect information about the market, competitors, and customers. The finance department builds detailed models. Supply chain experts assess the reliability of the procurement model. We call this "analysis paralysis." It not only causes delays but also prevents companies from reviewing other ideas. Some ideas just fly off the shelves. A nimble startup may launch a social media campaign faster than you can put together your analytical report convincing your bosses that TikTok is a promising channel to explore.

But moving faster doesn't mean moving blindly and without direction. To leave the competition behind, the Venture Mindset relies on these three core mechanisms.

Do your spadework outside the four walls

"Don't come all the way here just to see me," said then Facebook CFO Gideon Yu to Yuri Milner. His message: Facebook had a standing line of eager investors and Milner was one too many. But a few months later, Milner's DST fund, an unknown quantity in Silicon Valley at the time, landed a Facebook deal with a more receptive audience: Mark Zuckerberg. Milner attributes his success to preparedness and expertise. In the mid-2000s, he became a strong believer in the social media space and started to hunt for winners around the globe. His goal was to meet with entrepreneurs and pick the team with the potential to execute the best solution. What made Milner different from a long list of other investors was his large, diligently constructed spreadsheet providing data on social networks all around the world, including emerging countries such as India and smaller countries such as Hungary. This approach prepared Milner well for many other deals, such as Flipkart and Ola. He describes this strategy as "tap into sources, build relationships, and prepare spreadsheets." Tap, build, and prepare.

Not surprisingly, in 2008 Facebook started to blip on DST's investment radar. Milner immediately crossed the Atlantic to meet with Mark Zuckerberg and his leadership team. Because Facebook was a white-hot startup surrounded by crowds of eager investors, his chances were slim. Milner knew that simply bringing capital was not enough, but he also brought with him his expertise and his insights into social media. One of these he later dubbed "Zuckerberg's law" (similar to the famous Moore's law): every twelve to eighteen months, the amount of information being shared between people on the web doubles. Zuckerberg later said of DST, "These guys really have a unique profile. They have a lot of experience that they can bring."

"I spend lots of time to come prepared to such meetings," Milner stated. That preparedness turned DST's $200 million investment into an eventual $4 billion gain. Definitely worth a transatlantic flight.

Buckle up your industry expertise before you fly

If you ever have a chance to fly with JetBlue Airways, pay attention to the screen right in front of you, full of entertainment and live TV. You can enjoy popular shows, stock market updates, and breaking news while cruising at 30,000 feet. It may be hard to believe, but before April 2000 the luxury of live TV was available only to owners of private jets. JetBlue was the first commercial airline to introduce flat-screen monitors in every seatback and to give its customers live access to DirecTV channels at no additional cost.

Although JetBlue has always been an innovator that introduced various tech features into its business, a disruptive change in its approach started in 2016, when the company founded JetBlue Technology Ventures (JTV), one of the first corporate venture funds in the airline industry. JTV was founded and led by Bonny Simi, a former student of Ilya at Stanford. Even by the standards of Stanford graduates, Simi's career was extraordinary: airline pilot, three-time Olympic athlete, TV reporter, and finally venture capitalist! What could be next? Flying taxis, making *The Jetsons* a cartoon-come-to-life reality?

One challenge that JetBlue faced was its small scale for an airline. Possessing only 5 percent of US market share behind American, Delta, and United, it could hardly hope to have a long-term impact without asymmetric thinking and numerous bets that could disrupt and instantaneously get ahead of the competition. Simi's bosses realized that the airline needed to leverage the creativity of outsiders, and Simi was put in charge of JetBlue's venture efforts.

Simi understood that, to succeed, you need a prepared mind and VC thinking. She already possessed tons of insights about the airline industry; now she dove into studying the VC ecosystem and examples of corporate successes and failures in disruptive innovation. In just a couple years, she and her team reviewed and analyzed virtually all travel-related startups, along with conducting data analysis of billions of itineraries and travel searches. Bonny Simi stormed the hall of fame of the VC industry by building JTV's reputation and leveraging its deep expertise. Every startup in the field of air transportation dreamed of being associated with JTV.

Simi and her team were extremely picky, and there is a reason for that. They knew the industry and its needs very well, since their minds are prepared to spot all possible flaws immediately. One idea they encountered was intended to help pilots plan their fuel consumption better before a flight. But Simi immediately realized that this is not the pain point commercial airlines face. In another case, Simi bumped into a startup called Lumo that built a solution to predict, track, and manage flight delays for travelers and businesses alike. Simi's reaction was "absolutely, that's one we want to do," while others were lukewarm. Simi's prepared mind quickly noticed Lumo's ability to predict air traffic. You need to be prepared before you fly.

Pick your battleground

Many VC firms even call their approach "Prepared Mind," such as Accel Partners (another early backer of Facebook). Partners constantly think about what comes next and then search for companies that fit the thesis. Such preparedness helps Accel to back teams and ideas at very early stages.

In 2005, Google's search dominance was a fait accompli, but for every Goliath there's a David. Theresia Gouw, a leading Silicon Valley VC, told us the fascinating story of how she found one. Scientists use research labs to train their minds. Minds of venture investors are sharpened in meetings. They gather with startups, experts, and academics—anyone in the field they are interested in. For Gouw, who was then a partner at Accel, one such expert was Philip Nelson, then an entrepreneur-in-residence at Accel and a world-known guru on search engines. From discussions with Nelson, Gouw realized that Google's Achilles' heel was a "parameterized" search. Indeed, if a user wants to learn about top attractions in Boston, a few clicks will produce a list of options. But if you search for travel options, say, from Atlanta to Boston, Google's search engine was unhelpful. Details like specific dates, time of day, and preferred airline were too detailed for a small search query. Google was simply not designed for such search requests. The same held true for job searching, real estate, and many other verticals. Gouw smiled at us as she recalled the moment of her triumphal revelation. The opportunity she seized upon: vertical niche need-specific search. This was the thesis.

Armed with her thesis, Gouw went to work. She selected the real estate search vertical. Leads came from all over the place and some she . . . googled herself. She met with dozens of companies, and the more she learned, the more she recognized what it would take to win. When she met the founders of online real estate marketplace Trulia, she was prepared. When Trulia went public some years later, it was Gouw's thesis-driven prepared mind that contributed to that success. Accel eventually made multiple vertical search investments, including in Kosmix (a vertical search solution for shopping) and Kayak (an online travel platform).

The corporate mindset can benefit from these principles. There are hundreds and thousands of ideas to evaluate and make a decision about. Boiling the ocean is not the optimal strategy; staying focused is one way to prepare your mind.

Concentrating one's effort in a specific domain, while making sure to stay outside the cage and move beyond the four walls, is an efficient way to evaluate thousands of ideas. It could have been an unbearable task for any of these VCs to filter out a couple dozen companies among 3,000 candidates. In the pursuit of innovative ideas, you need to be fast in separating gems from stones. Being fast also holds true outside the VC world. But what counts as fast?

3.5
When Every Second Counts

Let's return for a moment to the Stanford class where entrepreneurs pitch to student VCs-in-training. What often separates success from failure is twenty minutes of the pitch. This amount of time is quite similar to what a lucky entrepreneur would have in front of real VCs. Why do we say lucky? Because most entrepreneurs would not even be invited, and their queries may end up in the trash folder of the recipient's mailbox. But of course we know that these entrepreneurs are prepared, not just lucky.

Earlier, we shared the results of our experiment in which we sent fictitious cold emails to startup investors. Some emails clearly resonated better than others, with the positive response rate varying from under 2 percent to over 15 percent. Quite an amazing difference, which could be partially attributed to the carefully picked keywords that hit the right string.

Pitching to VCs may be tough, but compare that challenge to the position of screenwriters. Each year, somewhere between 50,000 and 1 million scripts vie for a very limited number of Hollywood slots. Quite a competitive space, isn't it? However, the "script funnel" is just like the funnel for entrepreneurs' pitches. Once you pass the critical flaw stage, your script pitch lasts about fifteen to twenty minutes. Thanks to research conducted by Kimberly Elsbach of UC Davis and Roderick Kramer of Stanford, we know what happens in the minds of decision makers. Elsbach and Kramer not only conducted interviews but also videotaped pitches to producers, which included the interactions between a writer and a studio executive. It turned out that producers often make a decision in a matter of minutes, or even seconds. (Another study found a typical decision time of 45 seconds.)

If you think fifteen minutes is too short to make a life-critical decision, then don't look any further than choosing a romantic companion. When *Time Out* magazine asked 11,000 people in cities all over the world how long it takes them to decide whether there is any reason for a second date, almost half of respondents insisted that they need no more than two or three minutes. Probably just enough time to order cappuccino, but maybe not enough time to finish it!

Fashion can certainly compete with Hollywood in speed. Catwalk shows are glitzy events at which fashion houses display their new collections. A producer selects just a few models from thousands who apply for the opportunity. When researchers asked producers how long it takes them to decide on a model at a casting, they were surprised by how quickly producers professed to do this. One producer even told them, "An instant! You know, you know, you know!" What guides them? Their prepared mind! Producers spend countless hours browsing fashion magazines and periodicals to develop a skill they call a "good eye." Producers also network actively with others in the fashion industry to gain valuable information on model selection and criteria. This is exactly what VCs do in the pursuit of startups before putting them on the investors' podium.

Do Hollywood or fashion producers hold the speed record? Nope. Thanks to a complex eye-tracking study, we have learned that job recruiters spend on average 7.4 seconds (!) to make an initial "fit/no fit" decision as they scan an applicant's resume and search for certain keywords in a type of pattern-matching activity. Like VCs, recruiters search for a limited amount of information to match candidates with the desired role or reject them straightaway. They start by reviewing main data points: name, education, current and previous title or company, and the starting and ending dates of current and previous jobs. Then they scan through keywords. This is it. Are seven seconds enough to hire a good employee? Not at all, but the goal is to exclude unpromising candidates so that they can more carefully review a smaller subset of candidates later. The next time you prepare your resume or apply for a job, put yourself in the shoes of a recruiter who will decide on your future by screening your CV in seven seconds.

We want to end this chapter with a note of caution. Being prepared does not mean to rely on mental shortcuts or to ignore facts. Skip the hard work and endless hours of preparation, and you immediately demonstrate prejudice and become biased. But even prepared minds can be biased, so be careful. Be wary of ignoring unusual startups, dismissing people who don't fit the pattern, and overlooking uncommon ideas. Biases may spread like a hard-to-eradicate virus. Race, gender, or background can skew one's way of thinking. Don't confuse the prepared mind with shooting from the hip. Sometimes you do have to slow down to make the right call.

MINDSET CHECKS

○ Do you regularly interact directly with entrepreneurs, executives, and experts to deepen your insights on developments in your industry?

○ Do entrepreneurs and other companies come to you with their ideas to get access to your expertise and network?

○ Have you defined areas, topics, and white spaces for your organization to focus on or skip altogether?

FOUR

Say No 100 Times

*Why you need to be selective,
but not in the way you may think*

4.1
How to Break a Lance . . . and Piggy Banks

"Break it, professor! Let's count them!"

You are one of thirty participants gathered around a piggy bank. Before the meeting, we have filled the piggy bank to the brim with pennies, so full that we can't force even a single additional coin inside. We play this game regularly in our corporate workshops, and ask the participants a simple question: How much money is in the piggy bank? Try to guess yourself (see Figure 5).

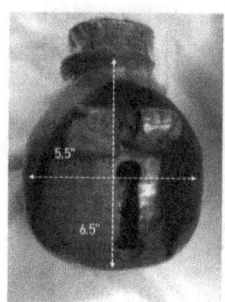

Figure 5.
That piggy bank "stuffed" with pennies. Each penny is 0.75" in diameter.

We give the group a few minutes and watch their fascinating strategies unfold. Some stare into the piggy bank. Some hold it in their hands, trying to guess the weight, and then go online to look up the weight of a penny. Some take photos of the piggy bank. Others open a calculator app on their phones.

Now it's time for a Piggy Bank Auction! Here are the rules. Each participant makes a bid indicating the price at which they are willing to buy all the coins inside the piggy. Everyone writes their bid on a sheet of paper, but only the highest bid wins.

Suppose the piggy contains 3,000 pennies, or $30, and you bid $20. If someone else bids more than $20, you do not win. Now, imagine you bid $20 and every other participant in the room bids *less* than $20. In this case, you win the auction. You pay us $20, and we pay you $30. You will pocket the difference and gain $10. However, what if you bid $40 and every other bid in the room is *less* than your bid of $40? Then you "win" the auction, but you have just become poorer by $10: you still get $30 from us, but now you owe us the $40 that you bid. You can win and yet lose at the same time in this game.

After everyone has written down a bid, the real fun begins. We ask everyone to hold their sheets in the air. The energy in the room becomes tense as thirty people lift their hands high above their heads, waving their bids. Then we ask only those with bids of $1 or more to keep their hands up. Then only those above $5. Then $10 ... $50 ... $100. As hands start coming down, people look around in astonishment. Some people's estimates were far lower than those of the people who still have their hands up. Finally, a gentleman in a dark blue shirt and silver-rimmed glasses is the last one holding a bid sheet up, with "125" scribbled in large handwriting. He is the winner, and everybody applauds. But is he? The piggy bank contains $12.74. In fact, the gentleman in silver-rimmed glasses is off by precisely $112.26!

This man won, yet in winning he lost.

Between the two of us, we have played the Piggy Bank Auction game hundreds of times. We have never lost money in the game. Not a single time. There is always someone in a group of twenty or thirty students—or senior executives—who bids more than what's inside the piggy bank. Only by submitting a bid above everybody else's can you become a winner, but your victory dance doesn't last long.

What you have just witnessed is a well-studied and powerful phenomenon known as the "winner's curse." The uncertainty plays an important role here. Every participant must guess the amount of money inside. Similar to evaluating innovative ideas, these guesstimates are all based on assumptions; they are all imperfect. Valuation, after all, is not a trivial exercise! Some guesses are well below the true value, while others are well above. Will the virtual reality idea become a hit like the internet or a flop like Clubhouse? No one knows yet. The same goes for the piggy bank contents. At the end, the game is all about the *maximum* estimate and the *maximum* bid (see Figure 6).

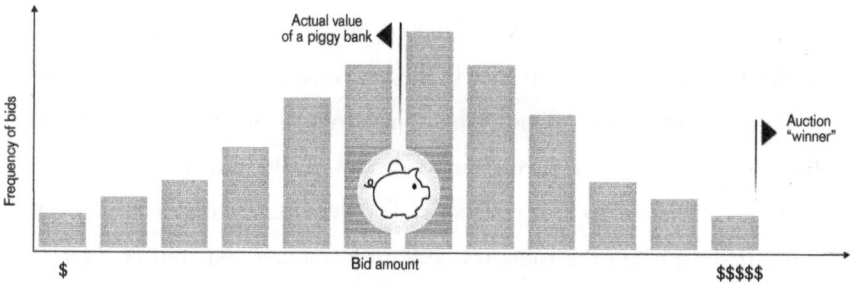

Figure 6.
Illustrative example of possible outcomes in a piggy bank auction

The winner's curse is everywhere around us, unseen but keenly felt. It helps to explain the failure of so many mergers and acquisitions (M&A) deals, for example. It also plays a prominent role in the VC world. In the

VC context, it is closely related to and reinforced by FOMO: fear of missing out. When investors consider making an investment offer to a startup, they are often concerned about being outbid by their more generous competitors. Should they raise their bid in the hope of owning a bite of the next Amazon or Microsoft, because if they don't they might miss this investment forever? Startups are like piggy banks, except that their true value won't be known for a long time. VCs try to estimate their potential value, and if they are worried about losing an opportunity, they may up the ante too high.

Of course, the more anxious an investor is, the more likely they are to overestimate the potential startup's worth. The higher the uncertainty and the hotter the overall VC market, the more intense FOMO becomes, making the winner's curse even larger. Many high-profile VC investments that ended in tears are the result of succumbing to FOMO. Consider the sudden rise and even more precipitous fall of the crypto exchange FTX in 2022, or the earlier rise and fall of another investor darling, WeWork. Or think of Ofo, a bicycle-sharing company from China. At its peak, it raised more than $2 billion from investors, only to promptly burst like an overinflated tire, leaving bikes dumped on streets as trash in its wake. FOMO is a common occurrence in the VC world.

In the Piggy Bank Auction game, the winner's curse gets worse when there are more bidders. If you win in a room of 100 bidders, chances are that you are about to lose your shirt. The winner's curse is also much more painful when the time available to formulate your bid is severely compressed. If we gave our participants half an hour to do more thoughtful calculations, no one would bid $125 for a piggy bank containing $12.74 in pennies.

In a competitive situation under severe time pressure, emotions run hot. Psychologically, we tend to associate winning the bidding battle with winning the actual war. We are afraid of missing the idea of a lifetime, so we rush to invest in anything that looks like the one. However, in any piggy bank–like situation, the best reaction is to step back and assess all available information, recognizing that, more often than not, rejecting the deal altogether is the best course of action.

If you think that the winner's curse and FOMO portend danger only for venture investors, think back to the last time your annual budget was debated and arguments like "now or never" were brought up. Or recall when you wanted to hire a specialist with multiple competitive offers and your HR staff suggested sweetening the deal. Or when a potential acquisition deal was on the table and the board and top brass stretched certain assumptions to increase the valuation. In all these situations, reluctance to step back and, if needed, reject the opportunity may cost you dearly.

Psychologically, we all want to close the deal, even at the risk of overpaying for a piggy bank full of coins. Realizing the prevalence of the winner's curse in our lives is a step in the right direction. It is particularly prevalent in the world of disruptive innovation, as great ideas come only once in a blue moon. VCs have developed rules of thumb and processes to keep the winner's curse in check. They are very disciplined about saying no far more often than you may think.

4.2
Saying No Is in Their Blood

How could someone reject an opportunity to invest in a $10 billion company and still win big?

Bill Maris of Google Ventures (GV), a VC arm of Google, holds a degree in neuroscience. He worked as a researcher at Duke University's neurobiology center before becoming a biotechnology investor and a startup engineer and founder. After joining Google early on and founding GV in 2009, he saw the potential of healthcare startups, including 23andMe (of DNA testing fame) and the cancer-centric Flatiron Health and Foundation Medicine, to name just a few. The last two were acquired by Roche for around $2 billion each, bringing a solid return to Google Ventures and a great reputation to Maris.

In 2013, another opportunity landed on Maris's desk. A healthcare technology startup claimed it could disrupt the traditional medical testing lab industry in the same way that the iPhone disrupted mobile phones. Recall the last time your doctor sent you to a lab to have blood drawn. Remember all those tubes collecting blood? Now imagine having no need for a doctor or clunky medical equipment. Instead, a single minuscule drop of your blood finds its way into a palm-held device. You then select options on a user-friendly app to run a specific blood test.

Theranos, now a defunct company, had been founded by a Stanford dropout ten years earlier. By 2013, Theranos boasted an impressive list of large-scale partners such as Safeway and Walgreens. Logos of big pharma names were prominently featured in the company investor pitch deck. Momentum ran high, with many talking up the next trillion-dollar opportunity. Indeed, the company checked off many boxes that a typical venture investor would require. However, one red flag caught Maris's eye. Theranos's board of directors featured remarkable celebrities: Henry Kissinger and George Shultz, both of whom had been US secretaries of state; General James Mattis, a celebrated US military commander; Richard Kovacevich, a former CEO of the Wells Fargo bank. An impressive list by all accounts. But oddly enough for a life sciences company, the board didn't have a single healthcare expert. And even though Theranos had already raised substantial funding, none of the investors were from reputable biotech VC firms and not a single investor was on the board. All this ran contrary to Maris's VC mindset.

His next step was to test Theranos's product, which at the time promised to run lots of simultaneous tests from a single drop of blood, even though the equipment was not yet small enough to get into your palm. It still sounded like a miracle. Maris sent a mystery shopper, a member of his life science investment team, to Walgreens to take the blood test. The result was not encouraging. When Maris's employee visited the drugstore, he was asked to go through the full venous blood draw instead of an expected single drop. After he refused, he was asked to come back a week later to give more blood.

Maris's concern was magnified by the secretiveness of Theranos's leadership, who evaded answering scientific questions and were unwilling to disclose details of their revolutionary technology. "It wasn't that difficult for anyone to determine that things may not be what they seem here," Maris recalled later. He no doubt feels happy about passing up the chance to invest in Theranos, which federal prosecutor Robert Leach described years later as "one of the most egregious white-collar crimes ever committed in Silicon Valley." In 2022, Theranos founder Elizabeth Holmes was convicted on four counts of criminal fraud and sentenced to eleven years in prison.

Was GV alone in declining the seemingly lucrative Theranos deal? No.

Years earlier, in 2006, another healthcare investor, Bijan Salehizadeh of Highland Capital Partners, also turned down a Theranos investment opportunity. As he was drilling down and trying to understand the technology, he felt that Holmes was unwilling or unable to answer most of his questions. A similar result unfolded when Holmes met with MedVenture Associates, a specialized VC firm that invested in med tech devices over multiple decades.

And David Singer, a partner at Maverick Ventures, confided to us that when he saw a slide deck for one of the earliest rounds of Theranos, he quickly concluded that "if they wanted to invade Europe it was the right group of people, but I didn't see any expertise at the company in building a sophisticated healthcare business." Amazingly, contrary to what many people might think, Theranos ended up having almost no VCs invest in them. What is common among the VC investors who looked into Theranos only to turn it down? Why didn't they succumb to FOMO? Theranos passed the preliminary "critical flaw" evaluation of many VCs, leading them to dive deeper into learning more. Wouldn't you?! If the one-blood-drop innovation was for real, it would be a great opportunity. But a questioning VC mindset led investors to scrutinize the idea and seek to understand all the nuts and bolts of the technology. As detailed due diligence brought up one red flag after another, their minds switched from opportunism to skepticism.

In chapter 3, we discussed carrying out a rapid initial assessment and training your mind to make fast decisions on cutting off projects *not* worth considering further. For the ones that pass the critical flaw stage, the VC mind switches gears. It is now time to pause, breathe in, and dive into details, lest the winner's curse and FOMO overwhelm you. This means identifying key assumptions; verifying them with experts, customers, and partners; making reference calls on the management team; and trying the product out, even if it means sending a mystery shopper. This is due diligence, VC style.

The famed Marc Andreessen surprised many Stanford students when he described his VC firm a16z's business to them in this way: "Our day job is crushing entrepreneurs' hopes and dreams. We have focused very, very hard on being very good at saying no." The Venture Mindset makes decisions to reject most ideas *quickly*, but for those it considers further, it does its best to inspect them *slowly*. Slow decision making, after the fast initial review, can become your lifeline.

How many deals do venture investors feel comfortable rejecting in their search for a long shot? How often do VCs say *no* on their way to a single *yes*?

Thanks to the research of Ilya and his colleagues, we know the answer to this question. For every one investment, early-stage VCs on average consider 101 deals. And this number is not the ceiling. Early-stage Silicon Valley VCs specializing in the IT space consider roughly 150 deals to make just one investment.

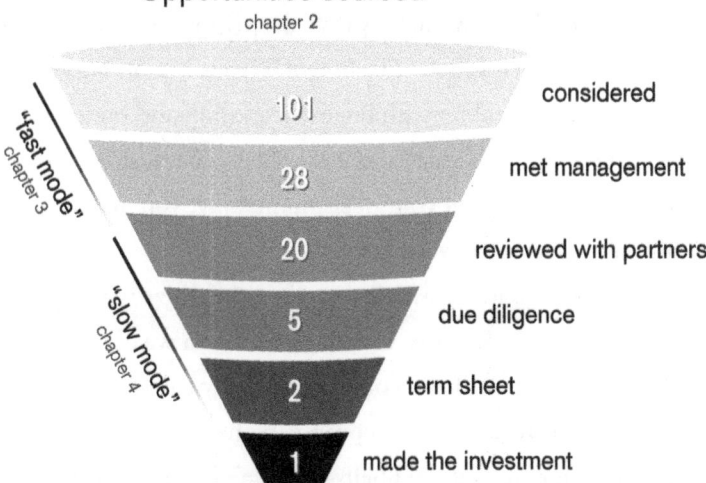

Figure 7.
Potential investments reaching each stage per closed deal

Figure 7 shows what we call the VC "deal funnel." We have already met the upper part. VCs have to source as many opportunities as they can so that the funnel is wide at entry. But the wider the funnel, the more challenging it is to consider each opportunity in detail. That's why VCs use the critical flaw approach. Out of 100 opportunities, VCs reject up to 90 after just briefly learning about the startup, reviewing the pitch, or meeting once with the team. A coffee chat with the management might take an hour, and many opportunities don't even reach this stage. Only about 10 of every 100 are seriously discussed among the VC firm's partners. These remaining opportunities are submitted to a careful, relatively slow due diligence process, as opposed to the fast critical flaw approach at the top of the funnel. It all culminates in only one investment. A hundred to one! All the rest don't make the final cut.

Look at these numbers another way. VCs start by rejecting nine deals out of ten quickly. Then, when they dive deeper into the remaining ones, they again expect to eliminate nine of ten! This is brutal, but this is how early-stage investors dealing with huge uncertainty and optimizing their sourcing make their business model work. If you are dealing with a high-uncertainty environment in your decision making, you may want to add this deal funnel strategy to your arsenal.

With this information in mind, you can sympathize with Ilya's friend Andreas, who is from Europe. Knowing that Ilya was an expert in all things Silicon Valley, Andreas complained to Ilya about startup investing. Andreas recently invested in a promising healthcare startup and lost quite a bit of money when it went belly-up. Ilya's first response was that in Silicon Valley startups fail all the time, even those that looked very promising and raised investors' adrenaline early on. Then Ilya asked Andreas how many startups he had looked at before betting his money on this one. Well, Andreas responded indignantly, he had met these guys and liked them, and the idea seemed promising, so he invested. In other words, his investment deal funnel was one out of one. That is certainly tempting your luck!

We've seen many commit the same error, especially outside Silicon Valley. Had Ilya's friend looked at dozens of similar startups and met dozens of founders in a relevant space, he might have found a more promising opportunity. For investors in disruptive businesses, not reviewing plenty of proposals before making a selection is like buying a lottery ticket: if you bet a small amount of money, the chances are against you; and if you bet your fortune, they are a death knell.

In a corporate setting, these mistakes are even more widespread. Our advice is simple: to avoid lemons, evaluate more cars. Expand your idea funnel and become disciplined about how you go through it, using different criteria at each stage. Of course, this advice is simple to formulate and difficult to implement. It is devilishly hard work.

4.3
Risk-Reduction Engineers

It takes just a few minutes to find and buy most items online. Netflix users spend less than twenty minutes to select a movie. It takes three to six hours to buy a car, from the time you walk into the dealership to the moment you drive away. But on average, the VC due diligence process takes a staggering 118 hours per investment. When MBA students, founders, and corporate executives hear this number, their immediate reaction is pure shock. Their shock deepens when they realize that these 118 hours are only for each investment that VCs ultimately approve. Add in the time spent on deals that never get completed, and investors likely spend well over 250 hours analyzing potential investments.

Ilya's colleague Brian Jacobs estimated that at Emergence Capital (the VC firm Brian cofounded) they spend 400 hours on due diligence for each new investment. These 400 hours include twenty minutes for each opportunity they decide to reject.

To make a decision, these hundreds of hours are condensed into a single, concise document called the "investment memorandum," or simply "the memo." The investment memo explains the logic of the investment in a well-structured way. It helps to position the deal within the context of other opportunities and portfolio companies. Most important, it collects answers to key questions, highlights risks, suggests any further due diligence items, and emphasizes what likely will remain unknown until the investment is made, regardless of the amount of effort expended. The key lesson you can draw from the memo's purpose for the Venture Mindset is this:

Don't hide risks. Bring them to light early on.

Investment memos are tools, not goalposts. They are concise. They weigh pros and cons, benefits and costs of the decision. They pressure-test the ideas. They identify major risks, assumptions, and unknowns.

They position the forthcoming debate in a balanced manner rather than stifling it. They are witnesses, not eager advocates. They are written with all the decision makers in mind and designed to be read before the group convenes. They are a starting point to spark debate. They often lead to a "no" decision. When was the last time you wrote or read such a memo?

Consider, for example, the investment memo written by Bessemer partner Jeremy Levine in December 2006, describing a proposed investment in LinkedIn, back then a new and fast-growing professional social network. The first feature that stands out is the memo's conciseness, at just eight pages. After discussing facts such as the management team and the market, Levine identifies major risks of the investment and paints various scenarios, from a complete disaster (in which everything falls apart) to a super-bright scenario (in which LinkedIn becomes a dominant global business social network). The purpose is clearly to inform and stir discussion among the partners. The memo is impressive in its honest and detail-specific assessment of an opportunity; certainly, it is not an attempt to convince the reader to rubberstamp the idea. The purpose is to identify weak spots early on and stimulate a frank discussion within the entire partnership.

You can judge for yourself how markedly different this setup is from the traditional corporate exercise, where the business case is presented to defend the idea rather than to challenge it and provoke further discussion. Sadly, to get a corporate project approved, the sponsors have to pretend to be extremely optimistic. And though everyone in the room knows that this optimism may be unfounded, championing optimism proliferates.

VCs are often described as big risk takers, so our audiences are frequently surprised to learn that VCs call themselves "risk-reduction engineers." VCs are disciplined about understanding risks and defining ways to reduce them—the very essence of due diligence. From the first meeting with the founders, VCs dive under the hood to assess the management team, business model, product, competition, and the startup's capital needs. However, they don't stop there. They call customers, suppliers, former investors, founders' ex-bosses, colleagues, classmates, and professors. VCs often work from a prepared document with a standard set of questions (e.g., about the total market for the product or the potential competitors), intermingled with startup-specific inquiries. For instance, what are the regulatory risks related to the new thin film layer that a startup's founders claim will extend the preservation of fresh oysters and other perishable produce for weeks? How does the management team plan to address these risks? To use the Venture Mindset, you have to wear a risk-reduction engineer hat.

Others outside the VC world have seen the benefit of preparing VC mindset memos. Amazon understood the benefits of such a structured approach to innovative ideas and introduced a similar practice in its daily decision-making process. The "PR FAQ" (i.e., Press Release and Frequently Asked Questions) is a six-page document that, in its structured design and intent, mimics VC investment memos. Alex wrote many such memos during his career at Amazon and reviewed even more. The first page is a fake press release, as if the proposed product has just been released publicly. It has all the attributes of a real press release: publication date (which indicates the envisioned launch date), a comment from a happy customer detailing specific lovable features, and another from the vice president in charge. In a single page, it presents a customer-facing portrait of the whole idea and gives the reasons for the team's excitement. The press release focuses on customers rather than on financial metrics or corporate benefits.

Whereas the press release is designed to be entertaining, the five FAQ pages address important, tricky, or even hotly debated issues surrounding the product. How will it make customers' lives significantly better? Why does this problem need to be solved right now? How will you measure success? What is the most contentious aspect of your product? What are the major risks and how does the team plan to address them? How big will the market be? How much time and capital will it take to build your product?

Memos are so powerful that we often ask teams in our corporate workshops to write memos on ideas for their own organizations. Like VC investment memos, they should identify not only advantages but also risks and concerns, while openly discussing the most critical assumptions and scenarios. This approach helps participants to identify previously unnoticed risks or flaws early on, before they commit months of work and millions of dollars.

Investment memos serve another often underappreciated purpose: they facilitate retrospective analysis. If the investment goes sour, scrutinizing the memo helps to find the potential reasons and missed flags, thereby uncovering patterns and improving future decisions. Similarly, if a rejected opportunity becomes a super success story, investors will pore over all the memo's details to identify why they missed their golden chance. A well-documented record beats memory every time. It is too tempting to say "I knew this deal would never work out" after the fact, and without documentation our pliable memories would be obliged to believe the claim. Once writing memos and keeping record notes on discussion becomes a routine, set aside time to review your failed or missed opportunities: like many VCs, you will learn more from those than from your successes.

When we meet with decision makers from different organizations, they find the VCs' ability to think fast and slow fascinating. Beyond having two modes, it is also critically important to shift gears from one to another at just the right moment. You can't afford to use the same middling speed all the time rather than accelerating or slowing down. This two-speed approach enables the Venture Mindset to process an unbelievable amount of information and still stay laser-focused.

4.4
Don't Clutter Your Funnel

If you drive too slowly in California, you could have to pay a fine of $238 and get one point on your driving record. Being too slow and striving to avoid all risk in the business world could be far more costly than that.

Although VCs try to reduce risk, they don't expect to eliminate it. They de-risk risks; they don't avoid them. What they do avoid is the analysis paralysis mode. Their meetings are short and focused. The longest Bessemer memo is around fifteen pages. Amazon limits its PR FAQ documents to a maximum of six pages, with no exceptions. In the VC world, an investment proposal rarely hangs around for more than a few weeks, whereas in the corporate world projects may be mulled over for months or even years. Corporations clutter their funnels, just as unhealthy food clutters arteries. Bureaucracy and indecisiveness are fatal aspects of the anti-VC mindset.

Take IBM, which in 1993 created, with rousing fanfare, a 150-person operation called Fireworks Partners to mimic a traditional venture fund and invest in startups in the multimedia computing business. This was a bold move by an eighty-year-old gorilla to drive innovation in a promising new sector. A couple years later, though, Fireworks Partners quietly disappeared. As Professor Josh Lerner of Harvard found, some of this fund's initial proposed investments were still in the internal review process when IBM gave up on the Fireworks idea altogether.

A corporate decision maker with an innovative idea knows that it takes so much time and effort to get just one opportunity past the finish line, the thought of repeating this arduous journey 100 times may be too painful. So they give up.

Ilya and his Stanford research fellow Amanda Wang experienced this traditional mindset firsthand when they conducted a detailed study of more than 160 corporate VC arms of large companies around the globe.

Here is one typical comment from the head of a corporate VC division, the company's forward-looking innovation leader: "Maybe our parent company understands the norms of the venture space, but quite honestly, if something came to us completely fresh with a six-week deadline, unless it was so obvious that I could get all-hands-on-deck support, I wouldn't ruin our reputation by pretending we could do it. I'd say this is for someone else." That executive was luckier than most; he at least believed his bosses understood the norms of the venture space. More than 60 percent of the time, Ilya and Amanda found, they didn't. A company's best investment opportunities and new growth engines are often wasted in this way.

Sometimes one press release is enough to signal danger. When IBM released information about its Fireworks Partners division, one article hinted at its future challenges. It was a one-paragraph announcement titled "The Reason for All the Fireworks!" that contained only 129 words. Remarkably, this paragraph listed five different IBM executives in charge of overseeing the new unit. It is hard to believe that every tenth word was a name of yet another executive responsible for the effort. On top of that, the text suggested that there were "likely to be plenty more" fireworks involved because they were still sorting out responsibilities in the "unfamiliar pecking order." Amanda and Ilya's research found a dazzling collection of corporate executive functions in charge of companies' innovation units. Not surprisingly, this slows down decisions further. The well-known proverb springs to mind: too many cooks spoil the soup!

We also find that most corporate VC units have to weave their way through multiple approvals and can get stuck at many points along the way: the corporate VC investment team, its head, another corporate senior executive, the investment committee (in which certain members have the power of veto), headquarters, or by the prospect of getting sent back for another round of approvals. Contrast this to the VC world's practice of a straightforward memo discussion.

Traditional organizations have great intentions. Companies establish innovation labs, generate a long list of ideas, and work hard to bring innovators inside. But then ideas get stuck in the funnel. The legal department asks for yet another review. Finance insists on yet another scenario modeling. The marketing team worries that the new idea may dilute the brand and suggests hiring consultants to analyze the impact. The road to hell is paved with good intentions. What were supposed to be tools to build a safe harbor become a deadly swamp.

Bureaucracy is like mold spreading across an organization. To be successful in innovation, get rid of the clutter. Reduce the layers. If we see too many executives responsible for innovation in any organization, we are always alarmed. Too many cooks. Too many meetings. Too many approvals. Not enough innovation.

The traditional decision-making process is wired differently from the VC process. Since a typical decision maker doesn't have to deal with the VC-like level of uncertainty on a regular basis, there is no need to review hundreds of ideas, and the selection process is focused, predictable, and incremental. Organizational processes, even in innovation and R&D units, are designed for projects and ideas with a low risk profile. In a stable environment characterized by incremental innovation, reviewing many opportunities and deciding quickly is less useful. In fact, having too many choices might be counterproductive.

Suppose you are asked to conduct due diligence on 100 suggested ways to improve your company's flagship product, a power saw. All these carefully constructed proposals have landed on your desk as a result of an innovation competition. You study one for a couple hours and find that, if implemented, it will increase the churning speed by 10 percent. That sounds good enough. Should you stop there or consider the other 99 proposals? The best among these remaining 99 may result in a sleeker, slightly more efficient, and marginally cheaper power saw than the first one you considered. But even the best one would not be a revolutionary new tool that would overturn your business model and put your company well ahead of its competitors (or so you assume—of course, you can never be certain of this unless you go through all the proposals). In a world of small, incremental changes, it would make no sense to spend hundreds of hours seeking the very best idea for a power saw; instead, just picking the first good idea and asking your dedicated engineering unit to execute it feels more efficient and cost-effective. The downside is that being overly focused on smaller, incremental ideas and not investing in finding bigger ones may hasten the day when the only strategy left is to overturn the chessboard.

Consider the case of R. H. Donnelley (RHD), once a multibillion-dollar corporation. Even though most US households have never heard of RHD, not so long ago its product was present and heavily used in nearly all of them. Do you remember that thick book called the Yellow Pages, with a yellow cover to match? The Yellow Pages were a business telephone directory that helped people find a service they were seeking in their local community and enabled service providers to advertise themselves. The name was legendary among investors as well as customers. More than half a million advertisers paid $3,500 a year for space in the Yellow Pages. As recently as 2006, RHD proudly announced, in its investor presentation, a steady growth in the number of its US publications, from a couple hundred to more than 600 in just three years. The total circulation had reached a mind-blowing 80 million copies. Not surprisingly, the RHD CEO's presentation to investors in March 2006 was titled "Positioned for Continued Success."

Yellow Pages directories went through many small, incremental changes over the years. For example, new categories were added (such as "feng shui," "Botox," or "mold remediation"). Did it make sense for RHD to organize innovation competitions? Perhaps not, if the implementation and evaluation would be costly and time-consuming. In fact, in their 100-plus-page presentation to investors in 2006, innovation was barely mentioned.

One slide on "Product Innovation" contained such impressive-sounding new features as "White Pages Color" and "Small Spine Advertising." But rather than just creating long presentation decks full of tiny expansions to their product, RHD executives should have been looking outside to see the coming storm. In this way, they would have realized that by 2006 a completely new business model, powered by online searches, had already commenced its powerful rise and was about to eat their lunch. Had they acted like risk-reduction engineers inspired by the Venture Mindset, they would have addressed that risk first.

Just three years later, in May 2009, R. H. Donnelley went bankrupt. Hitting all the fastballs but missing the curveball is always the risk when the VC mindset is ignored. RHD decision makers were well versed in traditional, incremental changes, but they completely missed the wave of digital disruption that struck like a tsunami. Incremental and disruptive types of innovation require different approaches, and you need to have your eye on both. Don't clutter your deal funnel with too many small ideas and incremental innovation, with too many cooks, or with too many layers of bureaucracy. Cultivate a habit of focus whenever approaching innovation.

4.5
The Power of Saying No Again and Again

Being selective and systematically rejecting most of the opportunities that come your way is not a privilege limited to venture investors, but a skill that anyone can master. One key goal is to efficiently reject most opportunities before you proceed to approve any. You will benefit from having multiple people involved, ideally people with prepared minds. Disagreement is your best friend in this case. Setting up the right decision-making pace and establishing clear rules make the process more predictable and efficient. Remember that the ratio of winning ideas to all ideas should be around 1 to 100. Anything less selective may create errors that will catch up with you later and may prevent you from finding that precious gem.

The Pulitzer Prize, one of the most prestigious American honors for journalists and authors, offers a good case study in how to say no again and again effectively. Must-read books such as *To Kill a Mockingbird* and the lead reporters who exposed the historic Watergate scandal have been among the award recipients. The participating judges read 300 books each out of thousands of submissions, or "entrants" as the organizers call them. The judges can nominate just three to the board. (There is that ratio of 1 to 100 again!) One former judge pulled the curtain when she disclosed that "not all books are read by the judges, nor do all books necessarily deserve close review." Pulitzer judges likely use a two-speed approach similar to that of VCs.

What about hiring? The same idea applies. At Google, where the chances to get a job are well below 1 percent, resumes are quickly "screened" at the first stage to create a short list of candidates. At the second stage, the remaining candidates are interviewed and reviewed with far more scrutiny. Many other companies follow the same approach.

Buying a house? Zillow reports that of every 100 homes quickly viewed, prospective buyers save information on thirty-two homes for further review. Only in four of these thirty-two cases do they contact the broker, at which point the true due diligence takes off. Again, we observe a fast-thinking mindset initially and slower decision making at a later stage.

One story that inspired us to say no more often ourselves is that of the young screenwriter and Emmy Award–winner Michaela Coel. In 2017, Coel received an attractive $1 million offer from Netflix for her gripping dramedy show *I May Destroy You*. Of course, she was tempted to sign with the leading streaming platform, but Michaela declined. As she carefully reviewed the terms, she realized that the company would not give her a percentage of the copyright. The move was risky. Shortly after, BBC and HBO offered Coel a much better deal that was more in line with her values and priorities. This is just another tribute to the Venture Mindset and its ability to decline deals lacking upside potential while searching for life-changing ones.

Be prepared to say no again and again. That's how VCs think; it's in their bones. VCs don't want to buy the first house or the first car. They want to look at 100 houses and take a dozen test drives. As you should grasp by now, this strategy is not due to indecisiveness or overinflated skepticism. To be successful in a VC-like environment, you must be prepared to say no 100 times and yes only once.

Extraordinary ideas and startups are rare creatures. You still have to say yes at least once. You can't reject *every* opportunity coming your way. A funnel of just one idea is bad, but a funnel of zero ideas is worse.

Don't get too skeptical

One time when we played the piggy bank game, the winner's reaction surprised not only our participants, but also us. As usual, the winner submitted an extremely high bid. The unusual part came when he insisted on receiving the coins stuffed in the piggy. We were puzzled, but we agreed that the request was fair and asked the bidder for his rationale. He explained that among billions of standard Lincoln pennies worth exactly one cent, there are a few rare coins with a value of thousands of dollars. In one instance, as a result of a production error in 1970, some coins were minted with a double die obverse (that is, the word "Liberty" appears as though the word has been printed twice, slightly off center). Those coins are among the most valuable coins in circulation today, with a retail value of about $3,000. And that's only the start! Even rarer is the 1969 Lincoln penny in which the entire head is doubled except for the mint mark. The value of such a rare coin is determined at collectors' auctions, and it could easily exceed $100,000. Not a bad return on a one-cent coin. It was a great reminder to us. Sometimes we all get too skeptical and may miss a precious and exclusive opportunity among the innumerable pennies.

MINDSET CHECKS

- How many new ideas do you screen each year? 10? 100? 1,000?

- Is your organization accustomed to rejecting ideas?

- Do you regularly conduct a retrospective analysis of successful vs. unsuccessful strategic investment decisions?

FIVE

Bet on the Jockey

Why VCs spend more time evaluating teams than you may

5.1
Second Chance

"*Super Founders* is actually my second book, guys," Ali Tamaseb told us over dinner at a traditional Persian restaurant in the heart of Palo Alto.

"Could that be the reason why it has been such a tremendous success?" Ilya parried, half-jokingly.

"Shall we call you a super writer, then?" Alex added, getting a loud laugh out of Ali.

Jokes aside, Ali's book *Super Founders* is thought-provoking. He gathered and analyzed tens of thousands of data points about venture-backed startups and interviewed more than 100 unicorn founders to better understand what leads to successful startup outcomes. "Super founders are founders with a prior startup founding experience that had a successful or modest outcome," Ali explained to us (while reminding us to try the local hummus). He then went on to describe some of the factors his algorithm takes into account.

Super founders are entrepreneurs who systematically build businesses with successful outcomes. The scale of each success doesn't matter much in Ali's calculations. What matters is the success itself. Ali's research suggests that, overall, super founders are at least three times more likely to succeed than other tech startups.

Ali's interest in super founders is not academic. He is a "unicorn hunter." With many unicorns already in his portfolio, he invests in advanced technologies from his Palo Alto–based VC firm, DCVC. Ali would consider investing in almost anything one of his identified super founders is working on, regardless of the industry, market situation, or competition. "Sometimes," he told us, "I even think that knowledge of the market, unless it is a very deep knowledge, may actually distract the investor from selecting the right investment strategy."

Is Ali's extreme trust in the skills and background of an entrepreneur representative of the VC mindset? Investors have to decide this with millions of dollars at stake every day. To see how they play their hand, let's turn to games.

In the early 2010s, the video gaming industry was on the rise. In 2009, Swedish enthusiast Markus Persson had embarked on a journey to build the best-selling video game in history. Just a few years later, he sold *Minecraft* to Microsoft for $2.5 billion. Another company—Supercell, founded in Helsinki in 2010—released two more games, *Hay Day* and *Clash of Clans*, in 2012. The company raised $12 million in venture funding at a valuation of about $50 million in 2011, but when the games immediately zoomed to the top of the charts, Supercell was overwhelmed with investors offering capital at a then mind-blowing (for a gaming company) valuation of $3 billion. The golden age of online and mobile games had truly commenced.

A storied VC investor, Accel Partners became part of the gaming wave. Accel was the lead investor in Supercell's early round. When a similar opportunity arose to invest in a small gaming startup called Tiny Speck, Accel jumped on the bandwagon. If only Accel's partners had known what a trainwreck Tiny Speck's game would soon become.

Two entrepreneurs, Stewart Butterfield and Cal Henderson, who had been obsessed with games since childhood, decided to develop a multiplayer online game. Butterfield described the new game to the media: "It's something I've wanted to work on since I was a little kid [when] I played *SimCity*." Not only did the founders name their new company Tiny Speck, but they also named their first game *Glitch*. "*Nomen est omen*," as the Romans used to say—name is destiny.

A year after Accel's initial investment, and after Tiny Speck raised another venture round, the company unlocked its game to beta testers. On September 27, 2011, it was finally released to the public. Four years of development, dozens of employees, a million cumulative hours of beta testing, tens of thousands of people waiting to try the game, and $17.5 million did not help as the game was soon locked once again for beta testing. Although the game attracted quite a few users, reviews were lukewarm, such as, "*Glitch* feels like a meal made up entirely of side courses" and "a little formless." Just as problematic, Butterfield and Henderson had decided to build the game using "flash" technology on a platform developed by Adobe, which limited the audience to desktop users. Mobile devices such as the iPhone were gaining momentum, but transferring the game to a new platform was too difficult. One employee at Tiny Speck later described *Glitch* as "expensive to build and keep and we had not attracted enough players to bear that expense." The forty-two-person team understood that "game over" was coming.

In November 2012, two years after Accel's first check, a "sad announcement from Tiny Speck" went online, starting with "This is a horrible day" and ending with "If there was a way to make it work, we would make it work. But there is not. . . . *Glitch* is over." Shortly thereafter, most of the team was let go. It could have been another startup failure story like so many others, for never was there a story of more woe than this one of Tiny Speck and *Glitch*. In fact, the story would have ended here, had Accel Partners not embodied the thinking of the Venture Mindset.

Even though *Glitch* was a terrible flop, Tiny Speck still had a nice pile of money left in the bank as the founders clicked the button to send the sad last announcement—more than they needed for a farewell party. In fact, Tiny Speck had a whopping $5 million left. Quite a fortune to spend.

Staring at such an abysmal failure, most investors would have gladly shut down the company and taken whatever remained to salvage something from the trainwreck they were leaving behind. What would you have done? You could still have recovered about thirty cents on each dollar you had put into Tiny Speck.

VCs think differently. Even though Butterfield offered to wire the remaining money back, the Accel investors refused and told him to find something new, doubling down on their bet because they believed in the team. The original investment memo written in February 2009 by Andrew Braccia, the investor at Accel leading the Tiny Speck investment, said, "Tiny Speck is still primarily a team bet. They have failed with one another, succeeded with one another, and everything in between." These VCs were insightful enough to distinguish between "startup failure" and "founder failure."

So the founders started dreaming up a new idea. In the language of Silicon Valley, they *pivoted*. As Tiny Speck's team went back to the drawing board, they realized that, in the process of building *Glitch*, they had created many internal tools that could be useful to teams in other organizations. One such tool was a simple chat that helped developers and product teams communicate with each other. You could search through and organize these messages in threads, making it unnecessary to go hunting for someone's response to your question through hundreds of emails, text messages, and random chats. It was all in one place. The tool was also fully asynchronous, with messages still waiting for users even when they were logged out.

But pivoting from an adventure-seeking computer game to a B2B (business-to-business) communication tool? Ben Horowitz, a cofounder of a16z, which was also an investor in Tiny Speck, reacted to the new product forcefully: "It sounds like a really horrible idea." Nevertheless, the investors greenlighted the idea and the founders started again from scratch.

And this is how the now ubiquitous Slack, used by thousands of businesses from Target to McKinsey and even the US Department of Defense—the app that is now the industry standard for intracompany communication—was born. In less than ten years, the company pivoted from standing on the brink of annihilation to being sold to Salesforce for $27 billion. As you can imagine, those patient early investors earned a buck or two from this pivot.

Tiny Speck's rise from the ashes is a VC mindset story on steroids. What were the VCs betting on? The founders, not the product. Investors had given up on the gaming opportunity they had initially supported, but they gave Butterfield and his team the chance to pursue a seemingly orthogonal, unrelated idea. In the VCs' eyes, these two distinct endeavors had a common feature: the human element. Andrew Braccia of Accel, the largest investor in Slack by the time of its IPO, boiled it down to a simple principle: he invested in Tiny Speck because of the team.

Accel's confidence in the founders was buttressed by the knowledge that Tiny Speck was not Butterfield's first adventure. He had already pivoted in his previous gaming attempt. In another ironic twist, the previous game that never got past the prototype stage was called "Game Neverending." Butterfield turned it into Flickr, an image-hosting service, which was sold to Yahoo in 2005 for around $25 million.

Braccia's bet on the founders, Horowitz's decision to stick with them despite thinking the new pivot was a bad idea, and Tamaseb's super-founder philosophy all exhibit another principle of the VC mindset, which values investing because of *people* at least as much as investing in *projects*.

Many eventually successful companies, if not all, go through hiccups and pivots in their early stages. Tiny Speck's story is an example of a rule, not an exception. On Valentine's Day 2005, in a small Menlo Park garage in the heart of Silicon Valley, Chad Hurley registered the trademark, logo, and domain for a new dating service. Although the dating site failed miserably, users started uploading videos of all kinds. This is how YouTube was born.

An app called Burbn (mentioned in chapter 2) was built on the idea that users would check in at their locations, make future plans with friends, and earn points for hanging out with them. After Burbn failed, the team pivoted. They experienced numerous bumps, nearly scrapping the entire app after months of work. This is how Instagram was born.

Odeo started as a platform for podcasts in 2005 until "the shit hit the fan," as colorfully explained by George Zachary, the Charles River Ventures investor who led his firm's investment in Odeo. Soon after Odeo's launch, Apple iTunes moved into podcasting and razed the company's optimism to the ground. After countless brainstorming sessions and meetings, one of the cofounders, Evan Williams, proposed buying back the company from investors, returning to them whatever was left of the capital, and starting a new company. One of the investors, Mike Maples, rejected the offer. When Williams insisted, Maples said, "I will take money back on one condition: that you would allow me to invest in your next thing." Why was Maples so insistent? "You should be willing and able to separate the failure of the business and the founder," Maples told us. "And I felt it was more about circumstances than about Williams that the idea failed." This is how Twitter was born.

Traditional organizations place processes above people: they normally make investments not in people but rather in companies, projects, and business plans. At corporate headquarters, people fade behind financial numbers and project presentations. It's especially uncommon to see such determined trust in people and their talent *after* they have demonstrably failed. Would you have taken your money (or what was left of it) and run in these scenarios? And would you spend more time studying business proposal details or interacting with the founding team?

Of course, VCs do not trust founders unconditionally. They focus on identifying the reasons behind a company's failure or need to pivot. They are unhesitant to keep betting on the founders if they determine that the failure was not because of the founders.

5.2
What Do Horse Racing and Unicorn Hunting Have in Common?

How often can you spot a finance professor passionately making bets in an attempt to figure out the winning horse? When Ilya was visiting Singapore's racetrack, where the ardor of the moment combines with extreme heat and humidity to make you sweat profusely, he noticed that the horse's name—not the jockey's name—appeared first when results were shown. Horse names are also presented first at the Kentucky Derby, Happy Valley Racecourse in Hong Kong, and Royal Ascot in England. Ilya was puzzled. Don't jockeys matter as much in horse racing? Though he lost about $100 in Singapore and has not tried his horse racing luck since, Ilya gained something of greater value.

Back in the 1950s, legendary quarterback and newsman Jimmy Jemail had a feature called Jimmy Jemail's Hotbox in *Sports Illustrated* magazine. Hotbox asked its readers to respond to provocative questions like, "What sport provokes the most arguments in your home?" On October 8, 1956, Hotbox asked the question "How important is a jockey to a horse?" Letters poured in from across the country. Professionals and race enthusiasts alike shared their views. Horse trainers, handicappers, stable owners, stockbrokers, and manufacturers all expressed opinions. Surprisingly, there was wide disagreement. The importance of jockeys varied from 5 percent to 75 percent. Opinions ranged from "the jockey determines the outcome" to "the horse rider doesn't matter at all."

More recent evidence from horse racing enthusiasts attributes about 10 percent of a horse's performance to the jockey on any given day. Jerry Bailey, the Hall of Fame jockey who became a racing analyst for ESPN, summarized his thirty-year career, during which he won almost $300 million in prizes, in this way: "A great jockey cannot make a slow horse win, but a bad jockey can get a great horse beat." Len Ragozin's *Sheets*, a must for any horse racing enthusiast, published a devilishly detailed analysis for each horse, including factors such as horse speed, distance from the inside rail, and weight carried. The jockey played only a supporting role in Ragozin's analysis, listed among the downside factors. And Bill Benter's algorithm, which helped him win close to a billion dollars in Hong Kong races, tracked 120 different factors for each horse, treating it as far more important than the jockey. All in all, Ilya concluded, the horse is clearly the winner over the jockey when it comes to horse racing. But is this true for the Venture Mindset?

"Horse" and "jockey" are commonly used by VC investors to describe factors they consider when trying to distinguish likely hits from flops. "Jockey" covers all the factors related to the quality of the founders and the management team. "Horse" encompasses all the business-related factors, such as the product, business model, and market size. In 2016, Ilya and his colleagues looked under the hood to better understand how venture investors make decisions. We first asked hundreds of VCs what really mattered for them in selecting startups. For 95 percent of investors—that is, nineteen of every twenty VCs—the management team was an important factor. Many horse-related factors were also rated as important. But then we took a step further and asked what investors considered the most important or "make or break it" consideration.

Among more than 1,000 VCs responding, 47 percent—almost half—said the team was the most important factor in their selection process (see

Figure 8). The earlier the startup stage the VC is investing in, the more critical the management team becomes. But even late-stage investors still placed the team far above any other factor. All the "horse" factors, even added together, were of lesser importance. Almost any way we sliced and diced the VCs, the jockey factor still came out on top. Neither business model nor product, not even the market size, made it to the top place.

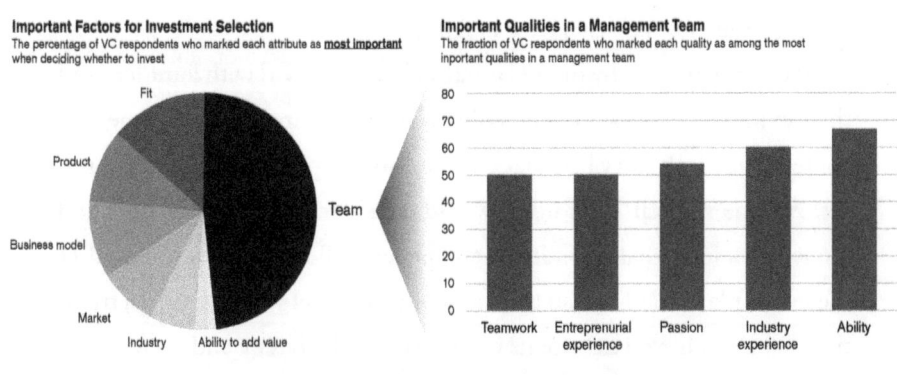

Figure 8.
Factors for investment selection and qualities in a management team

Why are VCs so different from the horse racing crowd? Because VCs know that ideas are a dime a dozen; execution of the idea makes all the difference. Most bright ideas will have many teams trying to execute them, but only one or two will succeed. Especially with early-stage start-ups, the horse cannot win without a great jockey. As General Georges Doriot, who started one of the first venture capital firms back in 1946, summarized it succinctly: "Always consider investing in a grade A man with a grade B idea. Never invest in a grade B man with a grade A idea."

One of the founders of Greylock Partners, Henry McCance, echoed this when he said: "This is a marathon, this is not a sprint; the rules of engagement are likely to change and you have to reposition your company. And if you have an A management team, they'll be able to do that; if you have a poor management team, no matter how good the initial product idea is, they will not be able to navigate it successfully."

We took the horse vs. jockey question one step further. Taking another angle, we asked VCs to look at the other end of their investment funnel and rank the factors that contributed to their successful and failed investments. Again, the team was by far the dominant factor. Choosing the right jockey is the most critical factor in success; betting on the wrong jockey is the most critical factor in failure.

We can now see why the VC mindset is so obsessed with founders and their experience, passion, and skills. It is hard to imagine the same outcome of the Slack story had Slack's investors not possessed the VC mindset. No one in their right mind would consider wasting *more* time and money on a team that generated a completely different business idea after the initial plan failed—or so the traditional mindset would say. In a traditional approach, you first focus on the idea and strategy and then search for and assign a suitable team. In a large company, the project and business plan are approved first, with high-level sponsorship from a VP or senior VP. Only after that does the high-flying executive start assembling the development team, reallocating roles within the company or hiring from outside. They then "supervise" the project (actually spending only a small fraction of their time on it). This design is the opposite of that taken by the Venture Mindset, where you start with the project leader or founder and then work backward to the business plan.

Organizations should design processes for successful internal start-ups to float up. And they can.

5.3
Build Your Racetracks

The code name "Project Caribou" was taken from a *Dilbert* cartoon. Everything about this product was like a joke from the very beginning. The prototype was built by a single person in one day. Then the team scaled up dramatically ... to two people. Just before the launch, the team rose to a brave dozen. There were no charts or task allocations as the team progressed. When potential users saw what was promised to them, they also knew it was a good joke. No one in their right mind would give away, for free, up to a hundred times more than any other product available on the market. When do you launch a "Caribou" joke? On April Fool's Day, of course. How can anyone pick any other date for such a product?

And so, on April 1, 2004, Project Caribou—better known as ... Gmail—was born.

These days, for many people Gmail *is* email. Gmail's story is especially instructive because Google didn't acquire it as it acquired YouTube or Nest. Gmail was ideated and built in-house. The product that almost 2 billion users love today started with a single engineer. His name is Paul Buchheit and his career at Google started in 1999, when he was hired as employee number twenty-three.

Gmail was a startup within a corporation. Paul Buchheit was, by all accounts, an amazingly capable jockey—motivated, creative, passionate, resilient. Gmail ran on a server at his own desk. He collected feedback and requests from its first users, who were other Google engineers. They and a couple engineers helping him were his extended venture team.

Gmail has been an overwhelming success, and it would be a natural temptation to equate this story with other startup success stories like Slack. But by doing so, you would miss the entire point, because Gmail was developed inside a big corporation. As with startups, the founder and their team are not enough to build the business. You need VCs to partner with them. You need racetracks for entrepreneurs to perform. Similar racetracks are needed for those with entrepreneurial spirit within companies as well. Scratch beneath the surface and you will find that, although Gmail was on the margins of Google's core search business, it was Google leaders' ability to design a racetrack that made Gmail possible.

Unlike a startup—where all the energy, effort, and resources are aimed at one idea—any startup within a company inevitably competes for resources and attention and is outside the daily worries of firm leaders. Therefore, the internal innovation process designed for such efforts greatly influences whether a project like Gmail is a viable possibility or a certain flop. Paul Buchheit's recollection here, after Gmail became a sensation in the email world, is illustrative. As he recalled in a 2007 interview, his bosses "asked me if I wanted to build some type of email or personalization product. It was a pretty nonspecific project charter. They just said, 'We think this is an interesting area.' . . . They were very general—just kind of saying, 'Yeah, we think there's something interesting to do here,' but it wasn't like they gave me a list of features. People really weren't sure what it was." Some years later, Buchheit, no longer at Google, was more direct: "It was an official charge," he said. "I was supposed to build an email thing."

As we dive deeper into one successful internal startup story after another, similarities emerge. Leaders listen carefully to ideas that their team members suggest, encourage them to work on many ideas, and then select those ideas with the most potential. The instructions are notably vague. Although there is no narrowly defined direction from above and the team can initially do pretty much whatever they want within broad limits, the leaders provide overall support. They also provide oversight to check in with the goals and milestones and to decide when to pull the plug if an idea fails. Buchheit acknowledged that many ideas he worked on at Google didn't pan out—as one would expect with risky internal startups.

Leaders also decide which projects to back all the way. One reason why Gmail became such a runaway success was Google's decision to be truly generous with storage space. Each email address got one gigabyte for free, which at the time was way above anyone's expectations. There was no longer a need to delete old emails or stay on the lookout for extra-large attachments. With Gmail's 1GB free offer, the era of email limitations was over. Of course, this decision, a super-expensive one back in 2004, was not made by Buchheit but by Google executives who bet on the Gmail horse.

Gmail is not the only product that emerged from within Google. Google News, Google Talk, and Google Scholar all started as small independent projects within Google and later became scaled businesses. They were not designed and kickstarted by any centralized unit somewhere up the management chain. They were not planned and thought through in any detail by the senior leadership or board of directors. They all happened due to the prevailing Venture Mindset within Google that made the confluence of several key ingredients possible. Google had talented and highly motivated individual employees, along with a process by which internal startups were encouraged to blossom and take high risks that could end in failure. Like other large companies, Google could afford to have many horses racing at the same time. Its executives realized that within a corporate environment, a good jockey and good horse are not enough; you also need racetracks in place to support them. What Google did was to design, perhaps informally at first, a racetrack that allowed jockeys and horses to race efficiently. Jockeys could switch horses, many horses did not reach the finish line, and some horses got a huge vitamin boost to run faster. Google had built an intrapreneurial factory.

The word "intrapreneurship" was coined only in 1978. Several years later, *The Economist* picked up the newly minted portmanteau, which combines the prefix "intra-" (meaning "internal") with "entrepreneurship," for one of its feature articles. But the term took the popular media by storm only when Steve Jobs used it in his 1985 interview with *Newsweek*. He shared that the Macintosh had been built by a team of intrapreneurs—a group of people "going in essence back to the garage, but in a large company."

Intrapreneurship can be practiced in all companies, not just technology ones. It requires the Venture Mindset, and as tech companies are more likely than others to inherit it from their VC backers, we may often find it there. But any company can design a racetrack for intrapreneurship—and some designs could be so successful as to transform horses into cars and the racetrack into a Formula 1 course!

Consider the Happy Meal. The world-famous Happy Meal started with a small experiment by an intrapreneur, Yolanda Fernández de Cofiño, thousands of miles away from the McDonald's headquarters. In 1974, Fernández became the first McDonald's franchisee in Guatemala. She observed that kids could not eat a whole Big Mac, because the meal was too large. Parents ended up overpaying only to throw away leftovers. Fernández came up with the idea of creating a children's menu with a smaller burger, smaller fries, a small soda, and a small ice cream. She did not stop there—she also bought toys at a local market and included one with each order to make it more fun. Happy Meals were a hit with Guatemalan kids and their parents.

This whole experiment took place without approval from McDonald's headquarters in Chicago. In most companies, this great idea would have stayed in Guatemala. But McDonald's held world conventions for all its franchisees, where ideas and experiments were exchanged and showcased. These conventions, if approached from the right angle, act like intrapreneurial racetracks. When McDonald's executives saw Fernández's menu, they bet more resources on this horse. Two years later, the Happy Meal was implemented worldwide.

It is tough to design a successful intrapreneurship culture. But one can start with some principles from the Venture Mindset checklist. Internal startups are run by highly motivated lean teams, without clear supervision from above, yet with tacit support and broad orientation of direction. Rather than forcing would-be innovators to go elsewhere, mimicking the startup setup makes intrapreneurship attractive to internal talent.

Placing people over process does not mean, however, that there is no process at all. Chaos doesn't necessarily translate into innovation; moreover, it can easily destroy ideas. The design should facilitate cutting through quite a bit of the internal bureaucracy and keeping the development team small, independent, fluid, and protected from internal politics. Intrapreneurs are motivated and energized; their success depends on their ability to solve a specific pain point for specific customers, often in a small setting. All this, however, is doomed to fail unless company leaders promote and scale up some of these initiatives.

For internal entrepreneurs to be successful, it is not enough to give them this name. You need the whole organization to support them the way VCs support their companies. You need to build racetracks for your jockeys to be successful. In a corporate setting, racetracks start with clear funding mechanisms, simple rules, guardrails, and milestones.

Products and the intrapreneurs behind them are all around us. Nespresso. Happy Meal. Gmail. Good intrapreneurs also tend to innovate again and again, becoming serial intrapreneurs. Yolanda Fernández de Cofiño did not stop with the Happy Meal; she also came up with the idea of hosting birthday celebrations at McDonald's. Paul Buchheit did not stop with Gmail; he also developed the first prototype of AdSense, a program for running ads on other websites.

Losing creative people like these may lead to trouble in the future. Bodexpress, a horse competing in the 2019 Preakness Stakes (the second race of US horse racing's Triple Crown), tossed his jockey right out of the gate—and then kept on running! Bodexpress was disqualified and, at any rate, was soon overtaken by other horses. The corporate world is even more punishing (not many horses manage to keep the same pace without their jockeys), yet the feedback loop takes much longer. Nurture your jockeys. Design and build racetracks for them. Help them attain their top speed.

5.4
Well-Rounded Square Pegs

You can't *manage* innovation; you can only *lead* it. Traditional organizations have plenty of managers, but often they lack enough builders and creators who can start things from scratch and pivot as needed. Yet larger organizations can offer innovators what no startup can provide. They can unlock access to extraordinary and immediate scale to implement ideas. Compare a large bank and a small fintech company. Or a large healthcare company with a biotech startup.

Armed with our knowledge of the Venture Mindset, we clearly see VCs looking for these three guiding principles in their teams.

Charisma and character matter

The eyes of Mike Maples, a famed investor behind a swarm of unicorns, lit up as he talked to us about the passion of founders: "They think of nothing else; they are totally crazily devoted to one end goal, they are desperate to solve the pain point of people." To visualize Maples's thesis, in the background of his Zoom there is a plaque that boldly states, "Practice reckless optimism," given to him by a founder he backed. Twitter, Twitch, Clover Health, Okta, and Chegg are examples of Maples's exceptionally successful bets. Bets on obsessed founders.

Alex Rampell of a16z swears by founders' charisma. He starts his founder due diligence by eyeing the people the founder has brought to the meeting and who has joined the team. If the founder of a fledgling startup—without customers, money, or a developed product—has succeeded in causing amazing people to drop everything and follow him, Rampell quickly gets interested.

Ilya can recall a long list of his charismatic students. One is recent graduate Rene Caissie. A maxillofacial surgeon from Montreal, Rene came to Stanford for a year of business studies and became immersed in the infectious entrepreneurial atmosphere. As Rene described his idea of building a platform that would offer personalized, dynamic health insights, everybody who listened to him got excited, feeling that "you want to work with this guy." A top computer science undergrad dropped out to build Caissie's platform Medeloop, leading hospitals signed on to try it out (before it was built!), and every expert Rene talked to wanted to become his adviser. Rene's contagious charisma is indescribable in words but palpably physical in his presence. As you evaluate founders, one key success ingredient to look for is whether they energize others and attract the best employees.

You can wear a Patagonia vest or a hoodie to look like a tech leader, but experienced VCs pay a lot more attention to smaller details. Here is a trick used by Kate Mitchell, a cofounder of Scale Venture Partners, to assess a founder's character and leadership skills. As founders visit VC partnerships to pitch their startups, they are in the selling mode. They are optimistic, friendly, confident, but always respectful to VCs. After the visit, Mitchell checks with the front desk to find out how the founder treated the receptionist while waiting in the lobby. Were they polite or arrogant, friendly or dismissive? As Mitchell told the Stanford class, "If I find out they were rude, I wouldn't invest. A founder must get the best out of everyone around them. If they can't treat a receptionist with respect, they will have trouble leading small teams to great entrepreneurial success."

Character matters. You are unlikely to learn about the character of innovation leaders from their CVs. This is why hackathons, competitions, and meetups source not only ideas, but also people. Character and charisma are tough to imitate. Thus, when it comes to innovation, the upside-down approach makes sense. Rather than starting with the idea first and then searching for managers to lead it, identify leaders first and let them innovate, form a team, and create the future at your organization.

Find misfits that fit

Ilya's student Tony Xu had no experience in logistics, optimization, or food delivery when he founded DoorDash. Brian Chesky and Joe Gebbia had college degrees in industrial design (and Chesky also had one in fine arts) when they cofounded Airbnb. They had no experience in the hotel or travel industry. The founders of Flatiron Health, a company dedicated to improving cancer care, came from Google and the technology sector. This didn't prevent them from building a successful company that was eventually acquired by pharmaceutical giant Roche. These and many other founders lacked industry experience, yet VC investors enthusiastically backed them. With incremental innovation, deep, intimate knowledge of your industry is critical to success. With disruptive innovation, such knowledge may often be a hindrance.

VCs often seek those who stand out in other ways. Xu and his cofounders experimented with food delivery based on group work at the Stanford business school and impressed investors with their flexibility, attention to detail, and ability to create a fine-tuned minimum viable product. Investor Paul Graham agreed to invest in Airbnb after Gebbia pulled out a box of Obama O's they were selling at the Democratic convention for $40 a box. Graham decided that if these two could convince people to buy cereal at $40 a box, they could also convince people to sleep in other people's homes. Another of Ilya's students, Mercedes Bent, is now an investor at Lightspeed, a premier venture firm. She describes what she is looking for in founders in a memorable phrase: learning velocity. "Successful startups scale exponentially," she explains. "Only these founders can keep up."

What VCs are looking for are well-rounded square pegs. Their goal is not to search for rebels, even though sometimes they find one. Their goal is to find misfits who would fit. Mike Maples says it loud and clear: "Startup founders are pattern breakers and the VC mindset is about breaking the mold rather than extending the franchise." Maples is even writing a book on this very topic (titled *Pattern Breakers*).

Contrast this to corporations, where lack of experience in a very specific industry or function often prevents people from getting in at all, let alone being invited to take a lead role in a new venture. Yet it takes both rain and sunshine to make a rainbow. Hiring new employees who don't fit all the criteria, such as an executive from a completely different industry, could be a key to reinvigorating a mature company.

What does the oil and gas sector have in common with Lego bricks? With 85 percent of its revenues coming from coal, the Danish fossil fuel company Dong Energy was the epitome of a mature company in a mature, conservative industry. Facing strong headwinds as fossil fuel prices were falling and S&P was downgrading the company's credit rating, in 2012 the board hired Henrik Poulsen as its new CEO. His resume had flashy highlights with roles in areas like global innovation and marketing for Lego. What his resume did not have was a prior exposure to the fossil fuel industry. Under Poulsen's leadership, Dong Energy, renamed Ørsted, became the world's largest producer of offshore wind energy, and by 2019 it was deriving 85 percent of its revenues from renewables. By the time Poulsen's tenure ended, in 2020, shareholders could cheer as well. Ørsted's market capitalization had more than doubled.

Poulsen's example fits well with the research results of Abu Jalal and Alexandros Prezas, who studied the impact of outside CEO hiring on the long-term performance of over 500 firms. Five years after the CEO succession, firms that had hired CEOs from unrelated industries had higher stock returns, profitability, and growth potential.

If your recruiters ignore candidates without relevant experience, then don't be surprised by the lack of diversity among your candidates or the lack of innovation inside your walls. Tristan Botelho and Melody Chang of Yale sent more than 2,000 fictitious resumes in response to actual software engineering job postings. The resumes had identical facts on education, interests, and skills. The only difference was whether applicants had startup founder experience. Interestingly, companies requested interviews with startup founders barely half as often as with nonfounders because nonfounders seemed to have a more standard background. If this is not an alarm signal to every corporation, then we don't know what is.

If the way candidates look, talk, and organize their work becomes an obstacle to an organization flourishing, it is time to rethink your corporate culture. For new things to emerge, you must have new ways of working.

Bet on the team, not the individual

Venture building is a team sport. To succeed, the founding team must build a first-class employee base and then scale quickly from a one-man show to a larger organization. "If you want to go fast, go alone; if you want to go far, go together," according to an African proverb.

Paul Madera, the cofounder of Meritech Capital Partners, carefully observes startup cofounders making their pitch, monitoring who is talking and how others react. For Madera, if one person dominates while others sit with sullen expressions, that's an inauspicious sign. He frequently rejects deals when he finds founders' interpersonal dynamics problematic.

Madera is far from alone. Y Combinator, a premier accelerator founders dream of getting into, tends to accept only companies with multiple founders who can balance one another and combine complementary skills. Would Slack have been as successful without Butterfield's cofounder, Cal Henderson? The Slack cofounders met each other in a very Silicon Valley way, with Henderson breaking into the email server of Butterfield's first gaming company. He was hired by the company shortly thereafter. Together, Henderson and Butterfield subsequently launched Flickr and then Slack. With full alignment in their vision and by pairing their complementary skills, they grew Slack from eight people to thousands of team members. Butterfield is a creative person in love with design; Henderson is an engineer who buries himself in code.

Too many traditional organizations hope that a single person from a large tech company can make the difference. A single person cannot. You need a team. By bringing multiple people with a new mindset in, you can kickstart innovation. Innovation is a team sport indeed.

5.5
You Can't Win the Race on a Donkey

"Bet it all on founders, ignore the rest" sounds like the headline of a clickbait article from the pen of a finance professor and a corporate innovation adviser. The reality is not as black and white. In addition to the jockey, most VCs give critical consideration to the market size, the business model, and the product. And most name at least one of these three horses as an important factor in deciding to invest.

Let's start with market size. Andy Rachleff, cofounder of Benchmark Capital and Wealthfront, offers this poignant observation: "When a great team meets a lousy market, market wins. When a lousy team meets a great market, market wins. When a great team meets a great market, something special happens." The size of the prize matters. VCs would not invest if the market—in the most optimistic scenario—is not big enough. As we write this chapter, SpaceX and other space startups are raking in billions of dollars because investors believe that the market—if these ideas succeed—will eventually be huge. The same holds for biotech startups building their products on the discovery of CRISPR and longevity aspirations. The potential market size is so humongous that even a niche idea may become a multibillion-dollar business.

What about the second consideration: the business model? "I always think about the value creation and the value capture," explained Cami Samuels, an investor at Venrock (whom we met in chapter 2), when we met over a poke bowl in her office. Cami described all the challenges biotech startups face when seeking to market a novel drug. For some life sciences products, one of the steepest hurdles is to reach primary care physicians and convince them to prescribe an innovative treatment to patients. The startup team may *create* value but may still not *capture* it. In her evaluation of startups, Samuels and other biotech investors work really hard to identify the value capture opportunities.

Over at a16z, fintech investor Alex Rampell echoes her sentiment: "The battle between every startup and incumbent comes down to whether the startup gets distribution before the incumbent gets innovation." In Samuels's world, an overwhelming distribution advantage effectively makes big pharma the gatekeepers of their sector. This gives them leverage in negotiations with a small and upcoming startup and often makes a biotech startup's path to success an uphill battle. This is why excellence in the laboratory (value creation) doesn't translate easily into high royalties and profits (value capture). Even a super jockey can't make a donkey jump over a fortress wall.

In short, the jockey is necessary but not sufficient for a startup's success. Moreover, what is relevant to success for small companies changes gradually as the company matures. As the startup grows and scales, the original management team needs to grow with the needs of the company. The skills required to create a product prototype and grow the team from three to twenty people are worlds apart from the skills needed to scale sales to thousands of customers and manage hundreds of employees. Some founders advance with the company; many don't. This is one reason why investors often insist on changing the leadership team at some point.

Steven Kaplan from the University of Chicago and his colleagues Berk Sensoy and Per Strömberg sank their teeth into this issue. They used a sample of fifty successful VC-backed companies to analyze the evolution of these firms' characteristics as they progressed from an early business plan to their IPO. What made their study extraordinarily insightful was their access to company business plans at different points in the firms' life cycle stages. They found that management turnover was substantial. Fewer than three-quarters of CEOs at the time of the IPO had also been in charge at the time of the original VC investment. Only about half of the next four top executives at the IPO had been top executives at the early stage. As firms grow, the balance between the jockey and the horse changes toward the horse. The firm's success depends less on the management team as the business scales up.

As organizations grow and mature, they strengthen themselves by developing smooth and predictable processes, well-established norms, and clear bureaucratic rules. This leads to the traditional mindset that puts horses well above jockeys in the pecking order. "Nobody's irreplaceable, including me," said William Clay Ford, the great-grandson of Henry Ford and the former CEO and chairman of Ford Motor Company. Modern business leaders largely agree with Ford on this point. In a normal environment, the role of managers and decision makers is to preserve the status quo, follow well-established guardrails, and from time to time tweak specs. These processes are mostly routine—so-called SOPs, or standard operating procedures—and well documented. After that, the business becomes a well-oiled machine supported by well-trained employees.

Think about your everyday decisions. Think of ordering an Uber or going to a nearby coffee shop. You don't care much about the names and qualities of people behind the service. You may vary your tips, but even those are decided pretty much mechanically. The same happens in an organization where the individual's roles are dominated by routine and by standardized decisions and tasks. It's more efficient to optimize the process than to trust an individual worker to reinvent the wheel every time the task is performed. McDonald's revolutionized the whole fast-food industry by introducing, adhering to, and constantly tweaking standards. Today it takes McDonald's only 112 seconds to cook and prepare a hamburger, with exactly 42 seconds on the grill. Think of Toyota's legendary quality, a direct result of "standard work," a fundamental discipline of the Toyota Production System. And consider Amazon and its library of airtight SOPs, which enable the company to hire 150,000 temporary employees during the holiday season to navigate peak volume seamlessly.

The idea that people are small screws in a well-organized process was developed with the rise of mass-scale manufacturing in the nineteenth century. Frederick Taylor was one of the founding fathers of scientific management. When he was at Bethlehem Steel, he calculated that on average each worker handled about 12.5 tons of pig iron per day. Taylor experimented with ways to organize production to increase worker output. One breakthrough came when Taylor motivated employees to increase their workload to 47 tons by promising a higher rate of pay. Getting a nearly fourfold rise in productivity for 60 percent more pay surprised Taylor and his bosses. The book that Taylor later published on optimizing human output in manufacturing was voted the most influential management book of the twentieth century. Even though Taylor's principles are about workers, the role of an individual worker is minimal. In the traditional corporate setting, workers can easily be replaced, swapped out, and anonymized (as they well know). It is the process that dominates. The challenge is that Taylor's findings regarding assembly-line times is no longer relevant in more innovative sectors of the economy and in more uncertain environments.

Taylor's method works well for incremental innovation, such as traditional corporate R&D processes. But creating a new entertainment show, building a new AI algorithm, or developing a radically new technological idea is quite different from loading pig iron or operating a conveyor efficiently. Although Taylor's ideas are still used profitably in many settings, the approach needs to be dramatically different in the world of disruptive innovation. In this world, people are not treated like screws and cogs, because their actions, though difficult to verify and measure objectively in an uncertain environment, can largely determine the eventual results.

The challenge is that, in most organizations, routine projects are so overwhelmingly common that the same mindset is then extended to projects in which the jockey plays a far more important role. Familiarity makes it hard to recognize opportunity. That's why companies adopting the "jockey first" model started springing up like mushrooms in the Silicon Valleys of the world. Traditional companies should take heed. Too often there are lots of great ideas, projects, and inventions going around in such companies, but relatively few people are capable enough to execute those ideas well. Ideas are relatively easy; execution is hard. Consider just one example from an era that now feels distant—the era of DVD players. Many predicted correctly in the late 2000s that the DVD format was quickly approaching the end of its life. But some leaders in the space failed to react promptly, and so they folded one after another, as was the case with Movie Gallery, which at its peak owned more than 4,700 DVD rental stores. Redbox, with its 41,500 DVD kiosks, tried to move into streaming—but belatedly, half-heartedly, and unsuccessfully. Of all these incumbents, only one company addressed the existential threat head-on. One reason was that it did not adhere to Taylor's principles. And it didn't just survive; it thrived. Guess who?

Netflix is a rare example of a company that managed to reinvent itself. It made a giant leap from being a successful DVD rental-by-mail company to being a successful online streaming company. And it didn't stop there. Netflix went on to give Hollywood a run for its money to become a leader in show creation. By now you shouldn't be surprised to learn that Netflix was a VC-backed company that retained its Venture Mindset. A particularly important principle was its commitment to "people over process." The level of trust in people at Netflix is extraordinary. Vacation time?

Unlimited. The company's expense policy? As simple as "Act in Netflix's best interests." Long hours? Won't get you a raise. Only A-level performance matters, not the amount of time invested. Netflix founder Reed Hastings titled his book *No Rules Rules*. At the core, his idea is this: "If you dummy-proof the process, you only get dummies to work there. That's why we're so opposed to that and focused on giving people great freedom. They'll make mistakes, of course, but you'll get a lot of great ideas." This trust in employees and producers has driven exceptional results. *House of Cards* (the most viewed show on Netflix when launched) came about because a director was given enormous freedom that would have been unprecedented at any Hollywood competitor. It took only thirty minutes for the CEO to sign off on the show.

Would Netflix have become so successful without a timely and smart bet on the new market of online streaming? We doubt it. Is the subscription business model instrumental to its success? Totally. Could the service survive technical glitches that would constantly annoy users? Duh. Obviously, the market, business model, and product do matter. But ideas are not mysterious creatures. They belong to people. They need a passionate owner who can make it a reality. People over process is the VC mantra. Netflix's main bet is clearly on the people and their ability to invent and develop. Hastings and his team found the balance between the horse and the jockey in their innovative industry. "The horse was good," Hastings said at an event in Mexico City, "until we had the car."

5.6
The Next Edison Could Be Sitting Right Next to You

One day in 2010, Thomas Houseman, Andrew Brooks, and Leslie Mead Renaud, three winemakers from the US West Coast, were arguing the issue of jockeys versus horses, but in relation to a liquid that has been made for thousands of years. It is a controversy as old as the winemaking craft itself: What is more essential to success, the "horse" factors such as soil (*terroir* in French) or the winemaker? The land reflects exposure to the morning sun, protective rock layers storing heat, nutritional elements in the soil, and, as winemakers from time immemorial have claimed, the touch of wine saints looking down from above. The winemaker brings the techniques and stylistic choices: how to crush grapes; whether to crush them at all; whether to supplement with acid, water, yeast, or nutrients; which barrels to choose; and how long to mature the wine in them. The jockey's decision choices are myriad, and all of them will change the wine's quality and flavor. Or will they?

In vino veritas—in the wine, there is truth. To find out the truth without arguing to their last sip of wine, the three winemakers decided to run an experiment. They would all try making wine from the same grapes that were picked at the same land plots in the same vintages. There were three winemakers, three vineyards, and three different vintages (2010, 2011, and 2012)—hence the name "Cube" for the project.

They chose Pinot Noir, one of the most difficult grape varieties and believed to be extremely sensitive to the terroir it is grown on. Think of the Burgundy region of France with its thousands of tiny wine growers, each cultivating a small plot of land, where moving just twenty feet to the left or right might make the difference between an astonishing wine that everybody is craving and merely a very good wine, even though both wines are made from Pinot Noir grapes.

Countless decisions later, six tons of grapes were transformed into wine, bottled, and tasted. James Laube, a reviewer from *Wine Spectator*, a premier wine magazine, and one of the tasters concluded that although the terroir was not completely irrelevant, "the decisions employed by the winemaker were the dominant factors," with even smaller decisions having "a huge impact on the final wine." Even for wine, it matters who is in the driver's seat or in the saddle.

From the wine cellar to the research lab. One exceptional model of intrapreneurship and the Venture Mindset is the Langer Lab at the MIT Department of Chemical Engineering. Led by Robert Langer, the researchers at this lab have filed more than 1,000 patents, licensed to more than 400 pharma and biotech companies. Langer became the most cited engineer in history (almost 400,000 citations and counting!). More than forty companies came out of the lab, earning Langer a spot on the *Forbes* billionaire list. We met Professor Langer and could have thought he was one of the students, not its head. He wore a gray T-shirt, joyfully introduced himself as Bob, and was bursting with ideas to each of our questions.

Langer's story started in a much less auspicious way. Early in his career, he could not land a job. He was advised to switch from chemical engineering and medicine to "oil and energy," was criticized by his more senior peers because "we don't believe anything you just said," and was once told by a senior scientist, puffing cigar smoke in his face, "You better start looking for another job."

Judah Folkman of Boston Children's Hospital, a big proponent of misfits, gave Langer a chance. Langer's personal challenges early in his career likely led him to build his lab on principles dramatically different from those of most other academic and corporate labs. Indeed, his lab is organized like a classic application of the Venture Mindset. In every research lab, people are important. But the 900 researchers who have come through his lab are actually considered the final "product" of the lab. Langer often brings in talent with unusual credentials. "I take a chance on people," he told us. "I have no predetermined plan besides the overall description of the field. I let people discover; I am just a guide." When one researcher approached him and asked what he'd like her to work on, Langer's response was as surprising as it was frustrating: "What excites you?"

Do you recognize the similarities between the culture in Langer's lab and at Amazon, Google, or Netflix? Langer believes that freedom and initiative will prevail and result in great inventions. When asked how he selects people for just a few slots from thousands of applicants a year, Langer responds, "I look for the best athlete." He then adds, "People who thrive here are people who want to be independent."

Langer focuses on impactful bets. Most of his patents and businesses may have been familiar only to experts, but 2020 changed all that. Among the more than forty companies Langer cofounded, one is Moderna, of COVID-19 vaccine fame. Langer believed in Moderna's potential ever since its founding in 2010 and he even predicted to his wife that it would be the most successful biotech company in history. He turned out to be right. Again, he was helped by his approach of encouraging his "intrapreneurs" to search and experiment. Like Google executives, Langer provided broad brushstrokes to his talented staff, not specific directions. His approach is not vague or formless, though. He runs a very tightly designed racetrack.

From technology businesses to fast-food chains, from corporations to smaller research labs, from winemakers to engineers—we all benefit from designing a process that prizes betting on people and their talent. Giving people structured freedom sparks intrapreneurial spirit. Design a racetrack system in which you bet on people, their character, and their passions, and you are more likely to win the race. People with ingenious ideas about how to reinvent the daily tasks they perform may have a more significant impact on your future than you could ever imagine. One of them might even invent a lifesaving vaccine or make your child's next meal happier.

MINDSET CHECKS

○ Do leaders in your organization think as much about "who" (the leaders) as about "what" (the business idea) when they launch a new initiative or project?

○ Has your organization built the "racetracks" (funding mechanisms, simple rules, guardrails, and milestones) for intrapreneurs to launch and scale new ideas?

○ Is your recruitment team focused on attracting people who are interested in ideating and building new businesses?

SIX

Agree to Disagree

Why you should encourage dissent and be wary of consensus

6.1
Monkey See, Monkey Do

"How come they don't eat pink corn?! I can't believe it," said a participant at one of our corporate workshops. She is the firm's head of marketing. She wasn't the only surprised person—everyone's eyes in the room were glued to an intriguing video on an experiment conducted in South Africa on the transmission of culture and group decision making. Not among people, but among *monkeys*.

Vervet monkeys, *Chlorocebus pygerythrus*, are highly social animals, living in groups of up to fifty individuals. "Our common ape ancestor millions of years ago potentially had common traits with us. Primates are a living link to our past," Professor Erica van de Waal, the enthusiastic leader of a large team of researchers across two continents, told us. In a South African reserve, van de Waal's team split wild vervet monkeys into groups. Each group was given two containers of maize corn sitting right next to each other. The first one was full of pink corn dyed with a coloring hue from a local African grocery store. The second one had blue corn. The difference, easily noticeable by the monkeys, was not just in color but also in taste. The scientists soaked corn from one container in aloe leaves, which made it bitter and distasteful. In the first group, only blue corn was made bitter; in the second, only pink. Not surprisingly, the monkeys turned their noses up at it. For half of the groups, the pink corn tasted terrible; but for the other half, the blue corn was unpalatable. The vervet monkey habitat was split into two zones, the pink zone (where pink corn was edible) and the blue zone. Soon the monkeys learned which food they preferred and became accustomed to eating corn of only one specific color.

Months later, the researchers stopped treating any corn, pink or blue, with aloe leaves. Although all the corn was now palatable, the monkeys had "learned" their lesson and stuck to the color of their initial preference. Baby monkeys, who had no exposure whatsoever to the bitter taste of aloe and no firsthand experience of the "bad" color, unwaveringly followed their mothers. They ate only pink corn in the pink zone and only blue corn in the blue zone. The rule stuck across generations and converged into a taboo-like tradition.

An even more eye-opening result awaited the researchers as they observed the behavior of migrants. Male vervet monkeys often migrate from one group to another. As the migrants arrived, they were very likely to adhere to their *new* group's preferences, instantaneously switching their behavior. Yes, these monkeys immediately adopted the "local tradition" and started eating corn of a color opposite to the one they had unhesitatingly preferred just a few days earlier. The group rules overshadowed their own experience.

Monkey see, monkey do. People, like monkeys, search for cues from their peers, copy group behavior, and adhere to group rules of conduct. But even though researchers have accumulated massive evidence on just how important groups are for decisions, behavior, and outcomes, we still tend to underestimate the influence of group thinking on our own judgment. A classic experiment, conducted back in the 1960s by professors

Bibb Latané and John Darley, is a powerful illustration of group-induced bias—this time with people.

Imagine you are tasked with completing a long survey, sitting alone in a closed room. Suddenly, the room starts filling with smoke. What would you do? Well, you would sound an alarm, wouldn't you? Indeed, this is exactly what most people in the experiment did individually. But what if you are among strangers, sitting in plastic chairs three feet apart, who are also completing the same tedious survey, their noses buried in the paper? If you believe you would still immediately alert everyone, you underappreciate the influence of others. The researchers found that people's behavior depended crucially on the actions of those around them. As accomplices were added who acted as though nothing had happened and continued vigorously scribbling notes on the survey, almost nobody raised an alarm even while ghastly smoke filled the room. People worryingly looked to their right and to their left, saw no reaction, looked surreptitiously again at the rising puffs of smoke, and . . . went back to working on their survey. Only one in ten took any action.

Well, might being surrounded by "normal" people, not accomplices, make a difference? Replacing actors with unsuspecting strangers did result in a higher reporting rate of the smoke, but still only one of three subjects took any action. Latané and Darley named this tendency to ignore signals of trouble in the presence of passive others the "bystander effect" and went on to study it in various forms for decades. The bystander effect is one of many undesired consequences of what we now call "groupthink," or the powerful effect of group-induced biases.

One profound finding of all the research on group behavior and decision making is that group members tend to minimize conflict and seek consensus. If everyone chooses a specific mode of behavior, the thinking goes, then I should follow. If everyone is in favor of the decision or does not explicitly argue against it, then I feel I must join in as well. Group convergence and group conformity are widespread. New or less experienced members search for cues to learn from the rest what color of corn to eat and whether a room filling with smoke is an ordinary event.

What if we replace corn and smoke with startups?

Business schools love making students work in groups, and Ilya's VC class fervently follows this recipe. Such activity is not just an educational tool for students; it's also a unique treasure trove for observations of how groups of exceptionally smart people make decisions. In one of these live cases, which we covered in chapter 3, we split students into twenty-four "VC partnerships" that decide whether to invest in startups that are actually raising capital in real time.

To refresh your memory, each partnership consists of six students. This nicely mimics the number of partners in larger VC firms. Students write a preliminary investment memo on each startup, grill the founders, conduct their due diligence, then determine which one (if any) they want to fund and submit their final investment recommendation. Importantly, the final submission must detail how their group's discussion proceeded and how they made their decisions.

Final decisions varied dramatically among the twenty-four teams. In one year, the most sought-after startup received only nine offers. All the other teams were adamantly opposed to investing in that startup and provided detailed justifications for their rejection. The same pattern repeated itself with other startups. For each one, some groups selected it as the most promising one while others considered it the least attractive. There is nothing unusual here, since picking breakthrough ideas is risky. Remember also that it was a *live* case: nobody knew the outcome, although we did our best to select worthy startups. With a bit of imagination, each could be viewed as a future DoorDash, Moderna, or Twitter. Naturally, we expect considerable variance in decisions *across* teams.

Surprisingly, what was remarkable was the almost complete nonexistence of disagreements *within* each team. Groups forcefully disagreed with one another, but students consistently *agreed* with one another within their six-member groups. How do we know this? We repeatedly asked students, in confidential surveys taken at different times, whether they disagreed with their group's decision or whether their group modified its decision-making process. Year after year, nine out of ten students expressed complete agreement with the decision. In individual interviews with students, many expressed surprise when they heard about an opposite response from a different team to "such an obvious great deal" or "clearly a horrible idea." The discord *between* teams contrasted strikingly with the like-mindedness *within* each team.

In fact, many of the twenty-four groups arrived at their decision early on. They then spent most of the time justifying their decision and arguing over details, such as what investment terms to offer their chosen startup. Teams were coming to a swift decision, but they weren't properly discussing the opportunity at hand or considering all angles to get to a good decision. Bias was steering their path.

How can such cohesiveness *within* groups coexist with such disparity *across* groups?

Let's observe together a resolution to this puzzle with our own eyes. When we ran an online executive workshop for a large European client during the pandemic, like Griffin from H. G. Wells's *The Invisible Man*, suddenly we could become invisible and visit one breakout room after another to observe and listen to the unfolding discussion without being heard or seen.

Let's watch the group members as they take their seats. Younger team members are vigorously scribbling some arguments on their notepads. One woman looks pensively at the wall, lips tightly pursed, in frozen concentration. Suddenly, a man in his forties wearing an expensive-looking brown jacket, who appears to be the most senior person in the room, kicks things off, asking another man, "So what do you think about this idea? To me, it sounds like a feature, not a product." The guy in a navy hoodie to whom the comment is addressed pauses for a second and responds with a nod. "Yep, it's more like a very niche solution," he says. "I think the unit economics is not clear at all, you know." A lady in a T-shirt joins in. "The idea is kind of cool," she says, "but the team seems to be off."

From our vantage point, we see that the three others, two younger scribbling men and the pensive-looking woman, are taken aback. One scribbler seems to want to say something but doesn't chime in. The discussion continues, but the decision has effectively been made. Soon, the team members converge, indicating absolute certainty about their decision. By this point, filling up their flipchart with pro and con arguments is a pure formality; the rejection of the investment proposal is a fait accompli.

In another room, the VP of retail kicks off the discussion. With equal rapidity, the group reaches the opposite conclusion from the first group. The same pattern repeats in other breakout rooms. In each case, one person, by virtue of their temperament or formal position or due to deference shown by other group members, establishes the tone for the whole discussion by starting the conversation. Like first impressions, this changes the dynamics and predetermines the eventual decision. Whoever may have had differing observations keeps their mouth shut and adapts to the team's direction. We did see some disagreements and even heated debates, but only on minor points such as how to present conclusions to the entire audience. On the main decision, conformity prevailed. Our conclusion: participants immediately stop eating pink corn and switch to blue corn. It is our nature.

We can call such group behavior "path dependence." Whoever starts the discussion tilts the group in a specific direction. If that person occupies a special position in the group to start with, by nature or hierarchy, those advantages add to the tilt. A negative opinion from that individual invites other negative opinions to pour in. Those who were initially positive are persuaded or decide on their own not to object, limiting their expressions to minor points. Dissent is an uphill battle, even in a student study group, and even more so among colleagues where one's career could potentially be at stake. These study groups, consisting of students or executives, are temporary structures; in the real world, the composition of decision-making groups is long-term and stable, making the group dynamics and path dependence even more pronounced. The preferred corn color is picked even faster.

But what if the taste of the corn changes? Do people, like monkeys, stick to their habits or do their tastes evolve?

In one of the in-person sessions we conducted with Stanford students, after the student groups had submitted their final investment memos, they received an email informing them that a well-known VC firm had made an offer to one of the startups. Because the partner who made the offer was on the East Coast, the startup would still be looking for a Silicon Valley investor. By Monday, the teams could update their offer if they wished.

This was not merely a trick by your clever Stanford professor, but a common occurrence. VCs like surprising their competitors by producing Friday afternoon term sheets; they know that reaching a decision or modifying a previously taken decision over the weekend is tough. The new information was valuable and very positive: it included the name of a famous seed investor, the investment amount proposed, and the founder's feelings about the valuation offered. In reviewing their original decisions, the teams that had made an offer to the startup should have considered sweetening their terms and those that had turned the startup down should have reconsidered. But just *one* student group modified their final investment memo. None of the other groups opted for any change whatsoever, maintaining that their original decision was the optimal one. Path dependence once again. After a group makes a decision, commitment to that decision justifies stubborn discarding of all new information.

After we complete breakout room exercises, we always ask participants to share their insights about their decision-making process and whether they would suggest any changes. Most respond negatively, adding that there was no need for a formal vote because "all the group members essentially agreed on the decision." Group members perceive their decision as straightforward, believing that they were on the right path. They were indeed on a path—the dependence path.

One experiment after another, one observation after another, brings us to the same conclusion: groups tend to reach a biased, easy-to-manipulate decision. People compromise, converge, and seek consensus. In a world of high uncertainty, the majority is often wrong, because the consensus conclusion is often formed almost by chance. This is why venture investors had to come up with different ways to make investment decisions. We can learn from VCs how to foster disagreements in groups, de-bias the group process, break the path dependence curse, and avoid reaching a consensus purely for the sake of reaching a consensus. How to agree to disagree.

6.2
Beware of Consensus

"Looking back forty years, every single great investment we made came with a lot of debates, disagreements, controversy," a Silicon Valley veteran tells us. "The deals that were obviously unanimous from the very beginning inevitably ended up duds." Reid Hoffman, a partner at Greylock, also says that his firm prefers investments where half the partnership says, "Ooh, that's a great idea," and the other half says, "Ooh, that's a bad idea." For example, a reaction to Hoffman's proposed Airbnb investment from David Sze, another partner, was "Look, every VC needs to have a deal they can fail on. Airbnb can be yours, right?" Other partners responded that the opportunity was a mistake, that it would become a drag on the portfolio and a waste of time. Bonny Simi, founder of JetBlue Technology Ventures, recounted that only one of their deals had ever had unanimous support; all the others had naysayers, and many investments were approved only after a long debate. And we now know how unanimity can negatively affect outcomes of VC investments.

Ilya and his colleagues collected data on decision-making rules and performance in hundreds of VC firms. One metric of performance was the IPO rate, or the fraction of portfolio companies of that VC firm that went public. The most successful VC-backed companies do go public, so the higher the IPO rate, the more successful the VC firm is.

We then compared two samples. In the first sample, we grouped all the VC firms that had a higher IPO rate than the median VC firm ("High IPO," or more successful sample). The remaining firms constituted our "Low IPO" sample. In our analysis of decision making and performance, we were particularly interested in firms insisting on unanimity, or those settings where all partners must agree for the investment to go forward. We found that High IPO VC firms were less likely to follow the unanimity rule. Statistically, the difference translates into a sizable difference in returns. This finding reinforces that unanimity is not the most efficient group decision-making process, especially when the uncertainly level is high and there are many unknowns. Whenever everybody agrees, or has to agree, on everything in the VC firm, it's not a good sign.

Compare this to a corporate meeting on the launch of a new product or on approval of the R&D budget. Presenters are here to get a formal sign-off on their request and not to debate. Time is used to convince the most senior boss in the room to give approval. Questions, if asked at all, are pure formalities, making certain the right boxes have been checked. Debate ensues only in cases of political misalignment or lack of "pre-socializing" with influential participants. Unanimous approval is the gold standard. Such meetings are designed to stifle debate. But what works for politburo-style consensus building in a traditional environment could be the kiss of death in times of uncertainty. "There is no 'I' in team," we often hear. But in fact "I" also stands for innovation.

At the other end of the spectrum, and equally dangerous, is a consensus-seeking culture that gets bogged down in relentless discussions and disagreements with no end in sight, and without coming to any decision. We are sure you have seen this type of meeting too. Such culture can prevent a company from making vital decisions on time. Consider the British broadcaster BBC, where many decisions required six or more meetings. At the Mattel toy company, under previous leadership, decisions on almost everything dragged on. Employees would spend weeks putting together elaborate presentations of 100 slides or more, detailing the minutiae of every upcoming product. A website redesign involved nearly a year of monthly meetings. By the time a decision was finally reached, the budget had already been reallocated to another project.

Not many VC partnerships can survive if they structure decision-making rules like this. Nor can any company facing turbulent times. For stability, go for consensus; for breakthroughs, rely on the VC mindset way.

VCs are not consensus seekers. They love arguing, fighting for their view of the future, listening carefully to others across the table, and kicking ideas around. The majority often rules, but that doesn't mean the majority is right.

Think of sports. In October 1990, the famous undefeated boxer Mike Tyson was preparing to fight a clear underdog, Buster Douglas. For many bettors, it was an easy and safe way for a Mr. Consensus to make some pocket money. Quite a few of them placed large bets, expecting marginal gains on an almost certain Tyson victory. One guy bet $93,000 in the expectation of winning only $3,000 at odds of 31 to 1 in Tyson's favor. Eventually, the odds reached an incredible 42 to 1. Not much gain, but it felt certain. But if you are a Ms. Contrarian and ready to go against the grain, your payout could have skyrocketed. The odds on Douglas were at 37 to 1, meaning that if you bet $10,000 on Douglas and he won, you would have walked away with $370,000. Of course, if Douglas goes down, everybody around will ridicule you. Interestingly, the largest wager on Douglas that night was only $1,000. Nevertheless, that night Buster Douglas knocked out the previously unbeaten Mike Tyson. The bookmakers paid out $37,000 to our Ms. Contrarian. You never know who wins until the match is played.

The same idea can be extended to investments. Consider Figure 9, where we visualize the tension in a 2×2 matrix. Your bet could be right or wrong, and it could be contrarian or done according to consensus. The wrong bet will result in a loss, and the only difference between the contrarian and consensus strategies is the amount of ridicule directed at the loser. For the right bet, though, the difference between the contrarian and the consensus could not be greater. As in the world of sports, so in the investment world: consensus bets yield small profits. The larger the herd and the stiffer the competition, the lower the returns. It's the contrarian bets that, if they happen to be the right ones, make an investor's name and fortune. "The consensus is built into the price," explains Ray Dalio, the legendary investor and the founder of Bridgewater Associates. "So, in order to be successful, you are betting against the consensus and you have to be right. That's the game."

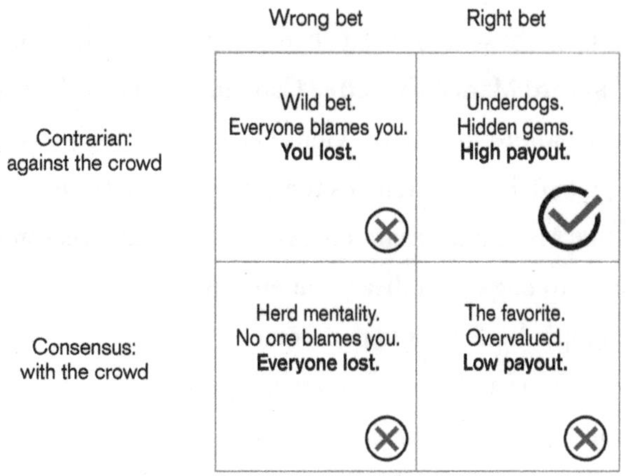

	Wrong bet	Right bet
Contrarian: against the crowd	Wild bet. Everyone blames you. **You lost.** ⊗	Underdogs. Hidden gems. **High payout.** ✓
Consensus: with the crowd	Herd mentality. No one blames you. **Everyone lost.** ⊗	The favorite. Overvalued. **Low payout.** ⊗

Figure 9.
Bets and possible outcomes

You may know John Maynard Keynes as one of the most famous economists of the twentieth century, but at King's College of Cambridge University he is also remembered as a contrarian investor. When Keynes started managing the King's endowment fund in 1921, he refused to follow a Mr. Consensus playbook. He sold off a significant share of the King's real estate to invest capital in stocks, which represented one-third of the portfolio by the time of his death in 1946. This was a very contrarian move, since at the time university endowments mainly owned land and fixed-income securities to preserve capital. Keynes managed to outperform the market by four times and multiplied every £100 he started with into £1,675 during those two dozen years.

You don't need to be a Keynes or a boxing gambler to adopt this strategy. Think of a nice house in downtown San Francisco. If it is well advertised, chances are slim that you will get a bargain. However, imagine the opposite when you're the only one who believes that a particular land plot is a promising site for a large office building and others think you're nuts. This may become the deal of the year (if not of your lifetime)—but, of course, only if you turn out to be right. VCs hunt for interesting, contrarian ideas.

This analysis of consensus versus contrarian approaches, originally described by Howard Marks of Oaktree Capital, has been fully exploited by VCs. VCs can't afford to join Mr. Consensus. The anticipated reward is not big enough to deliver the returns they are seeking. To succeed, they must be more like Ms. Contrarian. This is a fundamental reason behind VCs' willingness to engage in disagreements and controversies among themselves. It simply leads to better outcomes.

Not surprisingly, a variant of this matrix is popular among VCs. "The only way to make outsized returns in Venture Capital is to be right *and* non-consensus," says Andy Rachleff, a cofounder of Benchmark Capital. "You can't outinvest others by investing in whatever everybody thinks,"

Mike Maples told us. "You can't achieve that by acting the way other people act." Or as Bryan Roberts of Venrock succinctly summarized for us, "The worst thing that may happen is to have an organization where people say: 'If I'm wrong, at least I'm not alone.'"

VCs are not consensus seekers—they are disagreement seekers. "Conviction beats consensus," Alex Rampell declared passionately in our meeting with him. In an environment in which uncertainty about the future should give rise to different, often contradictory opinions, these opinions must be articulated.

Doing so is difficult. On top of all the group biases, an additional trap to avoid is the "you scratch my back and I scratch yours" pattern. One revealing example from a corporate environment is how the Performance Review Committee (PRC) worked at Enron, contributing to this company's ignominious demise in 2001. Each employee received a formal performance review every six months, with the employee selecting five coworkers, superiors, or subordinates to give feedback to the PRC. The process featured a lot of backroom negotiation. As researchers Clinton Free and Norman Macintosh found, "One manager described his conversation with another manager when he broached the subject of an imminent PRC as follows: 'I was wondering if you had a few minutes to talk some PRC.' She replied, 'Why—you want to cut a deal?' 'Done,' I said—and just like that we cut our deal. Business unit managers also made deals with one another, exchanging bad scores for both employees they wanted to dispose of, and for rivals they wanted to discredit."

The worst thing that can happen to a VC partnership, or any other group, is if one partner supports a deal led by their colleague while privately thinking the deal stinks, only because they hope the colleague will return the favor later and support *their* deal. Such mock consensus driven by political considerations comes at a steep price and becomes a slippery slope. One day, you will wake up in a Byzantine complex of intrigues and power plays.

As one VC told us, once you feel that you can't critique your partner's position safely, it's time to seek a way out. This principle holds true far beyond the VC world. Ray Dalio insists that any organization will win if it becomes "radically open-minded" and "replace[s] the joy of being proven right with the joy of learning what is true." He says it is the most valuable thought he could possibly share. Many VCs would wholeheartedly agree with him.

The VC underlying methodology therefore includes an easy-to-state principle: there is an obligation to dissent.

"I don't care a damn for your loyal service when you think I am right," General John Monash, a renowned World War I military commander, told his men. "When I really want it most is when you think I am wrong." In other words, it's your *duty* to speak up if you disagree with the higher-ups. To avoid missing billion-dollar opportunities, your organization must join the ranks of Monashes and make the obligation to dissent a part of its core values.

The principle is easy to state, but hard to make it work. Good intentions don't work by themselves.

6.3
Even the Devil Needs an Advocate

"I've searched all the parks in all the cities—and found no statues of committees," the famous British writer G. K. Chesterton reportedly stated. VCs are well aware of inefficiencies and biases in groups; they also know that these biases are particularly dangerous in a highly uncertain world. And they know that team members with prepared minds can make the right call if they design a process to avoid these blind spots. In our research and work with VCs, we observed many specific practices with which VCs equip themselves. The next time you huddle in a room with your team members, you'll be more likely to make a better decision with these four mechanisms we have learned from VCs.

Keep the team small

If you join a VC team meeting, you will notice something remarkable: the room is tiny.

Investors review deals in small groups. Many VC partnerships have three to five partners. Even with all the junior team members added, you will see an intimate and informal exercise. The meeting is designed to ensure that everyone who can contribute is expected to be present and everyone present is expected to contribute.

Innovative companies recognize that smaller teams outperform larger ones, as the communication quality, reaction speed, and individual motivation are far superior. Think of the famous "two-pizza team" size requirement designed at Amazon for teams working on a new product or service. The name is derived from the belief that the team should be properly nourished with two pizzas, implying an ideal size of no more than eight. Members of smaller teams also demonstrate higher accountability and reduced finger pointing later on. Many companies have followed the two-pizza principle, such as Intuit, a major provider of financial software. When the leadership at Mattel changed, one of the new principles was to permit no more than ten people in any decision meeting.

These principles correspond to the gut feelings of decision makers in many organizations and have extensive scientific backing. Back in the 1970s, researchers Richard Hackman and Neil Vidmar found that, for many tasks, the optimal group size was four or five. The greater the number of people performing a task together, the less productive they were. Next time you plan a decision-making meeting, invite only those who really need to attend, and even then ensure the number is below a dozen.

Juniors speak first

Have you been in meetings where the boss articulates his position and then asks, "What do you think?" Once the boss has spoken, it's hard to argue for the opposite position or provide a counterexample. This is the world dominated by HIPPO: the Highest-Paid Person's Opinion. Yet the information and opinions of others could be just as valuable, if not more so. Copying the behavior of superiors may very well be a survival tactic, but in the world of uncertainty it's detrimental.

VCs appreciate that if the process is designed in the right way, less experienced people can add considerable value. Meritocracy is key. Junior investment team members are often the people who have done most of the analysis: talking to customers, conducting reference calls, analyzing the market, preparing the investment memo. Especially in an uncertain environment, they possess lots of "soft" information that is difficult to formalize on paper. The "juniors first" rule encourages them to provide their assessment before any of the senior partners speak up. Strict enforcement of this rule creates a culture in which juniors are expected to talk first.

The junior-senior engagement dynamic is critical in many settings. In a study that should be better known, nine out of ten nurses confided they find it difficult to speak up to a physician, even if they observe that a patient's safety is at risk. You should favor the voice of disagreement over the silence of intimidation.

President John F. Kennedy took this principle one notch further during the fateful days of the Cuban Missile Crisis. Not only did he insist that everybody speak as equals in his team's deliberations, with neither rank nor chairman. He also skipped some meetings to ensure that his presence would not intimidate participants. Reading the transcripts of heated exchanges in the Oval Office regarding the Soviet threat, one cannot help but wonder whether it was these seemingly small but intentional actions designed to foster open debate in the Kennedy administration that avoided a nuclear Armageddon. Limiting your own power may lead to better decisions. That's a mighty lesson for any leader.

Assign a devil's advocate

To ensure that the opposite view is heard, many VC partnerships make it a standard practice to assign one person or a small team the role of contrarian. Laden with religious overtones, this term indeed originates from the tradition of assigning a person in the Roman Catholic Church to argue against the canonization of someone proposed for sainthood. Representing the devil, the *advocatus diaboli* was an official role within the Vatican administration tasked with finding evidence *against* the most deserving candidates for sainthood. Pitted against the candidate's advocate, the devil's advocate played an important balancing role in the canonization process. The Venture Mindset borrowed both the term and the practice from the church.

For example, venture firm a16z often designates a "red team" of people tasked with arguing against a deal. When Warren Buffett contemplates his biggest acquisitions, similarly to a16z he hires two advisers: one to support a case for the investment and the other to make the case against it. Some VCs apply the rule with more fervor than the Catholic Church, assigning *every* investment team member except the deal leader to a devil's advocate role. A roomful of devils! Quite a challenge to overcome.

One organization that uses the devil's advocate concept effectively is AMAN, the Israeli armed forces' directorate of military intelligence. After Israeli intelligence failed to predict the 1973 Yom Kippur War, a key idea that emerged from a postwar inquiry was to create a devil's advocate position, known as "the tenth man." That person's role is to disagree, raise red flags, and point out flaws in the group's deliberations and decisions.

An important conceptual and practical point is the difference between a devil's advocate and what is known as "authentic dissent." The idea of authentic dissent, popularized by Adam Grant in his book *Originals*, says that there are always devils among us and we should just let them speak freely. The leader is responsible for drawing out this authentic dissent. The idea does sound attractive, since assigning a devil's advocate seems less authentic, with people arguing for positions they do not necessarily hold themselves. However nice the intention of authentic dissent sounds, intentions don't matter—mechanisms do. If the organization has a culture in which people can freely speak their mind, the leader does not need to cultivate dissent. But if you start with an organization in which groups seek conformity and consensus, efforts to encourage authentic dissent may fail. Assigning a devil's advocate removes the social stigma associated with going against the grain.

Moreover, in cohesive and highly productive small groups, people may tend to think similarly on a number of issues, especially if they have self-selected to be in the group. The hope of authenticity may fail here. In contrast to encouraging authentic dissent, make everybody a devil. As examples of debate societies amply demonstrate, forcing people to take a position will lead them to pursue questions they otherwise would not have asked. Ask everyone in the group to come up with a reason not to invest. And ensure that you rotate your devils. If one person is constantly playing the negative role, the mechanism could backfire, as colleagues may get accustomed to it and ignore any criticism from this person.

Provide feedback in advance

In many VC firms, every team member shares their opinion on the investment opportunity after reading the investment memo, but in advance of the meeting. Importantly, these thoughts are collected independently:

you don't know anyone else's input yet as you are typing your own. This arrangement provides ample opportunity to submit negative information or a minority opinion. When the trove of collective reactions is finally revealed, the differences among group members are often substantial. The recognition of such varying opinions liberates the discussion.

Increasingly, companies use this mechanism in their hiring process. For example, Google's policy asks members of an interview committee to record their individual comments on each candidate before the meeting. Establishing such a process for other company decisions, especially large investment projects and strategic decisions, is not easy. However, embedding it is an integral part of the design, and creating a productive culture of disagreement is a must in an era of disruptive changes. To de-bias group thinking even further, some VC firms make the advance feedback blind. As a result, you don't know, prior to the discussion, what the HIPPO thinks.

Pay attention at the next meeting you attend. If *nobody* around you opposes a decision or raises critical issues, then perhaps people in your organization are not motivated to ask tough questions. If people spend more time reading attitudes in the room than reading about the proposed idea and critically evaluating it, don't expect new creative solutions to emerge. VC partnerships of such disposition can rarely survive beyond the first fund. Silence in the room does not mean consent; rather, it is a strong sign of potential disaster.

6.4
Lekkers: The Power of Going Against the Grain

After VCs have put so much effort into promoting dissent, they eventually do need to converge. Ultimately, some partnerships (especially smaller ones) do pursue unanimity, while many others require at least a majority to be in favor of the deal. It might appear that VCs eventually turn down contrarian ideas that don't pass the muster of group approval.

Ah, but we haven't mentioned Lekker! Lekker was a vervet monkey in Professor van de Waal's study described at the beginning of this chapter. He migrated to a group of the opposite corn color. That the monkeys around him were all eating the corn of *their* preference didn't matter to Lekker. He went straight to the container of his choice and munched on the corn *he* had become accustomed to. Untouched by bitter aloe, the corn did not bother him in the least. Was he simply afraid of food of a new color? "Not at all," van de Waal explained to us. "Lekker sampled a tiny bit of pink corn, but immediately switched back to the color of his liking. Lekker ignored the preference of the dominant female in the group." Lekker was a rebel, a monkey "innovator."

There were Lekkers in Latané and Darley's smoke experiments too. They were the 10 percent of subjects who stood up and sought help, despite being surrounded by conformists. And in the Stanford VC class, one of every ten students did disagree pointedly with their group.

Lekkers.

There are both monkeys and people who are ready to dissent, disobey, stick to their views, or rebel against the others. You know some Lekkers. Maybe you are one yourself. Many intrapreneurs and entrepreneurs we feature in this book are Lekkers. In a traditional environment, Lekkers are a pain. In a modern organization, Lekkers can be used to drive innovation, or they can be shut down and driven away.

One critical principle of the Venture Mindset is that Lekkers should be encouraged and given an opportunity to have their day. We call it "Lekkerism." We use the "-ism" suffix purposefully, because we hope to kickstart the "Lekkerism" movement into more organizational settings. Even though VCs strive to converge, they have also developed three specific mechanisms to enable Lekkerism.

Empower leaders with anti-veto power

You are likely familiar with the veto right. Some people (usually HIPPOs!) can overrule everybody else's go-to decision and put a stop to any action. US presidents have a constitutional right to veto acts of Congress. Five countries can each individually veto any decision of the United Nations Security Council. Smaller VC partnerships frequently give similar veto power to their partners. The veto rule reinforces trust among decision makers, especially if all of them have deep expertise in the same domain. Often, these partnerships require "enthusiastic consensus." They invest only if everybody strongly supports the investment.

But talk to Nagraj Kashyap. After working at Qualcomm, where he spearheaded the Zoom investment, Kashyap went on to start M12, the venture arm of Microsoft. One right he insisted on was "anti-veto" power. His team was welcome to go against him and invest in a deal he didn't like. And he could also go against his entire team and make an investment even if everybody else was opposed. The rationale was to catch unconventional investments; it was inspired by experiences such as his Zoom deal. One such investment was Kahoot, a game-based learning platform. Many experts were skeptical, and the internal team voted the investment down. Kashyap went ahead with it anyway. When Kahoot went public in 2021, it was a huge success—so huge that the returns on this deal exceeded all the capital their fund had invested in all other startups.

Amazingly, Kashyap designed a process that prevented himself from vetoing investment decisions. What he could do, however, was to go against his team and proceed with an investment even if everyone else was pessimistic. He denied himself a traditional boss's right to be a HIPPO to let both himself and his team members put a Lekker's hat on.

Let rebels make the call

"I don't believe in the consensus," says Bryan Roberts in his mellow voice over a cup of old Taiwanese tea in Ilya's office at Stanford. Bryan is a partner at the storied VC firm Venrock, which has been around since 1969. He takes another sip and tells us a story of how one opportunity was missed because a senior partner didn't like the startup name and the deal champion didn't push back. "That's like picking your favorite sport team based on their mascot!" he said, laughing. The startup was Yahoo.

Roberts introduced a process at Venrock that is designed to keep attractive but non-consensus deals from slipping through the cracks. Eight Venrock partners vigorously debate every deal, and then the partner who brought the deal in the first place makes the final investment decision unilaterally. "Our investors always ask me, 'How does your investment committee work?' Well, we don't have an investment committee. No voting. At all." Instead, Venrock lets each partner make an investment even if everyone else is against it. Other partners provide their perspective, question the lead partner's judgment, and play devil's advocate. But the decision is ultimately in the hands of one partner. Nicolas Sauvage, president of TDK Ventures, designed a very similar process after attending Ilya's sessions on corporate venture capital. "You can't expect everyone to agree all the time," he told us. "Moreover, we are not in the business of averages, but in the business of extremes. Truly innovative ideas and companies are rarely cookie-cutter ones. So as not to miss them, no one—including me—has a veto right on what our investment directors want to proceed investing in."

Imagine everyone in your partnership saying, "There can't be anything more boring than shaving razors" and "Subscription e-commerce is a dead end." Despite those words of discouragement, one Venrock partner still invested in a small startup called Dollar Shave Club. Many other VCs turned the company down. Roberts is certain they would not have backed Dollar Shave Club had it not been for their unorthodox decision-making process. The bet was spot-on: in 2016, the company was acquired by Unilever for $1 billion.

The VC world is full of stories when a single person had unique ability to see what others could not. The now ubiquitous PowerPoint may not have existed without the foresight of Dick Kramlich, then a partner at NEA, who, against the overwhelming rejection of his partners, invested his own money in the startup behind it. The company was then acquired by Microsoft and its product became the foundation for the product we still use today.

Professor Andy Wu studied cases such as Kramlich's in which dissenting VCs pursue investments individually after their partners do not approve. Wu found that partners at more than 500 VC firms made such angel investments. Even though they invest in younger startups with less educated, less experienced, and younger founding teams, these individual investments nevertheless generate on average the same financial returns as their VC firms.

To benefit from such Lekkerism, many VC firms give their partners the right to invest even if others disagree. This way they did not miss ideas as revolutionary as Zoom, Dollar Shave Club, and PowerPoint. What if you do the same in your organization and within your team? Like these VCs, consider giving people in your organization the right to make their own decisions, even if seemingly small ones, in the face of opposition. We can bet you do have Lekkers in your organization as well. What your organization might be missing is the way to let them demonstrate their counterintuitive instincts. Give them freedom and resources to act.

Minority rules

At Founders Fund, partners can cut a check for smaller deals, which are often at the earliest stage and thus the most uncertain, if they can convince just one other partner out of seven. As the investment size increases, so does the number of partners who need to agree. But unanimity is never required; even for the largest investments, two of seven partners can disagree and the investment will still go through. At a16z, each partner has a dedicated individual budget. The investment committee vigorously debates the deals, but it is the partner's responsibility to decide on an individual investment. If the proposed investment size is over their budget, then they need to convince other partners to share part of their budget to fund the deal.

How to introduce this mechanism to your organization? Next time a small group of leaders insists on the unusual idea, don't shut them down. Instead, give them a small budget to build a prototype or run a test. In uncharted territories, a minority could become discoverers of new continents.

Lekkerism does present one inherent danger. Imagine a partner insisting on a deal in the face of firm opposition. If the deal goes through but the company fails, it might be tempting to point the finger later on and say, "I knew it would happen." Some partnerships resist this tendency by demanding consensus from then on. As one investor notes, it's "Speak now, or forever hold your peace." VCs try to encourage their Lekkers when the new idea or company is reviewed, but, once invested, they then become the Three Musketeers, pursuing the "all for one and one for all" paradigm. Partners benefit together and lose together. If one partner's deals all end up duds, the entire partnership suffers. If one partner lands a deal like Google or Facebook, all partners benefit tremendously. Seeking disruptive ideas? Disrupt the traditional decision-making process in your organization and let rebels reshuffle the cards.

6.5
The Danger of Being Unanimously Wrong

One company that embodies many of our tactical tips to aid better decision making is Amazon. After phone interviews and in-person campus meetings, the hiring manager and a handful of other people (*keep it small*) get together to make a decision. Like many Silicon Valley companies, Amazon realized that the number of interviewers should be kept low, as adding more people to the loop reduces efficiency. Interviewers then submit their comments and a recommendation without anyone talking to one another (*provide independent feedback in advance*). Only then does the hiring team assemble as a group. One person outside the hiring team, with sufficient seniority and with experience from numerous interviews, is assigned a unique role called a "bar raiser." That person's single goal is to ensure that the candidate is better than at least half of their Amazon peers. Unlike the hiring manager, who usually wants to hire as soon as possible—because there is always more work than people—the bar raiser is independent and not under time pressure, often demonstrating a dose of healthy skepticism (*devil's advocate*). After the participants have read one anothers' notes, the discussion starts, with everyone in the room keeping in mind one of Amazon's sixteen leadership principles, which insists that leaders must "not compromise for the sake of social cohesion." Participants are expected to express their doubts and concerns. As with VCs, participants search for areas of disagreement rather than trying to avoid them.

After the group has read through and listened to all the comments, it is up to the hiring manager and the bar raiser to make the call. Both must enthusiastically support the candidate before an offer is made. But once the hiring decision is made, the situation flips: everyone fully owns the decision and no one complains about the outcome. Thus the name of this leadership principle: "Disagree and Commit"—similar to the Three

Musketeers attitude in VC partnerships. This well-scripted and detailed mechanism is one of the keys to Amazon's well-oiled recruitment machine.

Applying this kind of decision making to everyday decisions in your company can have a big impact. Take our decision around naming this book. The title and even the subtitle can greatly influence a book's appeal. We argued with each other and sought advice from our editor, publisher, agent, friends, and marketing professionals. Our process was intentionally designed to avoid the traps of groupthink. For example, the two of us felt psychologically that it was safer to accept an idea if it came from our tremendous editor, Lydia Yadi (who is *the* expert to trust in such areas). But we knew a trap when we saw one. We stepped back and agreed that all of us would first independently generate ideas (getting help from ChatGPT was permissible). We all then shared our top individual choices to create an extensive pool of title-subtitle pairs. At this point, the natural process would be to discuss the options and pick a winner together. But the VC mindset tells us that is a mistake. Instead, we agreed to pick our top choices independently. Only after that did we share and discuss our preferences. We agreed to be direct in our criticisms and deliberately avoided words like "my idea" to disavow the personal origin of any particular idea. We asked our friends to be devil's advocates. Our message to them was "Don't tell us what you like; tell us which option you really dislike and why, or suggest your own option."

Finally, after a vigorous—heated, but cool—debate, we ended up with five options. Each of us had a favorite. At this point, we shifted gears dramatically and, instead of voting ourselves, asked a cohort of Stanford students who had recently taken Ilya's VC class. Think about this step as an additional form of due diligence, like reference checks on a job candidate. Three days and 100 anonymous responses later, two leaders emerged. The other three options (which some of us liked) got a combined total of less than 10 percent. What a surprise! We presented two finalists to senior leaders at a Stanford executive program and the winner emerged. Finally, we made some small tweaks to the winning subtitle, which came directly from the founder of the Portfolio publishing house (thanks, Adrian!). This deliberately designed, multistage process resulted in the title and subtitle you see on the cover. Then we unanimously agreed on and committed to our selection.

VCs discuss, argue, debate, disagree, seek further evidence, and finally approve or reject the idea. The future of every individual decision is uncertain. As we are writing this, we have no clue whether we will beat Amazon's bestseller odds, but at least we know that we have intentionally addressed some of our biases throughout the creative process. "Sometimes I wish we would study more monkeys to learn about us and our biases," Professor van de Waal says with a sigh.

We wholeheartedly agree with her.

MINDSET CHECKS

● ● ● ●

- Is the culture in your organization consensus-at-all-costs, or does it give individuals autonomy to make risky calls?

- Are your meetings designed to promote debate and open to disagreements?

- Does your organization support innovative rebels (Lekkers) or does it suppress outliers?

SEVEN

Double Down or Quit

Why you should pull the plug faster and more often

7.1
Venture Casino: Fold, Call, or Raise?

The meeting place was squeezed between Jewish, Japanese, Italian, and Greek cemeteries. Not the most auspicious location to test our luck. "What a hellhole this place is!" says Alex to Ilya as an old red Chevrolet with a broken rear window cuts us off, nearly grazing our car. "I didn't know it is even legal to play poker in California."

The two of us are driving to Lucky Chances Casino with $50 in our pockets. We expect to lose all our money to Richard Harroch, an experienced poker player who has invited us to grab dinner together, teach us some poker tricks, and talk VC. We are losing money for a good cause: we know VCs feel at home in Lucky Chances and casinos generally.

"Venture capital is high-risk poker," declared Michael Moritz, the legendary Sequoia Capital partner. Our host Richard certainly agrees. He is a managing director at VantagePoint Capital Partners, a VC firm near San Francisco. He also coauthored the bestseller *Poker for Dummies* and has played in more than 100 tournaments at the World Series of Poker. "Knowledge of poker is helpful when it comes to VC decisions, particularly investment decisions and negotiations for M&A exits," he tells us as he takes poker chips from a bag. "You have to make great decisions in both arenas, and do so with incomplete information."

Hungarian-American prodigy John von Neumann was an early poker devotee. A force behind the development of modern computers as well as the Manhattan Project, von Neumann was looking for gaming models to describe economic decision making. He was unimpressed with both roulette and chess. Roulette is gambling in its purest form. No skill is involved; only *luck* matters. Chess and Go are on the opposite end of the luck-to-skill spectrum. These are games of pure skill, with both players possessing identical and complete information at any time after the game commences. This is why you see no chess championships in Las Vegas casinos and no roulette championships anywhere.

"Real life is not like that," von Neumann once complained. After diving into poker's mechanics, he found it more promising and concluded: "This game is the perfect model for human decision making." His own poker skills didn't benefit him financially, but studying poker helped him coauthor *Theory of Games and Economic Behavior* in 1944, laying the foundation for what has become the celebrated field of game theory. We now apply game theory to problems as diverse as Christie's auctions of old master paintings and nuclear war strategizing.

On the surface, poker is a deceptively simple game. In the most popular style of poker, called Texas Hold 'em, each player has to collect the most valuable combination of five cards out of seven available: two in their own hands, to which only they are privy, and five communal cards laid out on the poker table and available to everyone. Each combination has a different value, determined by the strength of the cards and the relationships between them. Whoever has the better combination wins and collects the pot—the accumulated bets of all players. The game seems simple, but the betting process and how information gets revealed make poker both extremely nuanced and exhilarating to play.

A round of Texas Hold 'em starts with each player receiving two cards. As everyone is peeking privately at their cards, once somebody bets you have to make the first decision: fold (quit this round), call (match a bet made by a prior player), or raise (increase the bet). Your choice at this stage of the game is in part dictated by the two cards you have. Some are much better because they make you more likely to assemble strong combinations at later stages. Your choice can also be dictated by other players' actions. You can't see their cards, but you observe their decisions to fold, call, or raise.

After betting on the first round concludes, three communal cards are revealed. The players now possess far more information about the combinations they can hope to assemble. Players have to decide again: fold, call, or raise. Then one more card is revealed. With this information, players again must choose to fold, call, or raise. Finally, the last communal card is revealed and again the players have to make a decision. Until the very end, players are uncertain about their chances of winning the pot. Finally, cards are revealed and the strongest combination wins.

Poker is a game of luck and skill. Players, armed only with incomplete information, have to decide when to call, fold, or raise. They should know the odds, be able to read other players' cues and predict their behavior, and react to the developing situation on the spot.

Many fascinating books have recently been written on poker's surprising links to psychology, business, and politics. But VCs have been using poker strategies for a long time. Or, as we prefer to think about it, poker players were among the first to have developed an acute VC mindset.

7.2
One Round at a Time

So how does poker relate to the Venture Mindset?

Until now, we have discussed how VCs source and evaluate ideas, identify risks, and decide to invest. Then the game begins. The first bets are typically relatively small. As with the limited information you have from the first two poker cards, VCs face huge uncertainty about startup prospects at this stage. In VC parlance, these stages are called "seed" and "Series A" rounds. Not only is the amount of funding provided to a startup in these rounds fairly small—at least relative to the size of VC funds—but VCs also know that if the startup does well, it will need more funding, or a bigger bet. Like champion poker players, who fold at least 75 percent of all starting hands, VCs also frequently fold if the information feedback from their initial investment is unfavorable.

Time passes. Three poker cards are revealed. In the VC world, this is the time when the first customers start using the product, the first financials hit the books, the technology is further developed, and the startup team succeeds or fails to attract the right talent. Fold, call, or raise?

If you are still in the game, the next round is coming, both for poker players and for VCs. One more card is revealed. Perhaps an expansion to a new country was problematic; the first professional CEO was successfully hired; new services were launched, though they didn't grow as expected; regulators are scrutinizing the legality of the offering; competitors are launching similar products. Fold, call, or raise?

Traditional organizations rarely act like poker players. They tend to wait for all the cards to be revealed before making a call. Indeed, the more information they have about the market and customer feedback, the lower the risk is. But they risk losing the momentum. When innovation is at stake, they may not even be invited to the table. The game is simply played without them, because others know they don't make a call.

In one such VC game, Sequoia Capital played its hand so well that it became Airbnb's biggest IPO winner. Well-established hotel chains felt the pressure too late and scrambled to create alternatives years after Airbnb had already gained momentum, becoming *the* marketplace platform for short-term stays. Making a call early on made the difference. Over more than a decade, Sequoia accumulated a stake eventually worth more than $10 billion in Airbnb. Like an experienced poker player, Sequoia made decisions sequentially, as more information became available. Its bet earned Sequoia a seat in the hall of fame for the best VC deals of all time. No bluffing was required. What was behind such an impressive win?

A tree starts with a seed. The first time the Airbnb founders, Brian Chesky and Joe Gebbia, met with Sequoia in 2009, their early website, airbedandbreakfast.com, had been functional for less than a year. As you recall, after multiple investors had turned them down, the founders sold cereal to Barack Obama and John McCain fans at Democratic and Republican presidential conventions for $40 a box, earning $30,000, enough to help them survive. Imagine Chesky and Gebbia's relief when they picked up a $600,000 seed investment led by Sequoia Capital. The valuation of the company was around $2.5 million.

In 2010, what started with renting rooms in apartments became a platform for renting out whole summer houses, boats, castles, and even private islands. "We are in more cities than Starbucks!" Chesky proclaimed with pride. With the founders now ready to launch their iPhone app, it was time to raise more capital. VCs use letters of the alphabet to determine each subsequent round of funding. Airbnb was ready for the first letter.

Series A. Some cards are revealed: Airbnb is present in 8,000 locations with 700,000 nights booked by November 2010. Reid Hoffman from Greylock Partners meets the founders and makes a bid. Hoffman values the company at an impressive $67 million (up from just $2.5 million a year earlier). Sequoia Capital must decide. Fold, call, or raise? Sequoia doubles down by investing an additional $1.9 million.

Series B. In July 2011, Airbnb announces its ten millionth booking. Complaints about guests are rising; one host's place is completely trashed. The company starts facing regulatory scrutiny. Not all the newly revealed cards are good ones. Still, the valuation hits $1 billion. Another VC firm, a16z, didn't want to miss what might become a "once in a lifetime" opportunity, and so it took the lead in the funding round.

Series C. In February 2013, many in Silicon Valley are shocked as Founders Fund raises the pot, investing $150 million at a $2.5 billion valuation. The raise is so large that the fund has to ask its own investors for permission to make such a huge bet. Sequoia calls by participating in this round.

Series D. Airbnb is still not profitable, but enough cards are already on the table to show investors they have a royal flush on their hands. Sequoia and others raise again! In April 2014, Airbnb is valued at an astronomical $10 billion.

A VC game can have more rounds than poker. Airbnb fundraising continues into Series E, F, and G. On December 10, 2020, Airbnb is listed on Nasdaq at a valuation of almost $40 billion. Soon the valuation surged past the $100 billion mark. Who could have expected that Sequoia's initial investment of half a million dollars would result in such a pot? You know the answer.

The founders and their VC backers went through eight rounds of funding, raised billions of dollars of capital, and waited more than eleven years for the IPO. New investment projects can be ravenous cash-burning machines. Even the most successful ones often need to go back to investors and raise more money, again and again. If the company is doing well, not only will it raise another round, but each round will be much larger than the preceding one. An average unicorn raises more than five funding rounds. Uber raised at least fifteen funding rounds between 2009 and its IPO in 2019; Facebook had at least twenty funding rounds between its founding in 2004 and its IPO in 2012.

If any VC committed the capital for all rounds to such bets on day one, we guarantee that they would quickly go bust. Unfortunately, many traditional companies ignore VC thinking and do exactly this when they commit to a large-scale investment project with so much information not yet known. Or even worse. They wait for all cards to unfold, but by then it is too late.

Figure 10 visualizes possible startup fates. Only one path leads to a successful result. The rest are all failures or so-so outcomes for founders and investors. Such charts are called "decision trees," with each arrow representing a branch. You start on the left with the hope that you will reach the right (IPO or M&A) at the end of the journey. Some trees are small; others grow like venerable redwoods.

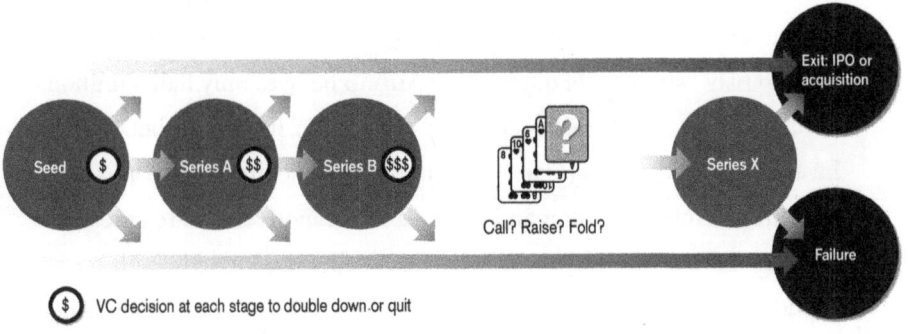

Figure 10.
Funding rounds are designed to provide entrepreneurs with enough capital to get to the next milestone and give VCs flexibility to double down or quit.

At later stages, startups are less risky and, as in poker, you know most of the cards by that time. There is still a chance to lose, due either to new cards as they are drawn or to cards held by other players. Sometimes, you can lose in a heartbeat.

Jawbone, once a hot startup with a product that measured people's heart rate and steps walked, was backed by the same big VC names as Airbnb—Sequoia Capital and a16z. In 2017, after fifteen rounds and almost $1 billion raised, it went bust.

Sometimes the very last card on the table upsets players. When a group of early-stage VC investors backed a promising California-based solar company called Solyndra in 2006, they expected a long wait. Solyndra raised many rounds, at increasing valuations, before attempting an IPO in summer 2010 at well more than $1 billion in value. The IPO failed miserably and Solyndra filed for bankruptcy a year later. The tide turned and the investors lost the entirety of their bet.

The poker card analogy helps us understand why VCs think in rounds. There may be no free cheese in the mousetrap, but you can approach it slowly, sniffing the air cautiously before sticking your nose in. The first investment is just the beginning of a long game. Think of it as a "pay to play" strategy. Sequoia's first Airbnb bet was only half a million dollars, a very small fraction of their eventual $240 million bet. Smart investors plant the seed (hence the name of the opening round) and nurture the startup with more and more cash. As more cards are revealed, they process the information and decide to call, raise, or fold. With every round, they can double down or quit. They keep their options open. And so should you.

7.3
Your Options Matter

If the concept of thinking step by step in rounds seems unnatural to you, you are not alone. In one workshop after another, the smartest and most experienced senior executives initially seem stumped by this concept. Our default mindset is not wired to think in stages or to envision the future as a number of sequential steps, with the current decision limited to a single step, while taking the whole journey into consideration.

Our instinctive default methodology is to make an irreversible decision and put the problem out of our minds. To end the process of cognitive dissonance. To find that easy comfort zone. It feels intuitively right to commit to the project you pushed into earlier, even if new information tells you otherwise. It feels right to support the startup team, especially if you have made the decision to invest in the first place, even if they are exhibiting subpar performance. But in poker, as in VC investments, the smart strategy is exactly the opposite. To win in the long run, you must be flexible and ready to change your mind every time you collect more information. You must be prepared to double down. You must be prepared to quit. This is the Venture Mindset.

Start with an experiment. The first iteration will have a very limited functionality, small scale, and often ridiculously high costs. "If you're not embarrassed by the first version of your product, you've launched too late," said Reid Hoffman of Greylock and the founder of LinkedIn. Such launches with reduced functionality are called the "minimal viable product" (MVP). Or go with the "minimum lovable product" (MLP), pioneered by Amazon. With the MLP approach, larger companies realize they can't disappoint customers or simply close the shop. Their bet is bigger because they are risking trust from existing customers, so making the product "lovable" from the beginning is critical in order not to break that trust. Delaying the launch is better than disappointing users. If the MVP or MLP works and resonates with users, you add more functionality. Test. Scale to more users. Test again. Add new regions or countries. Test some more. At each stage, the project either unlocks the next tranche of capital and resources or it is shut down. This approach allows you to derisk as VCs do. There is no longer any need to break a lance over a risky business idea.

Smart VCs value flexibility over commitment. Most business school students do not study this in their classes. Traditional finance concepts are built around making take-it-or-leave-it investment decisions, emphasizing commitment to the chosen course of action. Just think of multiyear cash flow projections accompanied by metrics such as net present value, internal rate of return, and return on investment. These common methods assume that the company is committed to the project, independent of the new information revealed along the way. There is little place for studying flexibility in the modern business school curriculum. The classes that executives take reinforce this traditional commitment mindset.

Yet the idea of flexibility is in fact known and widely studied in finance and economics. The academic term for flexibility is "real option." "Option" refers to the idea that a decision maker has the right, but *not* the obligation, to take a future action. "Real" means that the concept of an option applies to actual projects and businesses, not just fancy financial securities. For the Venture Mindset, real optionality is a matter of life and death. Both shutting down unsuccessful investments and continuing to support successful ones are critical to success.

Consider a16z's investment of $250,000 in Instagram very early on, when Instagram was still Burbn, a location-sharing concept. When the company raised its next round, a16z decided not to participate, partially because they were already investors in a competitor, Picplz. Their initial investment's return of more than 300X would make others envious, but for a16z it was a lost opportunity to earn even more. If you don't double down, then you may still win, but the win might be small and negligible. You can't play too safe and stay in the game. Referring to both poker and VC, Richard Harroch told us, "You won't survive for long if you fold all the time."

There are some industries in which real optionality has been used successfully. We often astonish our executive participants when we point out that, in the pharmaceutical industry, *each and every* drug investment has a negative net present value early on. Most drug candidates fail at various stages of development. They may fail the safety assessment or the efficacy test, or the drug may have a significant side effect, or it may be less efficient than existing drugs.

If a pharma company applied the take-it-or-leave-it style to its drug candidates, it wouldn't be around for very long. Rather, at each stage, the company retains flexibility to keep investing in a specific drug or to shut down the project. The optimal strategy for a pharma company is never to commit to developing a drug no matter what. By shutting down the project, the company can reallocate its valuable resources—scientists, equipment, money—to other, more promising or still uncertain projects.

Mining is another industry in which real optionality is a must for survival. Consider iron ore mining. The profitability depends on the market price of iron ore. If the price collapses, mines become unprofitable, as happened in 2014. Many existing iron ore mines were mothballed. However, mine owners are constantly monitoring global prices. The Roper Bar mine in Australia, which closed in 2014, reopened in 2017 as metal prices recovered sufficiently. Without taking this real optionality into account, most mines would never be built in the first place, because their expected value would be negative under a full-commitment strategy.

Or consider Hollywood. The popularity of any movie on its opening weekend involves a lot of luck. Successful movie studios therefore embed real optionality in almost any decision they make. For example, they hold back a large portion of their marketing budget so they can decide whether to spend it after the opening weekend. If initial revenues fall below expectations, the marketing budget can be cut or eliminated altogether. Another real option strategy is limited release. For example, the movie *My Big Fat Greek Wedding* was shown on only 100 screens upon its 2002 release. As the film gained popularity, the executives slowly expanded its distribution footprint and advertising budget. Eventually, the low-budget ($5 million) film reached thousands of screens and grossed $240 million in the US alone.

The common theme for all these decision makers, from poker pros to VCs to Hollywood entertainers, is this: reacting to new information is critical to survival. Unless you implement the same flexibility mechanisms in your organization, it is unlikely that you can build a billion-dollar business internally. Don't bet on your actions; bet on the option to bet later by making small investments. That way, you can double down later. It is hard for a traditional mindset to split a single large decision into multiple smaller ones, but this is exactly what the VC mindset does. Thinking about writing a book? Start with a sample chapter or blog post first. Reader feedback will inform you about the next best step. Considering a global expansion? Divide it into multiple waves, keeping your options open as you go. Implementing this flexibility is of course easier said than done. Too many forces, from our unconscious biases to organizational designs, conspire against us. The fold, call, and raise rules seem easy to follow . . . until they aren't.

7.4
The Slippery Slope of Decision Makers

Climbing to the very top is just within your reach. Especially when you're so close.

Rob Hall scaled the summit of Everest four times. In May 1996, he was leading a large group of climbers who'd paid Adventure Consultants, the company that Hall cofounded, to join him in his fifth ascent. Just 250 feet below the summit, the group met unexpected challenges. In the forty-foot stretch known as the Hillary Step, the climbers failed to fix the ropes quickly enough. It was now 11:40 a.m. and they had to restart the fixing process.

At that very moment, Hall should have known he had to turn everybody back. The weather at the summit was very likely to turn bad in the afternoon, and they would have no chance to start their descent within the permitted safety time. To make matters worse, they did not have enough oxygen in their tanks. But the summit was so close; they "were absolutely determined to bag the top." They began fixing the ropes, and the first group member reached the summit around 1:25 p.m., far off schedule. One by one, they continued their slow ascent, with some still reaching the summit by 3:00 p.m., now long past the time all of them had to be on their way down. As expected, the weather turned foul and oxygen tanks were depleted. Frantic rescue efforts could not save eight climbers, who did not make it down; the others were saved in the nick of time by the bravery of Sherpas and rescue teams.

Rob Hall and his group are not exceptions. Hundreds of climbers have died trying to summit Mount Everest. Prudent climbers often take great risks when they are very near the summit. With such a large payoff so close, it feels as if just a little extra risk is warranted.

What do mountain climbers and business decision makers have in common? Our human nature resists reversing course and cutting our losses, even in life-or-death situations—and especially if we think we are so close to being on top of the world. Economists and behavioral scientists have named this phenomenon "escalation of commitment" and have researched it thoroughly in different contexts, from military conflicts to group decision making.

Examples of escalation of commitment abound. This bias skews our reasoning, sometimes with fatal results. In poker, if a player with two favorable private cards is disappointed to find the first three communal cards unhelpful, the intuitive push is to continue the chosen strategy in hopes of a miracle at the next turn, rather than folding. A common mistake among amateur players is to treat giving up as a bad strategy. The single biggest difference between inexperienced players and pros is that inexperienced players don't fold frequently enough. It's hard for anyone to admit a mistake or accept that the hoped-for fortune is not going to materialize. We are all afraid of changing course. We get attached to our previous decision. We simply want to be right—even though we already suspect that we were wrong.

Nick Leeson might not have heard about escalation of commitment when he joined the Barings Bank at age twenty-two in 1989. Over its 233-year history, the venerable Barings Bank had helped the United States to purchase Louisiana and counted Queen Elizabeth II as a client. In 1992,

Leeson moved to Singapore to head Barings' derivatives office there. His London bosses were pleased by his trading activity, which soon was recording extraordinary profits. At times, Leeson alone was accounting for 10 percent of the whole bank's profits.

The reality outside the accounting books was quite different. When the market moved against the trading positions he had taken, Leeson was sitting on a loss of $1.7 million. Now he had a tough choice: he could report the loss to his superiors in London and face the consequences, or he could try recouping the loss by making a larger bet. He chose the latter. Since doing so violated the bank's risk rules, he started using a secret account. He was unlucky and soon faced a larger loss, making it all the more difficult to face up to London. From this point on, whenever he lost money on a trade, he placed a new, larger bet. Bigger losses, bigger bets. Quickly, the secret account accumulated over £20 million in losses. In one year, that climbed to more than £200 million. Then, in January 1995, a strong earthquake in Kobe shook Japanese financial markets. Leeson tried recouping all his losses by betting on the recovery of the Nikkei stock exchange. In for a penny, in for a pound. Leeson could not stop, just like an alpinist with the summit of Everest in view.

By the time his secret trades were discovered, Leeson's losses of £827 million became an insurmountable lesson for this bank with such a glamorous history. Barings went bankrupt.

But surely this is an aberration. Leeson's example is a powerful one, but it does not apply to most of us, right?

We often ask executive participants in our workshops to complete a survey that invites them to make an array of investment decisions. We are by no means the first to do this, but we continue to be surprised every time we see the results. Here's one of the investment decisions.

Two years ago, you made an investment decision on behalf of your company by investing $500 million in a project. So far, no *profit has been realized. You are now looking at what to do with your investment. You can abandon the project or inject more money into it. The cost of investment is $100 million today. If the investment is successful, your company's gross profit will be $1 billion in one year. If your investment fails, the company will not make any money—that is, your company's gross profit will be zero. The probability of your success is 5 percent.*

Take a moment to think before reading on. Make your decision. What is it?

The rational response is straightforward. After all, if you multiply $1 billion by 5 percent, your expected *gross* profit is only $50 million. Your expected net profit after subtracting the investment cost of $100 million is thus a *loss* of $50 million. In short, it's a terrible investment decision. Putting the cash in a bank would be a better move. Even if the bank pays you no interest, you at least retain your $100 million. But what about the initial investment of $500 million? As every economist will tell you, that $500 million has already disappeared. It has sunk down the drain and should not be taken into account. The only good decision here is not to invest further and to write off your losses.

But this is not what many senior executives decide here. On average, almost half the participants decide to proceed with the investment, ignoring the low odds and unfavorable math. Executives subconsciously hope that a $1 billion cash miracle can help them recoup the $500 million they have already lost. Their hope is magnified because the task description makes the decision very personal, using the words "you"/"yours" nine times. It is now *your* fault if *you* miss the chance to recoup *your* losses. Of course, once we walk through the math, everybody agrees it is a bad decision.

Personalization is key to this escalation of commitment. If instead participants are told not "you" but their colleague or predecessor made the first investment decision, they almost never throw good money after bad. People escalate their own commitments, not someone else's.

We've also noticed that different organizations respond to this problem in different ways. On some teams, fewer than 25 percent are sucked into saying they would make this unwise investment; for others, the percentage is much higher. Leadership and corporate culture matter a lot in making escalation of commitment worse. In one off-the-charts workshop, an eye-popping 80 percent of participants said they would make the additional investment. The executives giggled politely when told they were outliers. Later in the evening, one executive waited around while others drifted away for a cocktail reception. "I'm not surprised," he said. "Our boss doesn't allow failure. The boss's rule is that you can do whatever you like, but once you have started, your investment project has to get completed. Otherwise, he says it's a waste of money." The boss's fixation on never abandoning a project had heightened the company's propensity to make bad escalation decisions. If only the boss knew how much waste he was generating with this never-say-no-more mindset.

Escalation of commitment is particularly dangerous for VCs. As our veteran poker buff and VC investor Richard Harroch says, "A hand that turns out to be weak is analogous to an underperforming company." He further explains, "You need to be careful about the intuitive desire to chase a miracle by throwing good money after bad. Cutting your losses at the right moment is critical for poker players, VCs, and corporations." Not only does the desire to recoup losses sink even more money in a failing investment proposition, but it also deprives the VC fund of much-needed capital that could be invested in better-performing projects.

Cutting off funding of the beloved idea or business is emotionally hard. "Will I betray these people if I stop funding them?" you may ask. It's easy to convince yourself that six months and another $10 million just might turn your company around. Since the world of innovation is so uncertain, it's always possible to continue hoping for a miracle to justify going forward. The stress can be stifling, and often these brave investors run out of oxygen.

It is even harder to close a project in a corporate setting, as it could be perceived as a weakness, mismanagement, or failure. Fortunately, VCs have developed specific mechanisms to address the danger of escalation of commitment. To learn their tricks, join us in playing another popular game—not in a casino this time, but on television.

7.5
Who Wants to Be a Millionaire?

Fifteen—only fifteen—questions stand between the player and £1 million. You probably already know the rules of the incredibly successful TV show *Who Wants to Be a Millionaire?* that originated in Britain. As the player answers a tricky question by picking one of four options, the audience takes a deep breath. If the answer is correct, the next level is unlocked and the value goes up. For the second question, it rises from £100 to £200, and if participants nail the tenth question, it reaches £32,000. Whenever participants see the next question, they can decide whether to attempt an answer or quit and take home whatever they have already earned. If they answer all fifteen questions, the prize is £1 million. But if they give just one wrong answer, they lose. This game is eerily similar to a VC investor's decision whether to make a follow-on investment and take more risks or whether to quit. Remarkably, the TV game resembles the VC dilemma more than the show's creators might ever have imagined, due to the additional options available to participants.

The first person to win £1 million on *Millionaire* in the UK was Judith Keppel in 2000, followed by David Edwards and Robert Brydges in 2001. These three winners had one thing in common: on the way to the

£1 million prize, each of them used *lifelines*. There are three lifelines in *Millionaire*—Phone-a-Friend, Ask the Audience, and 50-50—and these first winners used all three of them. In case you haven't watched the show, we'll explain the game and how it applies to the Venture Mindset.

Phone-a-Friend: Don't double down alone

Here is a question worth £125,000: "Complete this stage instruction in Shakespeare's *The Winter's Tale*: 'Exit, pursued by a . . . '?" Tiger? Clown? Bear? Dog? Judith Keppel didn't know. Do you? Luckily, she still had an unused Phone-a-Friend lifeline. On any one question of her choice, she could call a friend for thirty seconds and ask for advice. Judith called her friend Jill, who was 100 percent sure the correct answer was "bear." Jill was right.

VCs are also often unsure about their follow-on decisions. And if they do feel certain, they know they could be suffering from escalation of commitment bias. Like Judith, they also call friends—their partners.

Recall that VC firms are organized as partnerships. All partners are highly engaged in the follow-on investment. Not only do they have to approve the deal, but we have seen some of them often deliberately play the devil's advocate role to balance out the lead partner's proclivity to escalation of commitment. By doing so, they also create a culture in which automatic agreement with the other person's view is not the status quo. Rather, other partners try to identify reasons *not* to invest further. In some partnerships, partners not involved in the investment must sign off on the follow-on round. Requiring the consent of people who are more distant from the project reduces the role of "you" and makes it easier to cut losses earlier if necessary.

Lightspeed Capital is well known for funding startups such as OYO, Snapchat, and Grubhub. It oversees over $18 billion in assets, with the majority of investments made in preexisting portfolio companies. Like other VC firms, it doubles down a lot. However, no check can be written without a sign-off from a "reinvestment team."

"Everyone's baby is beautiful," says Michael Romano of Lightspeed, "especially when you've been involved in some of these portfolio companies from a seed or Series A." James Ephrati, the head of the reinvestment team, has the charge "to independently challenge the follow-on decisions" and "to challenge every single one of Lightspeed's investment assumptions." The reinvestment team collects their own data, makes their own predictions, calls customers, and independently comes up with a recommendation, often challenging the valuation or recommending that the firm skip the follow-on round altogether.

Unless you do as Judith Keppel and smart VCs do by involving people in your organization who are external to the project in high-stakes follow-on decisions, you are at a high risk of escalation of commitment. Bring in other executives to decide whether to fund the next phase of a critical project. Get in touch with internal experts and ask them to join the team from time to time to help you make a better decision. Ask yourself if the new subscription program is on track or if it has no future whatsoever. Have someone in the room who launched a subscription program previously. Involved in a deep-tech AI initiative? Well, you can't make a prudent decision to continue investing without the tech expert in the room who is not a part of your day-to-day team.

Bringing friends into the room may even become your secret sauce. Pixar developed the concept of Braintrust, a diverse and fluid group of creatives. They are advisers who have no formal authority but lots of experience, and they offer multiple perspectives. Braintrust can be thought of as conducting a peer review or getting a second medical opinion from a panel of doctors. Hit movies like *Toy Story 2* would not have been as successful without Braintrust.

Phone a friend. Set up your Braintrust. As in the TV show, it's up to you whether to take their advice, but whatever you do, avail yourself of an unbiased perspective.

Ask the Audience: Seek the outsiders' perspective

To tackle his £125,000 question, the second millionaire winner, David Edwards, used a different lifeline: he sought the outsiders' view. He asked the audience for help. When that lifeline is requested, everyone in the studio picks up a small device to choose their answer. In a beautiful illustration of the wisdom of crowds, the player sees the distribution of support for each answer and has to make the final choice. Such wisdom helped Edwards, as he went with the 62 percent of the audience who selected the right answer. In fact, the audience's preferred choice is correct more than nine out of ten times.

Smart VCs also ask the audience. In their case, the audience consists of other reputable investors who are asked to put in money along with the existing investors. The distinction between existing and new investors is important. The new ones don't have skin in the game yet and are thus not exposed to escalation of commitment. Finding new investors ready to commit money is another way to attenuate the role of "you."

Founders are often required by their VC investors to find new lead investors; otherwise, existing investors won't put in more money. Both Alex and Ilya have received calls, Alex from his Stanford classmates and Ilya from his students, who were disappointed that the venture fund that led Series A in their startup agreed to participate in Series B only if a new investor was lined up to lead the round.

Importantly, this requirement is not about the lack of capital, but about keeping oneself in check. Many successful VC firms impose an important rule of thumb here. Existing investors look to new investors not just to affirm investor appetite for the company, but also to independently price the value of the company. For example, storied software VC firm Hummer Winblad rarely invests in the follow-on round unless new investors also commit. Another investor, Versatile Venture Capital, states clearly on their website that, after the initial check of up to $1 million, they would need a new investor leading the round for them to participate at later stages. Indeed, Ilya's research has shown that rounds led by new investors are more likely to result in better outcomes and higher VC fund returns.

We can see the power of the Venture Mindset at a large German electric utility, RWE. After the company had spent more than €10 billion making big take-it-or-leave-it decisions about capital expenditures—on shaky assumptions of ever-increasing power prices—the new CEO, Rolf Martin Schmitz, overhauled the entire decision-making process by implementing many of the mechanisms we've been discussing in this book. One example was to resolve a "strategic deadlock with the power-generation business—the cash cow of the company for years but now with a broken business model," as admitted by company CFO Bernhard Günther.

To reduce escalation of commitment, RWE set up a red team and a blue team to come up with different proposals, one staffed internally and one staffed externally. The internal team came up with an expected incremental approach. The external audience presented a more radical proposal, one that the company's board eventually adopted.

In our experience, many companies miss the opportunity to utilize the audience point of view successfully and incorporate it within their decision processes. Bringing in outsiders is often resisted by company insiders. Why would anyone from the outside know better than the team that has spent months or years on the project? This may be true of a traditional business idea, but the moment you enter uncharted territory, you need to bring external experts to evaluate. Use that lifeline. You need that collective outsiders' wisdom. Are the pilot results impressive and are customers giving rave reviews about the new product? Cool! Now bring in independent consultants. Even better, attract external investors to share the risks. Be like Walmart, which brought in the famous VC firm Ribbit Capital to collaborate on fintech initiatives. Be like Alphabet, which brought in outside investors for its self-driving division, Waymo. Be like a smart VC.

50-50: Quit often enough

It is easy to say no to the idea the first time you see it, but it is way harder to do so when you are "in the game." This is when the "50-50" principle becomes handy. Robert Brydges, the third UK contestant to reach the *Millionaire* quiz summit, used a different lifeline to answer that last, £1 million question: "Which scientific unit is named after an Italian nobleman: Pascal, Ohm, Volt, or Hertz?" Do you know the answer? Brydges wasn't sure. He used the 50-50 lifeline to eliminate two of the four options. Once the field was cut to Ohm and Volt, Brydges picked the correct answer. Alessandro Volta, inventor of the electric battery and hydrogen lamp, is believed to have said, "You must be ready to give up even the most attractive ideas when an experiment shows them to be wrong." VCs can't agree more!

The 50-50 lifeline reminds us that the funnel in the VC world is cruel. At each stage, only about half of all startups make the tough jump to the next round. The chances of surviving all these grueling stages and succeeding are slim. Only about one of every sixty VC-backed startups becomes a unicorn.

A typical VC strategy gives a startup just enough capital to function for the next twelve to eighteen months. The idea is that, over the next twelve months, investors expect the startup to reach its stated milestones, with six months added as a buffer. The essence of the 50-50 approach is to be willing to fail at any stage. Persistence is valuable, but so is pulling the plug.

Knowing in advance that half of their bets fail at each stage, VCs use the portfolio approach by cutting their losses early. As Marc Andreessen put it, "The approach of a venture capitalist is buying a portfolio of long-dated, deeply-out-of-the-money call options." What Andreessen means is that if he and other VCs committed to every startup they invested in, they would soon be out of money. Instead, they use the portfolio approach. By concentrating on the most promising ideas, they hope to ultimately grow one or two with disproportionally high returns. As in poker, the VC way is to double down on winners and quit on losers.

Ilya was once shown a portfolio of innovative internal projects by the CEO of a very large company. All seemed to be successful on paper. Ilya's feedback to the CEO? If a large percentage of your initiatives make it to the next stage, this could be either because you don't take enough risks and so they are not innovative enough, or because you don't weed them out early enough and are prone to escalation of commitment. Practice the 50-50 approach: aim to support only half of previously funded ideas in the next round.

Do as McDonald's did when it introduced its McPlant burger in partnership with Beyond Meat in eight restaurants. A few months after the burger's late 2021 test launch, they expanded the experiment to 600 locations. But then they pulled back later in 2022, as new data came in. They liked it at first. They liked it the second time. Then they folded. Launching a new product is not an on-off switch; it's a road with many traffic lights, each one unlocking the next block.

Who Wants to Be a Millionaire? was itself a bet at one point. When Paul Smith, the founder of a small entertainment production company called Celador, pitched the show under the title "Cash Mountain" to leading TV channels, he didn't have much luck. Everyone rejected it, one executive after another. Then, in April 1998, Smith met with David

Liddiment, the newly installed director of programs at ITV, a UK television channel. Smith brought with him four envelopes containing £250, £500, £1,000, and £2,000. Would the cash help?

Smith's creative idea was to play the game with Liddiment and ask him questions with four possible answers, in the same way the real show would be played. If the ITV executive answered the question, the prize would double and then the next, more difficult question would be introduced. Using his lifelines, including opening his office door and discussing a question with his staff, Liddiment pocketed £500. The game intrigued him, but did ITV immediately go all in? Nope. TV broadcasters follow the Venture Mindset. The show started with a pilot, then followed with ten shows. Once it became clear that *Millionaire* was becoming the single most popular non-sport TV show in Britain, it got a regular spot. Smith soon became a millionaire himself.

7.6
Killer Instinct

VCs, poker players, £1 million prize hunters, and TV producers have a common trait. They all split a long, risky path into stages, tweak their direction as they progress, and prepare themselves to quit when they see danger coming. Successful companies do the same thing, especially with their riskiest ventures.

Suppose you are instructed to launch a new business that will deliver orders to customers in less than one hour. Without a focus group. With a small team. In ninety days. Sounds like a herculean task, doesn't it? Amazon VP Stephenie Landry and her team accepted the challenge and announced the launch of Prime Now in New York City. In the end, it took 111 days to build, not ninety, but it became operational on December 18, 2014, just in time for Christmas. The last order on Christmas Eve was delivered at 11:06 p.m. in only forty-two minutes.

Prime Now became Amazon's success, and ultrafast delivery is now available in thousands of locations around the world. Few realize that it was only one of many ambitious projects Amazon ran at the same time. Amazon placed many bets. This one worked. In many other instances, Amazon decided to quit. Amazon Wallet was launched the same year as Prime Now, only to be closed in a few months. Amazon Restaurants, a one-click meal delivery service that debuted as part of a Prime Now app, was discontinued. The list of failures is long: Amazon Local, Amazon Surprise Sweets, Amazon Spark. This list is longer than that of the products that stuck around. Home runs matter. Strikeouts don't.

Though the ultimate goal is always ambitious, each step is like another VC round: a check to make sure the direction is right. The New York City launch was only the first milestone to test the Prime Now idea. Amazon continued with a more widespread rollout, and it was ready to quit if the new milestones were not reached.

Many decisions may surprise those not accustomed to the Venture Mindset. Prime Now was initially launched in just one zip code. The Prime Now warehouse was across the street from the Empire State Building, at a location more suited for investment bankers in expensive suits than for warehouse employees packing bananas. It took a mere sixteen days to turn an empty space into a functioning pick-and-pack station. Costs per delivery were running high. A stand-alone, simple Prime Now app was not integrated with the main Amazon app. These decisions by themselves would not make much sense to any logistics expert. But once you view the project as a testing ground, speed and simplicity of the test matter. For any such test, identify a specific question you aim to address, then ask yourself whether the test is simple and clear enough to ensure a fast resolution. Remember, you are running the test not to convince your organization to continue funding, but to address key risks, tweak the project as needed, and then construct larger-scale tests to learn more.

When a biotech startup conducts its drug experiments, it is not very concerned about the cost or how to scale up the solution. The first goal is to ensure that the drug works. Similarly, to try out a new idea or product, the goal is to design an experiment to test and verify the main assumptions. For Prime Now, Amazon's goal was to test whether customers liked the idea of ultrafast delivery. They did. But what if they didn't? What do you do then?

When you receive an email with the subject line "What is the target *kill rate*?" it may raise red flags. But this was a harmless follow-up question after a workshop with the leadership of a large US corporation. The company had invested heavily in numerous experiments and trials but could not benefit much from any of them. In the workshop, senior leadership proudly announced the number of initiatives and new ventures launched in the past few years, only to be puzzled by Alex's question: "And how many were shut down?" The uncomfortable silence revealed the truth. None. New products and services stayed around like zombies, were counted and recounted in corporate reports, and consumed precious resources and attention from senior leadership.

Like VCs, you need to develop a disciplined portfolio approach to when and how to quit your projects. Although the notion of a "kill rate" may jolt you, don't let it deter you. Prune your flowers; don't let a thousand bloom. Keep your shears handy. Keeping too many bets open for too long may prevent you from committing fully to any one of them. Too often, innovative ideas get just enough funding to keep their creators busy within a corporate environment, but not enough to have any impact. You can find such a rosarium of ideas within innovation labs, full of people in hoodies and jeans writing fancy stuff on transparent glass walls. Visitors (including the authors of this book) are frequently taken to such labs to showcase a company's commitment to innovation, its entrepreneurial mentality, and whatever other buzzwords are currently in fashion. Granted, the labs do look exciting. But unless any of the ideas receive enough attention and capital to scale some of them up, they just become innovation artifacts, not growth drivers. Smart VCs don't keep a garden full of weeds. The bets must become products that are tested and launched and then either scaled up or closed. VCs routinely let many startups fail and cut losses early to double down on potential unicorns. This rarely happens in innovation labs. An organization simply can't afford to take care of all the ideas it has generated. Not surprisingly, according to a recent report by the Capgemini consulting firm, the fail rate for such labs is 90 percent.

But not all corporate labs work this way. The Google X moonshot factory built a "serial killer" business model to ruthlessly weed out ideas. "Hey, how are we going to try to kill our project today?" asked Astro Teller, the leader of Google X (or Captain of Moonshots, according to his official title), during his TED talk. At Google X, hundreds of ideas are simultaneously floating through the funnel, with the vast majority of them being weeded out.

First, ideas are investigated by the rapid evaluation team, whose motto is: "If we can get to a *no* quickly on an idea, that's almost as good as getting to a *yes*." The team begins by writing an epitaph on the tomb! In an exercise known as the "pre-mortem," the team imagines everything falling apart and brainstorms what factors might have caused the failure. Soon, after spending just a few thousand dollars, the team decides whether going forward is worthwhile. The graveyard of ideas is enormous at this stage. Nine out of ten ideas (even more than 50-50!) get a "kill" verdict.

The surviving ideas progress to the next stage with the freedom of spending more money and time building a prototype and addressing the riskiest parts of the problem. This is also when possible commercial successes are evaluated. What about lighter-than-air flying buoyancy cargo ships? They would reduce infrastructure costs to ship goods around the world. Sound promising? Yes, until you realize that you need to spend $200 million just to get the first data point. The outcome? Kill.

Only 3 percent of ideas make it to Google X's Foundry step, where the goal is to test the idea as a business. At this point, a nimble team of fewer than a dozen people looks for a fit between product and market. "Within a year, we either de-risk the project to a point where we are ready to grow it," says Foundry leader Obi Felten, "or we kill it." Half of businesses won't survive. For the ones that make it, their "adult life" finally begins with a nod from the leadership.

You don't need to be Google to apply the same VC mindset–driven approach. Build, stage, quit.

7.7
Time to Quit

The "once and forever" mindset is so entrenched that it is hard to imagine an alternative. Think about the career choices we consider for ourselves or want for our kids. We should be spending lots of time choosing a career because it's a key decision in life. Or is it? Think instead about your career as a selection of real options you create. Think about developing new skills, knowledge, and contacts as new doors open to you. Value the flexibility available to you before you make a lifelong commitment.

Parents frequently ask us what their children should study to be successful in life. This is a traditional, commitment-entrenched mindset question. By the time their children graduate, whatever they study, the demand for new jobs will have changed in unpredictable ways. Who could have predicted twenty years ago the demand for experts in big data? One response we give to anxious parents is that the most important skill their children can develop is to learn how to learn, because whatever they learn now, they will need to relearn ten years down the road in our unpredictable, disruptive environment.

One main reason that US university education is renowned, unlike university education in most of Europe and Asia, where students select their discipline upon applying to college, is that US students don't need to select their major until their third year, after they have had a chance to explore many different subjects. Ilya knows many Stanford undergraduates who took advanced history, biology, and computer science classes in their first two years and who worked as research assistants in places such as autonomous vehicle labs before finalizing their major. Their European counterparts lack this flexibility. Students do not get admitted to, say, Goethe-Universität Frankfurt; rather, they apply to a specific department—chemistry, or Islamic studies, or meteorology. At age seventeen or eighteen, you are expected to make your final choice. It's a vivid example of commitment without flexibility.

The son of one of our US friends thought he wanted to go to college in the UK. But after his UK college trip, Kyle decided that he didn't want to be locked into a major from the beginning. This was a good move since he shifted from mechanical engineering to economics as a UCLA freshman. Many European young people don't have Kyle's luxury of choice.

Does flexibility come at a price? Of course. Making multiple bets takes time, and by staying focused you may get to the desired outcome faster. But consider how we conduct our lives. We often are ready to pay a premium for flexible airline tickets that we can cancel or change at the last minute. We choose hotels with cancellation options. Flexibility pays off if uncertainty is very high. We should act the same way in other uncertain situations.

Of course, a combination of luck and skill can make your journey smoother. John Carpenter, the first $1 million winner on the US version of *Who Wants to Be a Millionaire?*, easily answered all fifteen questions without asking for any help along the way. He was lucky to get a question about which month had no federal holidays; as an Internal Revenue Service agent, he could have easily recited the whole list of federal holidays. He used a lifeline to call his dad on the $1 million question, just to say he was about to win the top prize. But in the world of innovation, even John Carpenters need lifelines. Like poker players, we need to ask ourselves repeatedly: fold, call, or raise?

MINDSET CHECKS

○ Is your organization designed to run experiments and fund initiatives in tranches, or does it prefer to go all in right away?

○ Do you have mechanisms to regularly defund and close initiatives that do not work?

○ Do you regularly consult with external stakeholders and experts at key milestones of projects?

EIGHT

Make the Pie Bigger

What's wrong about incentives that VCs get right

8.1
In the Same Boat

His grandfather Dobramiro was a slave from Croatia who gained freedom only upon the death of his Venetian owner. His father, Pancrazio, was a ship helmsman. With such a humble background, no one could have expected Zaccaria Stagnario to become one of the wealthiest people in Venice in the early years of the thirteenth century. His climb to the highest social and political circles started in 1199, when he signed a contract with one Giovanni Agadi.

"In the name of the Lord God," the contract begins, "I, Zaccaria Stagnario, declare that I have received from you, Giovanni Agadi, 300 pounds of Venetian pennies that I shall carry in the ship from here to Constantinople to do business there and in any other place that seems good to me." Venice was an important medieval hub for trading between East and West. The contract provided for Stagnario to take this huge amount of capital on a trade voyage to Constantinople, without any other commercial instructions or strings attached. How could Agadi be sure that Stagnario would seek to multiply his capital? The secret lay in profit-sharing incentives.

Here's what the contract went on to say: "[Upon my return], I am to give and deliver here in Rialto to you your entire capital of 300 pounds of Venetian pennies together with three parts of whatever profit God shall give us with just and truthful account and without any fraud. I am to keep for myself the remaining fourth."

Modern-day VCs would recognize this text instantaneously, even if their contracts do not invoke God. Once Stagnario returned the initial capital, he would keep one-quarter of any profit. Agadi bore all the risks. The chance of losing his capital was high, but the sky was the limit for the upside. Stagnario was as interested in the success of the venture as Agadi. Such contracts had a special name: *colleganza*.

Economic historians view colleganza as *the* key business innovation of medieval times that unlocked the potential of long-haul overseas trade. It allowed ambitious startup merchants without any capital to enter the commerce game and make a fortune. Merchant voyages were enormously profitable if successful, but they were also extremely risky. Death from illness or shipwreck was common, seas were infested with pirates, and if the weather did not cooperate, the merchant might arrive to his destination a month late "to find the market was over for the year and be forced to dump his goods at fire sale prices," as Diego Puga and Daniel Trefler emphasize in their study of colleganza contracts. "Luck and also the business skills and effort of a travelling merchant could make the difference between huge profits and huge losses."

Aligned incentives ensured that merchants would make their most diligent effort to come home with huge profits. The colleganza innovation not only helped merchants like Zaccaria Stagnario to prosper but was also instrumental in making Venice a powerful maritime player, expanding social mobility, and allowing newly minted wealthy people to challenge the traditional elite. Some researchers even believe that it had a major impact on the formation of the Venetian political system and its parliament.

Centuries later, maritime ventures remained risky. The sperm whale-hunting business in New England uncannily resembled the Venetian voyages. The requisite startup capital was enormous, at around $20,000 to $30,000 in the 1850s. This amount was ten times the value of a typical American farm, at a time when an unskilled, unenslaved worker was paid less than $1 a day.

Similar to colleganza-supported voyages, whale hunting took years to succeed or fail, and losing a ship was an ever-present risk. An estimated one-third of all the whaling vessels that sailed from New Bedford, Massachusetts, never returned. Foul weather, a raider, damage from a whale attack, or a fire could have doomed the ship. What was promised in return for all the struggles? Extremely high returns. Ships returning to port after long whale hunting expeditions could snare a profit of well more than $100,000.

"In the whaling business they paid no wages," says Ishmael in Herman Melville's *Moby-Dick*, "but all hands, including the captain, received certain shares of the profits called lays." All hands took the risk, all hands exerted the effort, and all hands shared the profit.

But there also was a place for new people sandwiched between the owners of capital and "all hands." The owners of capital were often distant from the whale-hunting business. They had capital but no skills. Captains had the will and skills to navigate long voyages but no capital. What was needed was someone in between: agents.

The agent's role was to set up whaling partnerships, find capital, and then work with each captain to prepare for a voyage, acquiring the best equipment and making sure the right crew was in place. Agents often advised the captain on the scope of the venture and hunting grounds, but day-to-day hunting decisions were left to the crew. For their pains, agents partook in the partnership profits, holding between one-third and one-half of shares.

The crew was motivated in the same profit-sharing way. The captain's share of net proceeds, or "lay," varied between 5 percent and 10 percent. And the captain wasn't the only crew member who stood to gain from the venture's success. First mates, second mates, third mates, and harpooners would each receive their fair share, from 2 percent to fractions of a percent. Among the thirty or so crew positions, everyone, right down to the most junior boys under the mast, shared in the profits. Whales were divided up years before actually being caught, with detailed contracts—in much the same way that returns on investments are divided these days with unicorns.

8.2
A Rising Tide Lifts All Boats

Modern-day VCs and startup employees would immediately recognize the environment of incentives lived in by whale agents and hunters or by Venetian merchants of yesteryear. They all bear extremely high risk, exert great effort, and earn outsized jackpot returns when they succeed. VCs are intermediaries, connecting innovators with good ideas but no money to investors with money but no ideas. The modern-day equivalent of the colleganza contract is a limited partnership agreement, according to which VCs are entitled to the two-tier compensation scheme called "2 and 20."

The "2" of "2 and 20" is the fee, out of which VCs get a salary and bonus for managing the VC fund. Often, the annual management fee is 2 percent of the capital provided by investors. This management fee does not depend on fund performance. The fund's investments may be booming or going bust, but the same management fee continues to be paid out. Most VCs view the management fee like an appetizer at a fine restaurant. The main dish is the second component, "20."

The "20" refers to the share of the overall fund profit that VCs earn. As with Zaccaria Stagnario's contract in 1199, the VC fund first has to return all the committed capital to investors. Then VCs earn 20 cents on each dollar of profit. This is called "carried interest" or simply "carry." The 20 percent figure is a common arrangement, but many VCs take home 25 percent, like Stagnario, or even 30 percent, which is closer to whaling agents of yore. The term "carried interest" also comes from the sailing age, referring to the commission that captains received from selling goods carried on boats in adventurous voyages. Whether the percentage is 20, 25, or 30, the carried interest aligns the interests of VCs and their investors.

Similar to the whaling agents who ensured that the entire ship crew participated in the profit-sharing scheme, VCs want everyone working for the startups they invest in to expect to benefit from the upside. The Venture Mindset has found a workable incentive-driven solution. As a condition of investment, they insist that *everyone* who matters to the project's success becomes an owner, and they ensure that the share of the pie is meaningful. To paraphrase Gordon Gekko from the 1987 movie *Wall Street*, in the VC business, greed is *not* good. But it isn't that VCs are generous due to their charitable nature. By designing smart contracts, VCs make founders' upside essentially unlimited while protecting them against the downside risk. If they fail, the founders won't become rich, but they are not punished beyond that. VCs also make sure that the whole team benefits from success by setting aside a significant pool of equity for that purpose. A rising tide lifts all boats.

VCs achieve their goals through two powerful mechanisms. VCs *make* people work hard by providing incentives, but the incentives also *attract* innovative, talented, productive, risk-seeking, failure-tolerant people. As research has demonstrated again and again, these two mechanisms reinforce each other.

In one experiment, Australian researchers invited participants to play the popular "spelling bee" anagram game in which participants create words out of seven letters. Some participants were randomly assigned a fixed "salary"; that is, they were paid for their time, not for their results. The pay of other participants was determined by the points they earned (in the game, the most points are awarded if participants come up with a pangram, consisting of all seven letters). Those who were paid based on points used their gray matter more efficiently and came up with more words. Then the participants could decide whether they wanted to switch their compensation. The powerful mechanism at play here turned out to be self-selection: people decide which option to choose. As self-selection predicts, the more productive players selected pay-for-performance, while the less productive ones chose to be paid based on time. For the pay-for-performance group, the number of words increased even further.

In chapter 5, we met jockeys, members of a highly skilled and dangerous profession. Like startup jockeys, race jockeys have to exert a lot of effort to increase their chances of winning. In startups and races alike, investors and horse owners cannot easily verify the effort and commitment of jockeys. Sue Fernie and David Metcalf of the London School of Economics wrote a paper on jockeys' responses to incentives with the provocative title "It's Not What You Pay, It's the Way That You Pay It and That's What Gets Results." They found that horses ridden by jockeys who were paid a percentage of the prize money performed better than horses with jockeys who were paid a fixed retainer.

Coming back to VCs, consider just one day in the history of startups: November 8, 2013. On that day, as the New York Stock Exchange's opening bell rang, Twitter's IPO was announced and cofounders Jack Dorsey and Evan Williams added billions to their wealth. But Twitter's IPO also minted 1,600 new millionaires, many of them ordinary engineers and product managers who had been reckless enough to join Twitter when it was only a small startup. They boarded a whale-hunting ship and won.

Twitter's IPO was exceptionally successful, with demand for its stock almost doubling the share price on the first day of trading.

Although this achievement is remarkable, it is by no means unique. The total value of all US VC-backed unicorn liquidity events, such as IPOs, in just the year 2021 was more than $700 billion. The more than seventy-five IPOs that year, and many more over recent decades, have created thousands of very big winners. They joined the early backers of Twitter—VC firms Union Square Ventures, Benchmark Capital, and others—as beneficiaries.

These investors knew that people hoping for venture jackpots—founders and employees alike—needed to work hard, often for low pay. So as you embark on a long and risky journey, if you want the team to work hard and bring back a large prize, design incentives that let everybody share in the gains. Everyone who shares the pain must share the gain. Or you will miss the whale.

8.3
The Compensation Revolution

In 1957, Sputnik opened the space race, Asian flu triggered a pandemic, and the first Frisbee went on sale. The same year, the compensation revolution hit the road in California's "Valley of Heart's Delight," a name inspired by its fruit-ripening orchards. Unless you're a history buff, you may never have heard of this name, but you surely have heard of the valley. It's now known as Silicon Valley, and the new name came about in no small way because of the compensation revolution.

It all started with eight engineers who decided to leave a lab founded by William Shockley, a co-inventor of the transistor, who had just been awarded a Nobel Prize in physics. The PC was two decades away and the whole idea of a semiconductor was still quite exotic, but these eight rebels wanted to launch a venture in the semiconductor space. They had bright ideas but no capital. Arthur Rock, son of a Russian immigrant, who would go on to become one of America's first and best-known VCs, lent them a helping hand. After dozens of failed attempts, Rock secured the attention of an extravagant businessman, science enthusiast, and investor, Sherman Fairchild. Fairchild was a big shot, the largest individual investor in IBM at the time, and the founder and owner of many companies, such as Fairchild Aviation, Fairchild Industries, and Fairchild Camera and Instrument. The Allies used this last company's cameras to take aerial photos during World War II, and the Fairchild equipment aided in the making of aerial maps from Manhattan to the moon's surface.

Fairchild sensed that big ideas were brewing in the heads of the eight engineers and agreed to fund their enterprise, making each of them a shareholder holding about 7.5 percent of the company. The new venture was named (are you surprised?) Fairchild Semiconductor. His and Rock's intuitions were soon justified, as the small garage-based startup grew to almost $100 million in revenue and more than 7,000 employees in less than five years. Cunning Fairchild inserted a clause in the contract that gave him the right to buy out the company for a fixed amount of $3 million. Just two years later, he did exactly that as the company started demonstrating exceptional results. The eight founders each received a small fortune, and Fairchild was now in possession of eight salaried employees with fixed compensation. If you know anything about self-selection, you can guess what happened next. Within the next few years, all the founders left Fairchild Semiconductor to launch their own businesses.

Enter the Computer History Museum in Mountain View, California, and you can see a "Trillion Dollar Startup" tree. These eight founders, playfully called "Fairchildren," spawned hundreds of companies, including Intel, AMD, Applied Materials, Oracle, Apple, KPCB, Cisco, and Nvidia—six generations of ventures with all their roots going back to Fairchild Semiconductor. Fairchild Semiconductor's combined progeny is worth trillions today.

Why did the eight founders leave Fairchild? Because the company failed to provide sufficient incentives to retain them as employees. The eight, some of whom became VCs themselves and others startup jockeys, didn't repeat Sherman Fairchild's mistake that had caused them to leave the Fairchild business. They started implementing the practice of giving most of their employees company shares, eliminating the limit on the upside.

This incentive model soon became an industry standard for all VC-backed companies. Investors also insisted on setting aside a whole pool of shares for future (i.e., not yet hired) employees. In the 1960s, these proliferating employee stock option programs persuaded many engineers to relocate from the longer-established tech centers of Boston, New York, and New Jersey to Silicon Valley. Intel, founded by two of those eight original rebels, Gordon Moore and Robert Noyce, shocked many when it gave stock options to *everyone*. Moore and Noyce believed strongly that ownership was the best way to guarantee both loyalty and innovation. Today, Intel still grants stock to most of its employees. Other companies, such as Apple, swiftly followed suit. The compensation revolution started its triumphant march. Why is it so powerful? Why is it a revolution?

8.4
Incentives Drive Behavior

Economists love staging experiments with lotteries. Imagine being a subject in one such experiment, in which you have to make one decision after another. Would you choose to receive $40 guaranteed or take a lottery ticket with a 10 percent chance of winning $400? Will your decision change if the lottery prize is lowered to $200 or increased to $1,000? Your choices reflect your position on the risk preference spectrum. If you are indifferent between a certain $40 and a 10 percent of winning $400, you are risk-neutral. If you would rather have a 10 percent chance at a

$200 prize than $40 in hand, you are risk-seeking, and if the lottery pot has to swell to $1,000 to steer you away from a certain $40 in your pocket, you are risk-averse.

Would you expect startup founders to be more risk-seeking than managers of large companies? A group of McKinsey researchers conducted a global survey to shed light on the risk preferences of corporate managers. They asked 1,500 managers this question:

"You are considering a $100 million investment that has some chance of returning, in present value, $400 million over three years. It also has some chance of losing the entire investment in the first year. What is the highest chance of loss you would tolerate and still proceed with the investment?"

A risk-neutral decision maker should accept no more than a 75 percent likelihood of failure. That's because if you multiply the value of $400 million in today's dollars by a 25 percent chance of success, the outcome is $100 million, or the value of the initial investment. However, corporate managers, as a group, demonstrated a profoundly high degree of risk aversion. Nine out of ten required at least a 60 percent chance of *success* before they would make the investment. Are corporate managers a unique species?

Let's consider the bottom line first. The results regarding the extreme risk aversion of corporate managers are not a research fluke. Their risk aversion is confirmed by a preponderance of evidence. In our work with large companies, we see it every day. Intuition might suggest that entrepreneurs should be more risk-tolerant. But after years of comparing managers and entrepreneurs, researchers have concluded that the evidence is mixed. Of the twenty-eight academic studies we reviewed, half showed that *entrepreneurs* are more risk-loving than managers, and half showed that *managers* are more risk-loving. How could that be?

One person's risk preference could of course be markedly different from another person's. We're sure you can name some friends who are very cautious, conservative, and careful. In the same breath, you may recall acquaintances who are adventurous, rollicking, and high-spirited. Ilya knows an adventure-seeking skier who once crashed into a tree on his way down the slopes. He had to be rescued by a medical helicopter. A week after his discharge from the hospital, he was back to skiing. We all know such people. They could be managers, startup founders, or your hairdresser.

To explain seemingly puzzling risk-averse behavior by corporate managers, we need a tool. That tool is called a "payoff chart," and it visualizes the future outcomes for the investment project or company and your personal payout. Figure 11 shows a stylized financial outcome for the founders of a hypothetical startup. The horizontal axis shows the startup's

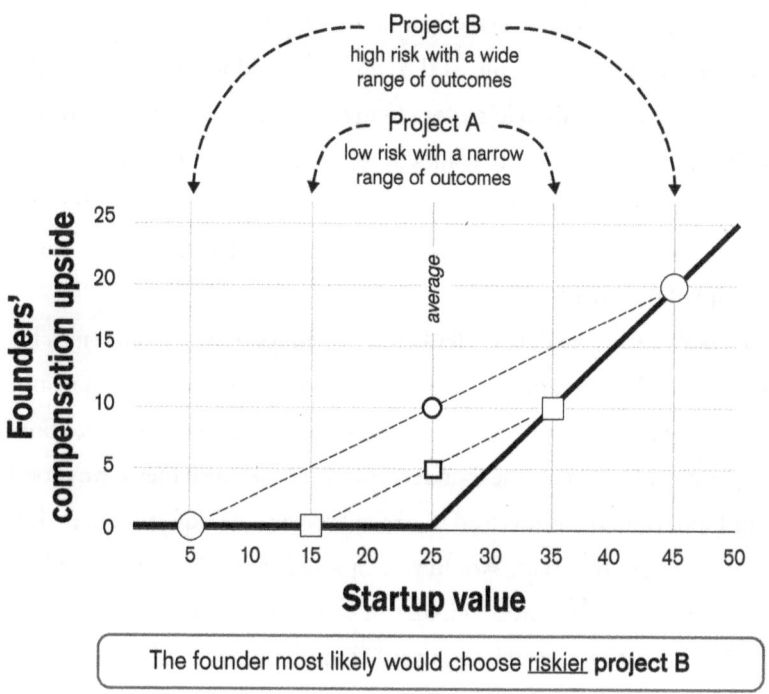

Figure 11.
Illustrative compensation model for a VC-backed startup

possible future value—say, the value at which it might be sold. The investor has injected $25 million. To the left of $25 million, the startup is unsuccessful, since it is sold for less money than what it raised. As we move to the right, the startup becomes more and more successful. The vertical axis shows the founders' payoff for all startup outcomes.

Consider the $5 million outcome. In the startup world, VC investors are senior to the founders: only after the investors are paid off do founders start benefiting too. Thus, for a $5 million outcome, the investor unhappily pockets the entire $5 million (but loses $20 million) and the founders get nothing. In fact, for any return of less than $25 million, the founders get nothing. You may surmise that getting nothing would incentivize the founders to avoid such scenarios, but we have not yet discussed what occurs in the scenarios to the right of $25 million.

As the startup value exceeds the amount of capital injected, the founders realize gains. For example, if the startup is sold for $35 million, the founders have $10 million left after paying back $25 million to the investors. If the startup's value becomes very large (beyond the $50 million shown in the figure), the investors also enjoy some of the profit, but the founders—as long as they own a sizable chunk of the startup—get the lion's share of the upside.

Of course, the founders prefer better outcomes to worse outcomes for themselves. Who wouldn't? But ask yourself whether the founders would prefer taking a risky action or a less risky one. The figure shows two possible investment decisions the founders could choose, once they have raised $25 million. Both decisions lead to two outcomes with equal chances, but the outcomes are different. Would you choose Project A or Project B?

Project A has a 50 percent chance of ending up valued at $15 million and a 50 percent chance of landing at $35 million. Project B's two possible outcomes, again each with a 50 percent chance of occurring, are $5 million and $45 million. Project A is safer, less innovative, and less volatile. The worst-case scenario won't see a large loss, but the best-case scenario won't see such a large upside either. Project B is more risky, innovative, and volatile. The worst-case scenario will see almost all the value disappear, but the best-case scenario will bring a very sweet payoff. Which action would the founders take? Which action would you take if you were in the founders' shoes?

If you were a founder, we bet you would select Project B. After all, if the startup is unsuccessful, the investors' money would be lost, not yours. But if it hits the jackpot, the sky is the limit. We also expect that corporate managers would choose a risky action *provided that* they were the founders.

The asymmetry in payoffs underscores the power of incentives. In startups, motivation is constructed to incentivize decision makers to take risks that can lead to outsized returns, as the case of Twitter vividly illustrates. Such incentives work particularly well in the world of disruptive innovation, where big winners can gain enormous benefits. The contracts between venture investors and founders have evolved to motivate entrepreneurs in this disruptive world. Such incentives increase the chance of failure, but they may also lead to jackpots.

What, then, about managers in a traditional large corporation? The traditional mindset works in the opposite direction, as Figure 12 shows by considering the same example. Imagine you are a corporate decision maker choosing between two investments, Projects A and B. These projects are identical to Projects A and B in the startup example, but, oh boy, the compensation of corporate managers cannot be more different.

Your managerial salary is fixed. You might own company stock, but in most cases an individual project is too small to have a noticeable impact on the company's market value. If the manager chooses a more innovative Project B and it succeeds spectacularly, the manager won't gain any more material benefit than with Project A. But if Project B fails, the manager could be punished severely. Your bonus is taken away, your chances of promotion are decreased, and your likelihood of being fired increases

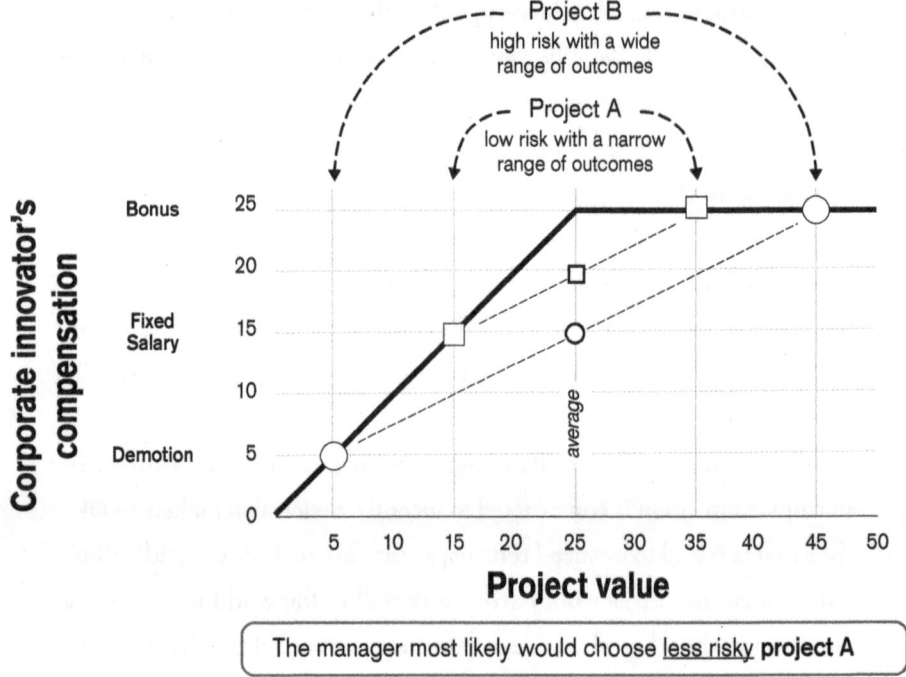

Figure 12.
Illustrative compensation model for a corporate project

uncomfortably. If you're like most corporate managers, you will pursue the safer Project A.

Let's reiterate the critical point. Figures 11 and 12 show the *same* choice of projects, and the same person could be making the decision in these two scenarios, but the decisions are very different. Financial motivation is a very powerful weapon.

We did simplify things in this example; reality is always more complex. One's corporate bonus might depend on project outcomes, and founders' stake in the profits might be diluted. But the critical insight of placing everyone in the same boat is very powerful and widely applicable. Corporate managers are risk-averse not because they are a different species, but because their financial incentives push them toward incremental rather than disruptive innovation. Finance office managers love incremental projects because of their shorter horizon, short-term cash flows, and transparent, unambiguous metrics. Engineers love incremental projects because they offer well-defined problems and well-designed processes. Sales and marketing teams love incremental projects because they appeal to existing customers and are complementary with existing business lines. But these preferences are all driven by incentives.

"Incentives drive behavior," we relentlessly tell our students and executives. The same people, when faced with different incentives, choose radically different actions. Over time, yet another powerful mechanism snowballs the effect. To see it in action, consider a study of more than 1,800 managers in Italian trade and service firms. Some of these firms paid a fixed salary; others carefully measured the manager's productivity and paid large bonuses for good performance. The managers who were by nature more risk-averse chose to work for a fixed salary. More risk-tolerant managers gravitated to firms that offered powerful incentives to try new things.

The organization that incentivizes more conservative behavior will attract people who are innately risk-averse. They feel at home in such an environment. Risk-seeking people will go elsewhere. Conversely, the organization that incentivizes more startup-like behavior will attract people who are naturally inclined to take higher risks. Self-selection is again decisive here: people decide whether to be in or out of the organization depending on what behavior it encourages.

8.5
You Get What You Pay For

Think twice before you set incentives. For an example of an incentive program gone seriously awry, consider the city of Hanoi in 1902. The colonial French administration, wanting to transform Hanoi into a modern European-style city, built a sewage system with an elaborate underground network. Unfortunately, the sewage also attracted rats that arrived on ships and trains from China. The situation soon became desperate as rats started climbing up the canalization pipes in the French quarter and out of toilets.

The colonial administration forcefully responded with a rat eradication campaign. They hired an army of professional rat hunters. On some days, up to 20,000 rats were killed. To bring the rat massacre to a successful conclusion, the authorities came up with a wonderful incentive scheme: they would pay one cent for each killed rat. To prove the kill, hunters had to show a rat tail. If you pay for tails—you get the tails.

Suspicions emerged when the French noticed rats running around on Hanoi streets with no tail. The locals had realized that by cutting off tails and letting the rats go free, they could kill two birds (rather than a rat) at once: they would get a cent per tail and they would leave the rats alive to keep breeding. More rats, more income. A new business venture emerged: importing rats from other provinces to Hanoi! Rat farming became a prosperous business model. The eradication campaign led to further multiplication of rats and had to be stopped, as the deathly bubonic plague hit the city. You pay for tails—you get the tails, indeed.

What large city tops the charts of the cleanest world cities? Singapore. The explanation is incentives once again. Singapore introduced draconian fines for littering. A cigarette butt may cost first-time offenders $300, with the penalty quickly reaching thousands of dollars for doing it again.

Or consider AT&T, which paid its software engineers based on the number of lines of code in their programs. AT&T executives presumably wanted better and more efficient codes, but what did they get? The longer the code, the better the pay. Software engineers produced very long codes, which resulted in slower and less efficient applications.

What might happen if you incentivized sales by rewarding larger revenue? In 2007, the home mortgage originator Countrywide initiated a "High-Speed Swim Lane" program, officially known by its acronym "HSSL," but which quickly became known among employees as "the Hustle." Loan officers were incentivized for high speed and high volume of loans. Bad loans quickly piled up, contributing to the financial crisis.

What could happen if salespeople were rewarded based on the number of customers they served? As Sears found out, repair shop employees in its auto service centers defrauded customers by pushing unnecessary repairs. What if the pay depends on the team size? Expect gargantuan teams. What if there is a penalty for low user retention? Expect a cumbersome process of unsubscribing and long call center wait times. What if the rewards depend on the growth in the number of users? Expect fake accounts—the rat tails of the modern world. Wells Fargo learned this lesson the hard way.

Finding the right incentives is exceptionally hard. Doing so in the world of innovation is even harder, since you have to encourage the kind of innovation you want: incremental or disruptive. The example of Thermo Fisher Scientific, a global lab equipment supplier, illustrates a smart approach to disruptive innovation. The company, which relies heavily on innovation, decided to crowdsource ideas about software solutions that could help people access advanced medical equipment. What is the best way to generate more and better ideas? Would you rather give a prize of $15,000 to the most innovative idea or split the prize into ten smaller ones, from $6,000 for first place to $600 for the tenth-best submission? In both cases, the total prize amount is the same. The company decided to do it both ways and split participants into two groups: one with a single large prize and another with many smaller prizes. Participants could decide to work in teams, submitting their ideas to a panel of experts who evaluated the proposals across multiple criteria.

The number of submissions and the overall scores for the "single large prize" and "many smaller prizes" groups were similar. But the novelty indicators, measuring solutions relative to what was already available in the market, were dramatically different. The "single large prize" winner was far more innovative. Participants vying for one large prize took more risks and thought outside the box; participants trying to win one of many smaller prizes opted to play safer. This is exactly what the competition designers wanted to achieve, and it is also what VCs expect from their startup management teams by making them focus on the larger prize. Searching for novel ideas? Keep this dynamic in mind.

Most of the time, a traditional compensation structure works well. You don't want your accountants to attempt risky projects. In the world of incremental innovation, with clear-cut mileposts, you want a measured degree of risk taking. But in the world of new businesses, disruption, and unknowns, the traditional incentive scheme works against companies. Tails will be brought, but not rats. This is when the Venture Mindset is required to succeed. The Venture Mindset tells you to achieve two changes at the same time: encourage upside participation while providing a degree of downside protection for the decision maker.

8.6
When Greed Is *Not* Good

Benjamin Franklin once quipped, "If you would have your business done, go; if not, send." All of us can save a few Benjamins if we follow his advice, and this applies particularly when we face exponential growth. Such growth does not figure into many of our decisions. We don't have to think "sink or swim" and are not daily on the brink of running out of cash. The entire VC business model is predicated on value creation rather than value extraction. It is about growing a huge pie rather than getting a larger slice.

The choice between a larger pie and a larger slice should be front and center in more businesses. In partnerships, such as consulting or legal firms, that choice is ever present. Partners are co-owners and the hard-earned profit is distributed among all partners at year end. The more earnings the partnership generates, the more cash each partner gets. But the more owners, the larger the denominator is, so the pie is divided among more people. Some partnerships decide to limit the number of partners while others take a leap of faith, hoping that newly promoted partners will make the pie bigger. Partnerships organized like an elite club that set the partnership bar too high start losing their best talent, as Fairchild Semiconductor did. The most ambitious of their employees open their own competing businesses or join competitors. Firms that open their doors wider to new partners get bigger and stay ahead of the competition. The strategy of growing the pie is one reason why the largest consulting firms have thousands of partners globally.

This concept is not limited to profit sharing. As Professor Alex Edmans has shown forcefully in *Grow the Pie*, keeping the focus on social value rather than exclusively on profits may surprisingly lead to more profits and better long-term decisions.

When faced with exponential growth in the context of disruptive innovation, you can align incentives by applying these principles of the Venture Mindset.

Make everyone an owner

Benjamin Franklin knew a thing or two about incentives. In addition to all the other hats he wore, he was also an innovative entrepreneur. In the early 1730s, he built a publishing and printing business, and his *Pennsylvania Gazette* became the most successful newspaper in the colonies. Franklin started to think about expansion. Because he could not travel from one city to another setting up businesses, Franklin came up with an idea. What if he were to send his most entrepreneurial employees to launch the business in other cities? He gave adventurous employees the requisite up-front capital and covered some operational expenses. They had to take care of labor, paper, ink, wool, oil, and any repairs. Like modern VCs, Franklin didn't ask for too much, to ensure that the new entrepreneurs had strong incentives to succeed. For six years, he would get one-third of the profit of their enterprises, with an option for them to become fully independent thereafter. Franklin founded the first franchisee system in America. He made his employees owners.

In an interesting study of the real estate industry, three researchers explored the power of incentives. They asked whether the same person would act differently when she is a real estate agent representing the client or when selling her own property. They carefully controlled for property characteristics, so that ownership was the only difference. The value differential they found was hefty. Real estate agents sell their own condominiums at a 3 to 7 percent higher price compared to when they represent the client.

For economists, the behavior of real estate agents is an example of the principal-agent problem, in which the agent (here, the realtor) does not fully internalize the interests of the principal (the property owner). The principal-agent problem is widespread in many settings: owner-manager, boss-employee, client-attorney. But it is particularly hard to address in a high-uncertainty environment, in which failure is the norm, not an exception.

That's why VCs apply the "compensation revolution" motto and make everyone the owner. This step, of course, is powerful far beyond technology companies. Starbucks introduced "bean stocks" given to all eligible employees, who are referred to as partners. Although being a barista may not make you a millionaire, bean stocks allowed many employees to pay off student loans, make a down payment on a home, or plan exotic overseas travels when Starbucks stock appreciated.

Placing everyone in the same boat can work even in a garage door business. The private equity firm KKR bought C.H.I. Overhead Doors in 2015 for less than $700 million and made all 800 employees, from truck drivers to senior managers, shareholders. This was unexpected and welcome news for the small town of Arthur, Illinois, where the company is located. The idea was the brainchild of KKR partner Pete Stavros, whose father was a construction worker. Since introducing the new incentive model, the company has steadily demonstrated improved safety, decreased waste, and increasing profitability. Even a traditional company can become a unicorn. In 2022, KKR sold C.H.I. to steel manufacturer Nucor for $3 billion. A multiyear journey paid off handsomely, and not only for investors. When Stavros announced the deal in Arthur, the crowd went ballistic. Hourly employees received on average $175,000, more than five times their annual pay, with a total reward pool of $360 million.

The Venture Mindset solves the principal-agent problem by making everyone a shareholder. Instead of looking for ways to get a larger piece of the pie, everyone is busy growing the pie.

The Venture Mindset also introduced vesting into employee ownership schemes, further incentivizing employees to stick around. Startup employees don't get their portion of shares right away but have to earn their ownership over several years as their shares vest. Those who leave too early forfeit their ownership. To benefit from a rising tide, you have to stay in the boat.

Solve the "1000 to 1001" challenge

Because VC-backed companies tend to be smaller, they have one distinct advantage over larger companies: attribution of success is easier in a smaller enterprise with one product line. Even rank-and-file employees can feel that their work increases the entire company's value in a material way. Whether you are a marketing manager or a supply chain specialist, everyone contributes to the same common goal: the company's "exit" value.

One thorny challenge at a large company is to link the contributions of individual employees to the company's valuation. We call this problem a "1000 to 1001" challenge. In his bestseller *Zero to One*, the famed VC investor Peter Thiel described the challenges of a company that grows from nothing into a great something. Building a company from ground zero is hard, but the impact is clear. The value goes from nothing to, say, $1 billion, making the company a unicorn. But what if a team within a large company delivers the same billion-dollar impact? Their contribution is diluted across a large existing business. This is a "1000 to 1001" issue. The impact is the same or perhaps even larger, but the reward is often disproportionally smaller, causing talented employees to leave. Often the ones leaving are the most entrepreneurial ones, the modern-day Fairchildren.

Waymo, a driverless car subsidiary of Alphabet, offers one solution. We sometimes jokingly ask, "Who is in the driver's seat of a Waymo car?" Our answer is: "Phantoms!" We are referring to the phantom shares given to employees. Waymo employees don't get incentivized with Alphabet stock because the market value of Alphabet is driven primarily by Google's search engine, not Waymo's results. Instead, they get "shares," the value of which depends on Waymo's own valuation and performance. These shares are phantoms, because Waymo is not an independent publicly traded company.

Although legal constructs may differ, the ultimate goal is to shorten the distance between each employee's effort and the company's valuation. This helps to bring "1000 to 1001" back toward "0 to 1."

Reward boldness

Silicon Valley is full of rags-to-riches stories. Have you heard of Charlie Ayers? He was a chef who competed against twenty-five other chefs to get the job at a small startup. The promised pay was only half of what he could get elsewhere, but the compensation also included stock options. After talking with friends, Ayers became convinced that the company was destined for growth, so he grabbed his lottery ticket and became employee number fifty-three at Google. His jackpot reportedly hit $26 million on the day of Google's IPO.

A graffiti artist, thirty-five-year-old David Choe, was invited to paint murals on the walls of Facebook offices and was asked whether he wanted to be paid in cash or accept company shares. Choe chose all stock, becoming one of more than 1,000 millionaires when Facebook went public.

You may discount these stories as cool examples that can't be replicated in a traditional organization. But they illustrate that, to align incentives, you need to ensure there are ways for all employees to participate and benefit. Creating examples of employee success will make others work harder to achieve theirs.

Speaking of millionaires—Wall Street stock traders and Google's and Twitter's early employees may easily come to mind, but "McDonald's has made more millionaires than any other economic entity ever, anywhere," says George Will of the *Washington Post*. That's due to its franchisee model in which the interests of all parties are closely aligned by intention.

Finally, imagine that you are the founder of a very successful startup. How much would you own when your company hits an all-important IPO milestone? When we disclose the average percentage, many are surprised. Only 15 to 20 percent of the shares are typically left for all the cofounders. The founders of Lyft, Box, and Pandora kept only 6 percent, 4 percent, and 2 percent, respectively. Why would people accept such arrangements? Because VCs and founders of VC-backed companies prefer a smaller slice of a larger pie rather than the other way around. Corporations should too. So should all of us whose aim is to promote the generation of innovative ideas.

MINDSET CHECKS

● ● ● ●

○ Do your teams and leadership benefit from the success of innovative projects?

○ Is the payoff significant enough to stimulate risk taking?

○ Are smaller teams working on critical projects valued in your organization, or is it only the scale and the size of the project budget that determine significance?

NINE

Great Things Take Time

What's the main killer of innovation

9.1
Fire Up Long-Term Thinking

It all starts with a fire.

Matagorda Island, located about 100 miles southwest of Houston, Texas, used to be home to Peninsula Army Airfield, a World War II training facility. Oilman and investor Toddie Lee Wynne owned the Star Brand Ranch on the southern end of the island and offered it for an unusual event: a rocket launch. The ambitious goal was to deliver payloads into orbit through the first-ever rocket launch pulled off by a commercial, for-profit company.

After multiple delays, in the late afternoon of August 5 enough liquid oxygen was pumped into the fifty-five-foot rocket to lift it off the ground, reach outer space, and qualify for the space hall of fame. A few dozen technicians crouched behind an eight-foot wall of sandbags waiting for this historic moment. At 5:00 p.m., as the igniter button was pushed, smoke appeared at the rocket's base. But as a main valve on the liquid oxygen tank failed to open, the pressure started quickly building up. A second later, before anybody could blink, the suborbital vehicle produced by two firms, one from Houston and another from Sunnyvale, California, exploded on the launchpad, setting off a brush fire on the surrounding grass. It took engineers half an hour to put the fire out.

"We're not sure what happened," blurted Charles Chafer, a disappointed spokesman for Space Services Inc., right after the disaster. But it was clear that the blast on Matagorda Island had foiled the hope of sending a commercial satellite into outer space for a paltry $3 million to $5 million per launch, or a fraction of NASA's exorbitant, monopolistic costs.

A year later, a successful commercial launch occurred. This time, the founder of Space Services Inc. received a congratulatory note stating, "You have shown the potential of private enterprise to perform even the most sophisticated technical feats." What made the note so special was its author. The note was sent by the President of the United States.

His name was Ronald Reagan. . . .

It was the year 1981 when that fire destroyed Wynne's Percheron, the first-ever US privately funded commercial rocket. Elon Musk was ten years old and living with his father in Pretoria, Transvaal, South Africa.

Twenty-five years later, in March 2006, another small island, this time in the Pacific Ocean, was the site of another attempt to turn a dream into reality. By now, Musk had become a wealthy entrepreneur by selling his stake in PayPal. Now, as the founder of SpaceX, he came to the distant Kwajalein Atoll in the Marshall Islands to see the breakthrough with his own eyes. What he didn't know was that about seven minutes before the launch, a small corrosion crack in the aluminum nut caused a fuel leak. The moment the main engine ignited, the leaking fuel caught fire and it was all over. One small, rusty nut halted the much-ballyhooed first launch of a SpaceX rocket, Falcon 1, which could have become the first privately developed, fully liquid-fueled vehicle to go into orbit around Earth. But Falcon 1's disaster did not end the hope. Musk would try again.

One year later, in March 2007, on the same atoll, the Falcon failed again—this time because of a rocket motor problem. Again, Musk was determined to try again.

SpaceX's third attempt was on August 3, 2008. The flight was critical, as SpaceX had entered into contracts to deliver payloads for commercial and government customers. Falcon carried a satellite for the US Air Force, nanosatellites for NASA, and a payload for a private company, Celestis Inc. Again, the Falcon failed. The media had a field day, blaspheming NASA and the Defense Advanced Research Projects Agency (DARPA), both of which had bet on the company.

The day after the third failed attempt, Musk left everyone open-mouthed when he announced that SpaceX had just received a $20 million investment from Founders Fund, a leading VC firm headquartered in San Francisco. SpaceX's first external fundraising happened not just after its third highly public failure, but also in the midst of the 2008 financial crisis that shook the global economy.

"The fourth launch . . . was the last money that we had for Falcon 1," Musk acknowledged years later. But finally, in September 2008, the fourth launch of Falcon 1 was a success.

Less than a year later, DFJ, another prominent venture firm, led an investment round that put $50 million more into SpaceX. The fifth launch, in July 2009, just a month after the DFJ investment, reached its goal as well. The tide turned. SpaceX opened the whole new era of private space companies, with Blue Origin and Virgin Galactic soon joining SpaceX in the sector.

On May 22, 2012, the unmanned Falcon 9 blasted off with a unique container on board. The owner was Celestis, the company whose payload ended up in the ocean after the third failed attempt of SpaceX. The container was full of the cremated remains of people who had paid dearly to deliver their ashes into outer space on a so-called "Memorial Spaceflight" mission. Among the remnants of 320 people were ashes of astronaut

Gordon Cooper and actor James Doohan of *Star Trek*. Celestis itself was a very special client. It was owned by Charles Chafer, who announced Percheron's failure to the world back in 1981, and a subsidiary of Space Services Inc., the very company that made that 1981 attempt. Chafer ended up fulfilling his dream only with the help of SpaceX.

It took less than ten minutes for Falcon 9 to reach orbit, but SpaceX's journey to gaining respect from experts, analysts, and the world took much longer. In the memorable words of Bill Nelson, the head of NASA, "Everybody pooh-poohed SpaceX."

Despite all the criticism and skepticism, the number of launches geared up. In 2008, there were only two launches, one of which was a failure. In 2014, there were six, all successful. In 2022, SpaceX launched sixty-one rockets, or more than one per week. By then it was an undisputed leader in space launches, even when compared to government agencies. The company did all this with a fraction of the budget typically allocated to government space agencies such as NASA, Russia's Roscosmos, or China's National Space Administration (CNSA). It was an exceptional achievement by a relatively small team of only a few thousand people. As a sobering comparison, Russia's Roscosmos employs more than 200,000 people.

If you were a risk-loving investor who put money into SpaceX back in 2008, you are worth a lot more now than you were then. Using one of the valuation metrics beloved in the VC industry, post-money valuation, SpaceX was valued at just over $400 million in 2008; fifteen years later, in 2023, it had skyrocketed to $137 billion, an increase of more than 300 times. Both Founders Fund and DFJ made not only a risky but also a very long-term bet. Recently, Musk admitted how extremely risky his bets were, acknowledging a "90% chance that both SpaceX and Tesla would be worth $0."

As we write this chapter in mid-2023, SpaceX is still a private VC-backed company and recently raised its Series N. That's right—SpaceX investors still bear the risk and are still waiting for a chance to convert their early bet into cash. Some half-jokingly argue that SpaceX may even exhaust the alphabet and still not make it to the IPO. SpaceX investors made a bet on the future and now wait patiently for the outcome.

The SpaceX story is a classic lesson in going slow to go fast. VCs bet on tectonic shifts that take time to mature and realize full impact. Going in early and with patience is the VC mindset's credo. Many corporate decision makers clearly see approaching tectonic shifts in their industry, too. Robots and generative algorithms will one day replace many employees. Renewables will encroach on traditional energy sources. Aging populations will place pressure on healthcare systems. But none of these changes happen within a single budget cycle, so decision makers kick the can down the road. This may continue for a while until the tectonic shift becomes unavoidable, but by then it is too late; the can has fallen off the precipice. Would the traditional mindset have invested in SpaceX back in 2008 or 2009?

We are often asked, "What does SpaceX have to do with us?" Space exploration is obviously a long-term bet, people say, but our sector is "short-term," be it footwear or auto parts or weight-loss products. We hope by now you've learned that in the Venture Mindset there are no short-term sectors. There are long-term trends disrupting every sector. Your neighborhood auto mechanic shop may disappear like the vinyl rental shops or corner travel agencies of yesteryear. Shoes are here to stay, but will the perennial struggle to find the right size and shape that supports your posture lead to a disruptive technological solution that will catch today's dominant players unaware? People will always worry about obesity, but will the next generation of drugs destroy traditional weight-loss companies? VCs and innovative companies are betting on these and long-term trends as we write these sentences.

In Ernest Hemingway's novel *The Sun Also Rises*, Mike Campbell is asked how he went bankrupt. In a memorable line, Mike responds, "Two ways. Gradually and then suddenly." In one sentence, Hemingway encapsulates the danger of ignoring long-term trends. Alas, we have encountered many Mike Campbells in the business world. Don't become one.

9.2
Grow from the Ashes

Among the many SpaceX VC investors was Sequoia Capital. In the 1970s, its founder, Don Valentine, picked the name Sequoia as a reference to the tree that grows taller and stronger with time and may outlive all of us. Among the seeds Sequoia has planted, 23andMe, Apple, DoorDash, and Instagram are just a few that have matured into tall trees.

California is the land where great things take time to grow. Go no further than the magical Redwood National Park. There you can find the largest, oldest, and tallest trees, not far away from Silicon Valley. The world's tallest living tree, named Hyperion, was discovered in 2006 by naturalists Chris Atkins and Michael Taylor. They initially measured its height with a laser, but to confirm its place in the Guinness Book, someone climbed the tree all the way to the top to measure the distance between a dropped tape and the ground. Hyperion took a leisurely 700 years to reach two and a half times the height of the Statue of Liberty. Of course, like any other sequoia, it started with a single seed. But a seed and time are not enough. Sequoias need fire.

Wildfires can be devastating, leaving behind thousands of acres of burned land. But as evidence of the complex equilibrium in nature, fires are also necessary for sequoias' survival and replication. Forest fires cause sequoia cones to dry out, open, and release seeds that give birth to future trees. Out of many cones and seeds, only an impossibly tiny share survives to rise over their peers.

Fires are devastating for cities, too. At 5:12 a.m. on April 18, 1906, San Francisco was hit by a major earthquake; soon, the entire city was engulfed in massive fires. The first shocks caused thirty-five-year-old Amadeo Peter Giannini and his wife, Clorinda, to jump out of their bed. Their house in San Mateo, seventeen miles away, was shaken but remained standing. Giannini was a newly minted banker who had opened the doors of his Bank of Italy in San Francisco two years earlier, in 1904. The fire was threatening to turn his dreams to ashes. Trains had stopped operating, so Giannini *walked* those seventeen miles to San Francisco. The bank building was in total disarray. However, to his relief, Giannini found the valuables and records intact. Giannini placed about $80,000—an enormous sum at the time—on a wagon borrowed from his stepfather, covered the heaps of banknotes with oranges to protect them from looting, and rode back home.

Most San Francisco bankers claimed they would need six months to restore their operations due to their collapsed buildings, trapped assets, and paperwork challenges. Giannini opened his bank the next day and started giving loans, one handshake at a time. His bank, now set up on the waterfront of the devastated San Francisco North Beach, consisted of a simple desk made from two beer barrels and a plank. Giannini believed that the city and its people would recover quickly. From the ashes more businesses and taller buildings, like sequoias, would grow. Giannini was prepared to give loans without physical collateral. He made a risky, long-term bet and won.

In his banking career, Giannini made many unconventional gambles. He served immigrants of wildly different origins, women, working-class customers, and farmers. He offered consumer finance products that were not common at a time when banks symbolized prestige and wealth. He gave smaller businesses what he called "character loans," based on an individual borrower's reputation. "The little fellow is the best customer that a bank can have," he said, "because he is with you. He starts in with you and stays to the end."

Some of Giannini's bets were so unconventional that he gained a reputation as "ruthless and reckless, an intimidating, fiery-tempered financial maverick who brought to his branch banking empire . . . a fierce competitive drive and the urge to dominate others." He was, some said, "California's well-loved and well-hated people's banker." The capital his bank provided had a lasting impact. He backed Walt Disney in times of financial troubles, and his bank financed Disney's first full-length animated movie, *Snow White and the Seven Dwarfs*. He was a banker of choice for California wineries. Giannini even financed William Hewlett and David Packard when HP was still in a garage. That garage is now a landmark and the official birthplace of Silicon Valley.

When A. P. Giannini died in 1949, his bank, with $6 billion in assets, was the largest in the world. It remains one of the largest global financial institutions, now known as the Bank of America.

The same story happens again and again. In the moment of fire, literal or metaphorical, most investors run away in panic, but a few continue backing new ideas and entrepreneurs. In late 2008 and early 2009, on the ashes of a more modern financial crisis, many companies sprouted their first shoots. Too many step back when a recession hits, valuations decline, or a "fire" spreads. But VCs know that the most revolutionary opportunities come at exactly those times. Think of Uber, Airbnb, and Square—companies that not only transformed the taxi, hotel, and payments industries but also enriched their early investors, who had the guts to invest in crazily bold ideas when the dust had not yet settled. SpaceX, Tesla, HP, Uber, and Disney have grown into record-tall sequoias. Many more companies of the same caliber, which we will recognize as grand successes only years from now, are being planted today thanks to the VC mindset.

It's hard to imagine a traditional company announcing massive innovation projects in the middle of a major downturn. Instead, we hear "downsize," "stay put," and "cut the risk." Where the traditional mindset sees downsizing, VCs see opportunities.

Bill Gurley of Benchmark Capital showcases this VC philosophy loud and clear: "Benchmark never changes our investment cycle due to economic swings." In his late-2022 post "Winter Is Coming," investor Fabrice Grinda described gloomy times ahead, but he finished with words of optimism: "The best startup investments of the last decade were made between 2008 and 2011. The macro that matters for startups is the one 6–8 years from now." As Sheryl Sandberg said, "If you're offered a seat on a rocket ship, don't ask what seat. Just get on." This kind of long-term thinking enables the Venture Mindset to overlook short-term fears of cash burn to see beyond the immediate horizon. You need a fire to give birth to the largest sequoias in the world.

9.3
Priceless Assets

"Dad, they all want to meet you!" Thus started one week of fame for Ilya when he became the most popular dad at his daughter's elementary school. It all started when she mentioned that her dad was the world's leading "unicorn expert."

Ilya is indeed an expert on unicorns—but not the one-horned mythical animals in medieval legends. Aileen Lee, a Silicon Valley VC, wrote a post in 2013 titled "Welcome to the Unicorn Club: Learning from Billion-Dollar Startups." This was the first use of "unicorn" to denote a VC-backed company with a reported valuation over $1 billion, most of which are extremely successful startups. Unicorns were still exceedingly rare in 2013. Lee and her team identified only thirty-nine private companies that belonged to the "Unicorn Club." Ilya and his team have been analyzing VC-backed unicorns for years, and the herd is far bigger now. At the time of writing, there were more than 1,000 unicorns.

The significance of unicorns shouldn't be underestimated. The cumulative value of all publicly traded companies in some countries may be less than that of a single unicorn. Moreover, the estimated total fair value of all private VC-backed unicorns is trillions of dollars. To appreciate the significance of this figure, consider that it exceeds the GDP of India, Brazil, or the UK and is close to that of Germany. The unicorn of myth has become reality in the VC realm. But it's not limited to VCs only. Today many traditional organizations have become unicorn-makers. Although it is hard to place a price tag on corporate unicorns, they impact the value of their parent organizations for sure. Just think of Amazon Web Services, Azure, Post-it, or Disney Parks.

Investors, CEOs, and board members are all curious about what makes a unicorn and, even more importantly, how to find, make, or breed one. Is it all about wide networks, talent, and bits of luck? Of course. However, one particular trait makes VCs such successful unicorn shepherds.

Patience.

The trouble with unicorns and other VC investments is that these are hard-to-sell assets. They are like old paintings you might have inherited from your great-grandparents. The painting just might be by a famous artist, but it is often not easy to authenticate and sell one. Investors buying stocks of publicly traded companies can sell whenever they wish. The life of an algorithmic quant fund's transaction is measured in milliseconds, if not in nanoseconds. Day traders, to justify their name, buy and sell routinely within any given day. But VCs are stuck with their decisions for years. They know that the capital they provide to startups will be tied up for a long time, even and perhaps especially in case of success. Rarely do they have a chance to get out of their unicorn stake quickly. To use professional jargon, their investment is very *illiquid*. Or more informally, they are stuck.

Illiquidity is only one of the challenges startup investors face. VC-backed companies also tend to burn rather than earn cash. They are typically unprofitable, and their worth lies in expectations of future greatness, not in today's revenues or existing hard assets. As a result, they do not pay dividends. In fact, they often bleed cash like streets overflowing with water after a heavy rain. The average unicorn raises more than half a billion dollars and then burns through this money with the hope of joining the ranks of successful public companies or being acquired at an astounding valuation. Often, they must wait years until their startup ownership can finally be exchanged for cash. This milestone is called the "liquidity event," but VCs use a simpler term: *exit*.

VCs call these events "exits" not because the company is exiting, but because VCs can finally exit their investments and hopefully realize some profit. For many early investors, the exit is the first time they see any cash come back. The IPO of Palantir Technologies in 2020 was a success for early investors. They sold their shares for a triple-digit return, but they had to wait sixteen years for it. Palantir is one of more than 230 unicorns whose early investors had to wait more than ten years. Among all the unicorns that have gone public, it takes on average nine years after their founding before the IPO bell is rung. Even for late-stage VC-backed companies, the average time frame is close to five years. It took ten years for MongoDB and Uber, twelve years for Eventbrite and Joby Aviation, fifteen years for DocuSign and Etsy. And as we noted above, SpaceX has remained a private company for more than fifteen years.

In a nutshell, the Venture Mindset requires great patience. It's hard to imagine worse assets than those owned by VCs. Seriously. Startups are risky and illiquid. These companies don't make any profit for many years, so investors must wait a long time to get their money back.

Performance of innovative businesses is often described as a J-curve or a hockey stick (see Figure 13). The curve illustrates the fact that most disruptive ideas initially generate only losses, with just a small fraction eventually getting on the exponential growth trajectory. In the VC world, the depth and length of the loss period are extensive and intensive. It always gets worse before it gets better. Nerves of steel are needed to live through the first part of a J-curve.

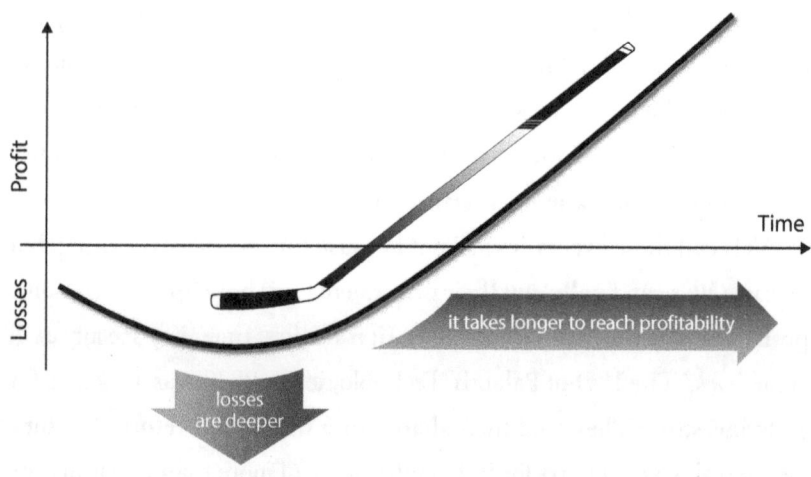

Figure 13.
Hockey stick or J-curve of a typical VC-backed company

Successful VCs are well rewarded for their patience. The silver lining is the average unicorn valuation of $4 billion at exit; the average exit valuation is more than twenty times the total amount of capital raised. Such returns are exceptional, however. VC investments are like a shiny Cinderella's coach with a risk of turning into a pumpkin at any time.

The patience requirement and the inability to step off the train mid-journey compel the Venture Mindset to think differently from traditional investors and decision makers. But what is truly remarkable about VC investments is that the closest equivalents to what they do—along many dimensions—are corporate projects.

Illiquidity, perennial lack of profitability, and long wait times are prominent features of both startup investments and many risky internal corporate investments. Countless executives in many companies we have worked with react to our description of the challenges VCs face by exclaiming, "Gosh, this is so eerily similar to the projects we need to decide on in our industry"—whether it is mining, construction, shipbuilding, or consumer products. You name it.

Being stuck with an idea or a business for a long time changes the mental model. Imagine renting a car for a week. You spill some cola as you open the door—no big deal, just use a tissue and the remaining drops won't bother you much. What gas will you fill it with? The cheapest. Who cares? You are a short-term user, and minimizing your cost per day is the main concern. But all this behavior flips if you are buying a car and plan to hold on to it for several years. You use different selection criteria, fix stains and scratches promptly, and use the recommended gas because you care about protecting your car's long-term value.

Long-term thinking changes how we behave. It makes us more willing to incur short-term losses. "Because of our emphasis on the long term," says Amazon founder Jeff Bezos, "we may make decisions and weigh trade-offs differently than some companies." Patience and long-term thinking free the mind from unnecessary limitations and push us to think about what might happen to the world in five, ten, or fifteen years. They force us to look beyond day-to-day routines. They drive VCs to search for strategic long-term bets on such business ideas as space tech, driverless cars, and CRISPR. On the other hand, these initiatives enjoy the luxury of not having to report their earnings every quarter. Their investors are often far more worried if their portfolio companies are showing profit too early. Is the company sacrificing further growth opportunities and potentially missing the chance to become a unicorn?

While traditional investors and decision makers focus on short-term profitability challenges, VCs think about long-term potential. They won't ask entrepreneurs about their current market share; they worry about the future market size. They look for future sequoias and are less perturbed by short-term fires. They also know that fires and earthquakes are often the best occasions to search for new seeds.

As these new seeds grow, they may disrupt the world, but as with sequoias, large changes may take time. It took more than sixty-five years for electricity to reach 90 percent of US houses. The telephone was a luxury accessible to only one-quarter of Americans even after thirty-five years of its commercial availability. A. P. Giannini had to ride a horse-drawn wagon to save his Bank of Italy assets in 1906. And only half a dozen years later, large American cities had more cars than horses on the streets.

What will replace the car in the same way that the car replaced the horse? Think of Uber or Lyft. The latter was called Zimride when Floodgate partners Ann Miura-Ko and Mike Maples decided to invest in this company in 2010. They had observed multiple large and long-term macrotrends. GPS locators in smartphones were becoming orders of magnitude more accurate. Enough people had smartphones to provide a critical mass of drivers and riders. "It was an inflection point!" exclaims Maples to us. "Make a bet years before and you may end up only with a hopeless dream. Wait longer and you miss it all." This long-term vision—not a desire for short-term profits—convinced them to invest, making it one of Floodgate's most successful investments. "Startup is an underpriced bet on the future because most people are not willing to pay," Maples explains further. "I lean in on the uncertainty: the more uncertain the future the better, as fewer people would be willing to chase it."

We wish people in more organizations, not just VCs, would take such stances. The paradox is that many organizations instead make bets on the past, not on the future, investing in ideas past their expiry date.

What will come next? Driverless cars? Flying cars? More efficient public transport? A network of remote offices connected via virtual reality rooms? No one knows, but VCs are investing in all these ideas. Many in the corporate world are skeptical, and rightly so: many ideas won't survive. But as we remind our students and executives, skepticism is better than hubris. "The horse is here to stay, but the automobile is only a novelty—a fad," the president of the Michigan Savings Bank reportedly told Henry Ford's lawyer, Horace Rackham, in 1903. More recently, in 1999, Steve Riggio, CEO of Barnes & Noble, declared, "No one is going to beat us at selling books—it just ain't gonna happen." In 2007, Microsoft CEO Steve Ballmer stated, "There's no chance that the iPhone is going to get any significant market share. No chance. It's a $500 subsidized item." "We do not see [technological changes] on the horizon for the last mile delivery at present," said Fred Smith, CEO of FedEx, in 2017. How did all these visionary decision makers miss the space shuttle into the future?

9.4
Looking Past Short-Term Gains

Thinking long-term is a choice.

It's 11:00 p.m., and Alex is still in the office of the COO of a large power plant. "The only thing that matters is the time horizon!" the executive grumbles, taking a sip of a Diet Coke. "You tell me what is the exit plan, and I tell you what to do," he concludes, squeezing the can and throwing it into the bin. We are at a kickoff meeting for a strategy planning project.

"Take my repair and maintenance program as an example," the executive continues. "My budget spending on boilers, well, boils down to whether we plan on selling the business three years down the road or in ten to fifteen years." With a shorter time frame, he then explains, he would care only about short-term profitability and would instruct his team to cut all possible costs to the bare bones. Attractive financials, in his view, would help to get a higher price from the next owner. But if he learns that the same assets will remain under his supervision for at least a decade, he changes his tack. Instead of cutting costs, he decides to retrofit and repair the plant.

People widely apply the same intuition to the hiring of talent, investment decisions, bonus programs, and many other business situations, particularly when uncertainty levels are high. Consider a firm's approach to training new employees. As you may have noticed, service quality varies dramatically across restaurants. Some personnel know very little about the menu or the wine list, because they are not trained or motivated to learn; neither the owner nor the employees expect that they will stay around for a long time. But if you expect a staff member to stick around, the effort and cost of training become more justifiable. Davide Oldani, the chef-owner of famous Michelin-starred restaurant D'O in Milan, opted to build a different culture from that of his peers who burn through staff rapidly due to long hours and intimidating treatment. Oldani's long-term aspirations guided him to pay his staff above-market salaries and offer continuous training. As a result, the staff turnover is exceptionally low: only three people have left in ten years. The Michelin Guide ranked highly the "professional and enthusiastic service" and recently awarded the coveted two stars to the restaurant.

Or consider employee bonus programs. The first question employees might ask is "Are we even going to be here by the time we receive the bonus?" Look around and you may be surprised at how heavily many decisions are influenced by the time horizon. Lots of decisions that sound advantageous in the short term may lead to disastrous long-term outcomes. Some may even cost you the company.

Who could have predicted that the promise to earn a billion dollars would be the beginning of the end? In a regular quarterly earnings call, a CEO suddenly threw a juicy bone to Wall Street analysts by promising that the company's social media business would hit the mind-blowing $1 billion revenue mark next year. Right out of the gate, four years before that momentous earnings call, the website had hit all the right buttons. It took only a few months to acquire millions of eager users from all over the world. Soon, 5 million people were registered on the platform. The next year, the website attracted more traffic than Google, as the number of users reached almost 100 million. The company even struck an exclusive partnership advertising agreement with Google worth $900 million, one of the largest deals in the history of digital media up to that time.

Then the tide turned. Parents started blaming the social media platform for suicides and sexual abuse of their children. The company was caught sharing user personal data with advertisers, including their names and profile pictures. Lawsuits started piling up. The website had bugs. Teenagers thought it was not cool enough and stopped registering. Spam messages, from random marriage proposals to friend requests purportedly sent by nude webcam girls, proliferated. "A place for friends" turned into a "massive spaghetti-ball mess." "Delete Your Account" became the motto behind users' anger.

If the story sounds familiar, think again. We are not describing Facebook but its predecessor MySpace. We last met MySpace in chapter 2, when we described how VC investor Paul Madera and his partners' due diligence on MySpace was cut short as the News Corp media conglomerate acquired it in 2005 for more than half a billion dollars. The CEO who said he would be surprised if the company had not reached $1 billion in revenue in a year's time was Rupert Murdoch. MySpace's revenue in the previous year was below $100 million. Soon enough, MySpace failed and was sold off for only $35 million.

Defeat is an orphan. Although it is hard to pinpoint one reason for the MySpace debacle, many agree that the $1 billion short-term promise Murdoch made in that infamous earnings call was the last nail in the coffin. "The boss said we have to make a billion dollars," recalled former MySpace vice president of online marketing Sean Percival, "so I guess we need to make a billion dollars." With the overarching goal of driving next year's revenue, executives concentrated on maximizing advertising income at the expense of improving underlying technology and making users want to engage. The deal with Google required MySpace to ensure that it delivered a certain number of clicks on Google ads per year, further exacerbating the short-term frame of mind. While Facebook was developing its product to be user-friendly, MySpace pages were slow, clunky, and full of annoying ads. The all-consuming focus on short-term revenue goals doomed the chances for long-term success.

The MySpace story had many losers, but there were a couple winners. Two VC funds, VantagePoint Capital Partners and Redpoint Ventures, invested around $15 million each in MySpace early on and cashed out when Rupert Murdoch's empire acquired the startup. The investors got healthy returns of 9X and 3X, respectively. But these investors were far from happy. Geoff Yang, a Redpoint partner, strongly opposed the sale to News Corp in 2005 and believes the new owner destroyed the value of a great asset. Most would be on cloud nine after tripling their money in a few months, but not Yang. His Venture Mindset focused not on short-term gains but on the lost long-term opportunity. He wished theirs could have been a long-haul journey.

The VC mindset message to leaders across their portfolio companies is loud and clear: make decisions that benefit the company's long-term value and demonstrate progress toward this goal in the next six to twelve months. Some progress is needed since VCs rarely offer more money before some milestones are met. But the emphasis is on a long-term trajectory, not a short-term return.

For traditional companies to enforce such long-term thinking is difficult but critical. One hundred people couldn't stop laughing when they recently saw one of our slides with a provocative message, which stated that a corporate VC initiative is truly working only if it survives at least two CEOs. The 100 participants were top leaders of a 25,000-employee bank, attending our "Digital Entrepreneurs" workshop as they prepared to launch innovative financial products. The bank CEO was among the people laughing. He had been assigned to lead the bank just a couple years earlier. Had many of the prior CEO's innovation initiatives survived until our workshop? You can guess the answer.

The average tenure of large US companies' CEOs is around seven years. The typical horizon for VC investment is five to ten years. Could this be a clue as to why so many corporate innovation programs fail?

Short-termism is sprinkled everywhere in the traditional mindset. Budgets are designed for one year. Payback time frames of more than a few years raise questioning eyebrows. Corporate executives love discussing the J-curve, but they tend to ignore its less exciting and often painful dip into the red. Almost four out of five senior finance executives would give up economic value in exchange for smooth earnings. When Ilya and his research fellow Amanda Wang studied more than 160 corporate VC arms of large global companies, they found that more than half were tasked with objectives shorter than two years and had their budgets approved either one year at a time or one deal at a time. This is a sad picture of a traditional mindset trampling the opportunities offered by the VC mindset.

VC-backed companies are protected from scrutiny by the Wall Street quarterly beat. VC investors do scrutinize their investments closely, but their scrutiny is geared toward a long-term horizon. They rarely freak out because of a quarterly loss, unless it indicates that long-term promises are off. Shai Bernstein now of Harvard reported in a 2015 paper that when private companies go public and start facing pressure for quick results from investors, their best inventors tend to leave, and the ones who remain produce fewer patents, compared to inventors at companies that had to stay private for unrelated reasons. Patents might not be the best measure of innovation, but they serve as a good indicator of a company's R&D efforts. Bernstein also showed that once companies go public, they plow less of their resources into far-sighted R&D investments.

Some well-established companies do know how to think long-term.

"We like things to work in five to seven years," said Jeff Bezos. He lives by this mantra and gives a long enough runway to let new businesses such as AWS, Amazon Go, and Alexa get up to speed. Regardless of the business complexity, the company pursues both long-term vision and high ambitions. "We're willing to plant seeds and let them grow," Bezos said. "We may not know that it's going to turn into an oak, but at least we know that it can turn out to be that big." Let the Venture Mindset inspire you. Complement your annual budgets with three- to ten-year plans. By extending the timeline, you will feel the atmosphere change in the room. By stepping back from your immediate challenges, you will make your next annual budget more attuned to long-term risks and opportunities.

Facing a conservative corporate culture full of skepticism? We often lead an exercise in our executive sessions that we call a "pre-mortem" exercise. We ask participants to imagine their company would not exist in five or ten years down the road and to identify the main factors that led to its hypothetical demise. We also ask them to identify a company that may be responsible for the dethronement. Then we finally ask what can be done to protect the business. These Venture Mindset exercises inevitably upend the tone of discussion.

Some companies in traditional industries understand the long-term game very well. Farm tractors and combine harvesters may not appear at first glance like the cool products of some newer tech companies. But John Deere, the leader in the farm equipment sector, started making long-term bets as early as 2002, when it first released tractors with autonomous features. The company realized that the world was sitting on a volcano, with the global population expected to erupt by an unimaginable 2 billion additional people by 2050. This increase could put even more people at risk of hunger, which already affects every tenth person on the planet. So in 2017 John Deere made a long-term bet by acquiring a company called Blue River Technology, which leverages the power of computer vision to do precise lettuce thinning. John Deere also made Blue River's CEO and cofounder Jorge Heraud the head of its automation agenda. More precision, less waste, and higher yield were the long-term expected results, but they take time. In 2022, John Deere announced another new bet on building a fully robotic, machinelike tractor. This "feet on the ground, eyes on the horizon" philosophy suits a company that is not looking for a quick buck. As an indicator of what horizon the company cares about, Deere's then chairman Sam Allen said in 2016 that he'd ask colleagues "where you want the company to be in 10–20 years from now." These bets are very unlikely to materialize in additional billion-dollar revenues for John Deere in the next year, but they may very well help the company succeed amid the agricultural technology disruption that is impacting this critical sector of the economy.

Is long-term thinking reserved only for large US players? Not at all. Kaspi.kz made a dramatic transition from a traditional bank to a successful multiprong tech company. This originally conservative financial institution from Kazakhstan (the country ridiculed not long ago by the comedian Sacha Baron Cohen as Borat) surprised many with its innovative business model and long-term focus. Company leaders were among the first in the world to realize that consumers prefer to manage their life with just a few taps on their phone. The resulting superapp, which combines payment services with e-commerce and financial products, made Kaspi.kz one of the largest publicly traded companies in Central Asia. With a "thinking long" mindset, companies can build lasting and innovative products.

You may not have used the Kaspi.kz app, but it's highly likely you've used Acrobat Reader or Photoshop, products of Adobe, the software giant with more than $15 billion in revenue. In 2013, the company faced an existential challenge when it announced that it would no longer sell the boxed version of its Creative Suite software, priced starting at over

$1,000. Instead, customers would have to buy a subscription and pay $50 a month. Users compared the model to "digital heroin" and revolted. More than 30,000 users supported a Change.org petition to reverse the transition. With the lower initial fee and angry users, short-term revenues took a hit. But Adobe's leadership was firm: they had made a long-term bet on the cloud and the software-as-a-service model. The switch to the cloud was a short-term pain with long-term gain.

It is exceptionally hard for company leadership to sacrifice short-term revenue or profitability numbers in exchange for long-term success. But it is not a challenge for C-suite executives only.

9.5
The More Marshmallows the Merrier

You might be aware of the famous marshmallow experiment, in which Stanford psychologist Walter Mischel invited four-year-olds to select a marshmallow, a pretzel stick, or a cookie chip from a tray. Once they had made their choice, the children were offered a stark choice: one marshmallow (or whatever they preferred) now, or two of the same kind if they would wait alone in that room for fifteen minutes without eating that one marshmallow, cookie, or chip seductively placed on a table near them. What would you have done?

Some children placed the marshmallow in their mouth immediately after the adult closed the door; others waited . . . and waited . . . and eventually, after fifteen long and painful minutes, got their well-deserved prize. Go on YouTube, type "marshmallow experiment," and you can find a modern reincarnation of the original study, in which kids struggle to conquer their desire to instantly plop the delight into their mouth. Fewer than half of all kids manage to resist the temptation, while the others succumb to the desire for immediate gratification. In one experiment, a boy carefully separated two halves of an Oreo cookie, licked the cream in between them, and then placed the outer pieces back on the table and waited to get his two cookies! Every kid wanted the extra treat, but some kids managed to wait patiently for the long-term result while many others preferred the short-term gain.

What really made this experiment famous was the subsequent studies conducted years later. Children who managed to delay gratification for fifteen minutes at age four had better outcomes in terms of academic achievement, social skills, and coping with stress. Children who rocked the marshmallow test had an average SAT score 210 points higher than that of the children who could wait only thirty seconds.

Half a century of subsequent research confirmed the original findings that children who exercised self-control did so in specific, predictable ways. They actively shifted their mind from the short-term gain—the delightful marshmallow—to other activities. Some looked away and closed their eyes. Some played with toys. Some kicked the chairs and the table. Some started singing. Some even took a nap. Staring at the marshmallow while thinking about the short-term and long-term rewards was not helpful. Embracing delayed gratification is not just about pure willpower but also about finding and implementing a coping strategy. Avoid thinking about the ultimate reward, stay patient, and you get twice as much. Those who were instructed to think about fun things could wait much longer. More recent experimental studies found other ways to cope. For example, placing kids in small groups helps them find better strategies to exercise patience.

Coming up with strategies that work against short-termism is challenging. Valuing immediate rewards over long-term ones is built into our decision making, for adults and small children alike. Discounting future rewards is a standard valuation mechanism in finance, based on the simple observation that $100 today is more valuable than $100 a year down the road. But what if people prefer $100 today to $150 in a year? Research has demonstrated that most people's decisions imply shockingly high discount rates. In one study, John Warner and Saul Pleeter used the military downsizing of the early 1990s to examine the decisions of more than 65,000 US army officers who could choose between a large lump-sum payment and an annuity. Most selected the lump-sum payment, even though the annuity compared favorably with the lump sum, based on prevailing rates at the time, implying a very high discount rate.

Impatience is only one side of revealed time preferences. Researchers use a special term, "hyperbolic discounting," to denote time-inconsistent decision making, in which immediate gratification implies a very high discount rate, yet people, when comparing two distant future dates, use a much lower discount rate. Hyperbolic discounting is behind many decisions. Impatient workers afflicted with "hyperbolism" search less diligently for a new job. A higher extent of impatient hyperbolism is correlated with obesity and alcoholism.

"The stock market is a device to transfer money from the 'impatient' to the 'patient,'" quipped Warren Buffett. Buffett and his long-term partner Charlie Munger are well known for delayed gratification. Yet in the liquid stock market, short-term gains may loom large. To thrive in their illiquid world, VCs learn to ignore short-term gains (a marshmallow today) in exchange for long-term success and eventually a profitable exit (two or maybe even ten marshmallows in the future).

Similarly to the strategies kids use in conquering their instantaneous desire to swallow a marshmallow, successful VCs don't constantly think about the exit future of their portfolio companies. Steve Vassallo, general partner at Foundation Capital, told us how back in 2014 he led his firm's investment in payment startup Stripe. A couple years later, the valuation had increased threefold and they received an offer to offload their shares. Some of Steve's partners may have been tempted, but not Steve. "It is a generationally important company," he told us. "We may have to wait more than fifteen minutes for that second marshmallow, but the payoff will be all the sweeter." The offers continued coming in as the valuation rose to new heights. As the marshmallow grew in front of his eyes, Vassallo waited patiently. Finally, he sold part of his stake at a valuation of $110 billion, making a return thirty times over. Vassallo draws two marshmallow-related lessons: "The discipline of saying not now is of vital importance, whether for tenacious kids or VCs. But you also have to eat the marshmallow eventually. Withholding forever is not an option either."

What matters more to VCs is the day-to-day work of helping entrepreneurs increase the company's value and meet milestones that position the company for long-term growth. They know that the exit will happen one day, but they concentrate on the journey, not the final destination.

The same applies to our life-defining decisions. Whenever former colleagues and students ask us about career options, our response is always the same. Focus on your long-term value and put less weight on short-term metrics such as starting salary or a signing bonus. Those are the adult equivalents of a marshmallow now. We all have to pay our bills and so salary can't be ignored, but don't get into the trap of short-termism. Exercise the VC mindset. Your career is probably one of the most important and exciting projects you are working on. Think long.

The next time you face an important decision, consider Captain James Cook's realization as his ship was approaching Easter Island in Polynesia. Cook and his men found barren land, three or four broken canoes, and a few hundred people, whose language they could not recognize, inhabiting this island three times the size of Manhattan. There was no sign of any trees. But they found hundreds and hundreds of large statues, "fifteen feet in length, and six feet broad over the shoulders," made of volcanic ash scattered across large areas. "We could hardly conceive how these islanders . . . could raise such stupendous figures," Cook wrote in his 1774 diary.

The statues hinted at a more prosperous and more populous civilization in earlier times. The island, once teeming with millions of trees, had lost them all. The Easter Island mystery has given birth to many historical puzzles and has played a prominent role in recent ecological disaster narratives, such as Jared Diamond's stories of why societies collapse. Many scientists believe that the slash-and-burn agriculture method practiced by Easter Island's farmers produced the disaster. In the short term, burning down woods made more land available to grow crops and support the growing population, but in the long term it took just a few generations for all the trees to disappear. Is human civilization currently living out a large-scale marshmallow experiment that spans generations, not minutes?

If you want to conduct a marshmallow experiment with Ilya or Alex, then sweets will not make the cut (unless it's a sweet wine). As a collector of fine wines, Ilya often brings friends to his wine cellar, a chilly place where guests inevitably wonder, "What is the most valuable bottle you've got here?" Ilya's answer: "It is the one that my great-grandchildren will open!"

Good wine requires patience. Whenever Ilya shares a 1941 bottle with his father, who was born in that year, or toasts his grandmother's memory with a 1916 Madeira, special moments are born. And not much can beat the delayed gratification of holding a glass containing the golden liquid of Rüdesheimer Apostelwein, the sweet wine made from Riesling grapes picked in the steep hills overlooking the Rhine in the year 1727 (the wine, tasted in Bremen Ratskeller in 2018, was delightful!). Of course, while some wines benefit from such extensive aging, most turn to undrinkable vinegar. Risks lurk at every corner and on every shelf. Hopefully, Ilya's grandkids and their kids will enjoy reading this paragraph as a message across time while they uncork a bottle of wine preserved for them so many moons ago. Or maybe they will prefer imbibing wines sourced from orbital wine cellars, if future space innovators take note of a recent study showing that red wine ages faster in space than on earth.

What is your long-term bet?

MINDSET CHECKS

○ Are stakeholders of your organization comfortable with making investments in ideas with a time horizon of five to ten years?

○ Is the long-term value of the project or initiative taken into account, or is the primary focus exclusively on short-term profitability?

○ Are management incentives centered on the business's profitability or its value?

Conclusion

"Are you ready for a shoplifting-like experience?" Alex playfully whispered to a group of executives as they were going down the aisles to the store exit. The executives were participants in the Stanford Executive Program (SEP), enjoying a weekend trip to Seattle. The store had no lines, no cash registers, not even any cashiers.

This was summer 2018 and the first Amazon Go store was finally open to the public. What a surreal experience as we grabbed products and left the store without interacting with a single employee! No hassle, no lines, no wasted time, but lots of fear among the major retailers. Will shopping ever be the same again?

Just a few days later, the same executives were taking notes in Ilya's sessions on disruption and corporate innovation, mastering the principles of the Venture Mindset. "Do not be fearful," Ilya concluded his message. "Take the lead in the innovation game." One of Ilya's students who had been on the Seattle field trip, Tomasz Blicharski, took that advice to heart. Just three years later, Żabka, the leading Polish retailer, launched its first cashier-less store under Blicharski's leadership. Two years later, a network of Żabka Nano convenience stores had overtaken Amazon in the European autonomous store race. Blicharski's title is managing director of Żabka Future. He and his team are literally responsible for the future. The best way to predict the future is to create it.

"I was inspired to take the risk, transform the company, and make it truly future-proof using the principles I learned," Blicharski told us five years later. "Cashier-less store is only one of many things we launched to improve the customer experience." It all started with the decision to save time for customers, opposite of retailers' usual dream: to keep the customer inside as long as possible. "Think of convenience stores as refrigerators. You don't want to spend too much time in your fridge, right?" Today an average visit to Żabka Nano autonomous stores takes less than one minute—fifty seconds, to be precise. How long was your last visit to your local convenience store?

Żabka became a flagship example of what technology and the Venture Mindset can achieve. Many executives are understandably fearful of the disruption onslaught; others become eager learners and brave builders. Innovative leaders of traditional companies learn from startups. More importantly, they learn from the venture capitalists who make startups possible, and they acquire the VCs' mindset. Rather than ignoring large-scale shifts, these leaders define them.

The automation battle in today's world is far from over. Żabka overtook Amazon in Europe, but Amazon is still a giant innovation machine. John Deere unveiled the first fully autonomous tractor in 2022, but it may soon face harsh competition from the likes of Tesla or Waymo. Microsoft is a generation older than Google, but it is now threatening the search giant on its home turf. Century-old Disney recently surpassed Netflix in subscriber numbers, but will it remain ahead in an unforgiving streaming war?

Traditional companies can and do strike back successfully at their younger challengers. They are often more capable, with ample resources, better access to capital, and a large customer base to help them outcompete VC-backed startups and other newcomers in their industries. However, what they are often missing is the right mindset—specifically, the Venture Mindset. The more corporate leaders take on this mindset, the more unicorns, decacorns (10X unicorns), and centicorns (100X unicorns) will emerge under a corporate roof.

In the world of innovation, there is no cookbook with clear-cut recipes for progress, but there are guiding principles and mechanisms that, if implemented, increase the chances of survival and success. These principles have been learned and perfected by the most experienced backers of innovation: venture capitalists. They should also be applied elsewhere. In this book, we have detailed the most important guiding principles. We have avoided minute discussion of how to apply these principles to a specific industry or particular technology, for several reasons. First, specific applications usually require customization, as we have witnessed again and again in our consulting work with many corporate leaders. Second, the success of each tactic is heavily affected by the quality of execution. And third, specific industries and technologies might be transformed or disappear not long after this book hits the bookshelves (if there are still bookshelves). Applications will change; the guiding principles of the Venture Mindset will not. We have discovered that building innovation internally, if done properly, can be as impactful as, or even more impactful than, lining up a series of acquisitions. Corporate venture capital teams may discover their own Zooms and bring momentous changes to corporations—or, if not done well, it could be a complete waste of time, effort, and money.

Venture investors are well aware that once a particular idea shows up on the cover of a business magazine, we are late in the game. For the general public, ChatGPT became a hit in early 2023. But the startup behind it, OpenAI, was founded in 2015 and, with VC backing, became a unicorn in 2019. The founder of the Impossible Burger plant-based meat company made the list of *Time*'s 100 best inventions in 2019; this VC-backed company was founded in 2011 and achieved unicorn status in 2016. VCs are quietly discovering ideas long before they gain wide attention. Both OpenAI and Impossible Burger were in Ilya's database of VC-backed companies at Stanford early on. Even large companies in adjacent industries mainly ignored or ridiculed them until it was probably too late.

What starts with ignorance soon becomes fear. In our workshops, we often show executives a simple heatmap of recent unicorns and unicorns-to-be in their industries. Such a bird's-eye view visually showcases where the change is happening, where VC money is flowing to, and what kinds of change a particular industry can expect in the coming decade or so. This simple chart often gives executives the shivers, because their reliable business sector with stable cash flows and happy stockholders is depicted as a vulnerable target for potential disruptors. But being an eager learner and a builder is far more productive than reacting with fear and defensiveness. If VCs can identify these emerging opportunities, why would you not do the same?

Ilya's research showcases that the main rule in the world of innovation is the absence of hard rules. Unicorns are extremely diverse, and it's hard to predict which startups out of thousands and thousands of candidates will become trendsetters. Many are based in Silicon Valley, but plenty are located in other geographies. The founders could be young dropouts or experienced former executives. Having a degree from a leading US academic institution certainly helps, but many unicorns are founded in other nations, or by US immigrants who arrived with degrees from all over the world. Being a former Google, Amazon, or McKinsey alum helps too but doesn't guarantee success. In this field, unpredictability is predictable. This is the beauty of the world VCs have mastered. And anyone can win by making the right bet.

The right bet starts with people, their decisions, and their mindset. Innovation often starts with rank-and-file employees rather than founders and senior executives. The legendary Steve Jobs was not even aware of the experimental project that led to the creation of the iPhone. Moreover, he almost rejected the idea, but the team working on it insistently convinced him to proceed. Howard Schultz was a marketing director at Starbucks when the idea of selling espresso-based drinks in addition to coffee beans struck him after a business trip to Italy. If the original founders of Starbucks could have seen the huge potential of a coffee chain, their history could have been quite different. Schultz instead founded his own company and then bought Starbucks, subsequently transforming it into the world's largest coffee chain.

Nintendo could have been just a manufacturer of playing cards. But because of Gunpei Yokoi, who was hired in 1965 as an assembly-line maintenance engineer, Nintendo became a legendary video game company famous for its Mario games and its own console. How did this happen? The grandson of a Nintendo founder noticed Gunpei Yokoi's creative talent. When Yokoi was asked, "What do you want me to make?," the response was: "Something great." And Yukoi did create great somethings, including the Game & Watch handheld system and Game Boy. Nintendo, founded in the nineteenth century, found a profitable pathway to the twenty-first century only because it reinvented itself multiple times. Many other companies, such as Disney, Lego, and 3M, have deployed the right mindset to reinvent themselves. We wholeheartedly believe that traditional companies can keep pace with the generational changes that require reinvention, but to do so they need both leaders and team members with the right mindset.

That's where you need to start—people and their mindset. Just as the operating system on your smartphone requires periodic updates, your people require an occasional reset. To do this, one of the companies we worked with ran a specially designed workshop for its newly appointed VPs. The rationale was that what had enabled the participants to become VPs may not make them great organization-wide leaders capable of reinventing the company. One family-owned business dedicated resources to establishing the mindset of the younger generation prior to giving them full control of the company and a chance to reinvent it. Many other organizations select a hundred or so of their current and future leaders for training designed to seed the Venture Mindset across all divisions and equip their most motivated people with the right tools. It takes a single person to spark an idea, but it takes many to make it a reality.

With a new mindset underpinned by the nine principles we have examined, employees, board members, shareholders, and owners across generations can see things from a different perspective. When Tomasz Blicharski realized that technology may transform the whole retail industry, he started searching for breakthrough ideas with a disproportionate impact. Some ideas, like the Żabka Nano store concept, worked. Many others failed, but that didn't dent his team's motivation. Why? *Home runs matter, strikeouts don't!* As Blicharski was sharing his story with us, he was about to board a plane, once again to Silicon Valley, where he searches for new ideas and inspiration. *Getting outside the four walls* is still his mantra.

In our journey, we've met many heroes like Tomasz Blicharski and shared some of their stories with you. We have learned that there is always a person and a team behind any innovation. JetBlue Technology Ventures would not have been possible without Bonny Simi and her *prepared mind*. A. G. Lafley empowered P&G to create a large pipeline of ideas just for a few to survive, *saying no 100 times*. Robert Langer's superlab would not be possible without his belief that *the jockey matters*. Nicolas Sauvage of TDK Ventures effectively uses the *agree to disagree* principle to search for novel ideas to innovate within an almost 100-year-old Japanese corporation. Astro Teller and his Google X team designed the process of *doubling down or quitting* to hit the next Google. *Making the pie bigger* worked well for manufacturer C.H.I. Overhead Doors thanks to KKR partner Pete Stavros. It took Jorge Heraud many years to announce a fully autonomous tractor at the Consumer Electronics Show in Las Vegas from the moment he started building Blue River Technology and its subsequent acquisition by John Deere. *Great things take time* indeed.

As you implement these principles, you can send your questions, observations, comments, and success *and* failure stories to us at comments@thevcmindset.com. We would love to hear from your front lines.

Mindset matters. To build a future-proof company, the Venture Mindset matters even more. Embody it and deploy it to transform your company, your life, and your world.

Acknowledgments

What does it take to write a book? Just as there is no single recipe for lasagna, each writing journey is unique. Here are our ingredients. Devote many years to research. Set aside three years of discussing, drafting, and rewriting. Examine tirelessly thousands of files scattered across hundreds of folders. Listen patiently to your coauthor. Get support from your family members. Stash away many cases of wine.

However, our secret sauce was a collection of colleagues and friends who dedicated their time to making this book possible. Without that sauce, our effort would have been futile. We are indeed lucky cooks.

We want to thank all our students, workshop participants, and corporate clients. We have learned more from you than from all printed and online sources combined. You asked us tricky questions, probed deeper into real-life examples, and challenged us to come up with practical tools to implement innovation in your organizations. Your curiosity inspired us to write this book in the first place.

"There is no easy-to-read book to share with all my employees, across my entire organization," one senior executive once complained to us, "so that everyone understands the importance of what you just told us about innovation!" We have tried to fulfill his request. We hope that everyone who wants to apply the fascinating lessons of the VC world now has a book they can read and recommend.

Turkish coffee, old Taiwanese tea, and even older Madeira helped our creative juices flow. But working with venture capitalists made all the difference. We are grateful to the hundreds of them who opened their treasure chests of experience in meetings, brunches, Zoom calls, and late-night dinners. Some went on record. A few preferred to stay anonymous. All put their money where their mouth is. Those meetings were precious. They could have made a book all by themselves. We would like to thank the whole VC community for opening their cache of tools and mechanisms that have enabled them to shape the modern world. Now this cache is available to a wider audience.

Although we can't list here all the VCs who helped us over the years, we would like to highlight Patrick Eggen, Nagraj Kashyap, and Sachin Deshpande (the protagonists of our opening story on Zoom), as well as Paul Arnold, Mercedes Bent, Claudia Fan Munce, Theresia Gouw, Brian Jacobs, Mike Maples, Kate Mitchell, Alex Rampell, Bryan Roberts, Cami Samuels, Nicolas Sauvage, David Singer, Ali Tamaseb, Steve Vassallo, and Ann Winblad. Special gratitude is due to Theresia Gouw and Brian Jacobs, who are not only successful VCs but also Ilya's partners in crime as co-creators of Stanford's course on venture capital and entrepreneurship.

We wrote the book about venture capital, but not for venture capitalists. We wrote it for decision makers, and many helped us along the way. We talked with leaders of large companies, midsize enterprises, and government agencies. Tomasz Blicharski from Żabka, whose story we tell in the conclusion, is one of many inspirational examples of what can be achieved with the Venture Mindset.

We wholeheartedly believe the Venture Mindset is applicable elsewhere, not just in the world of venture capital and business. Innovation is borderless. This is why we reached out to many experts in other disciplines—science, education, drug discovery, even gambling. Many were surprised to receive our inquiries. How would you have responded to an email asking to discuss the similarities between venture investors and vervet monkeys, or a request to teach a Stanford professor and a tech executive how to play poker? Fortunately, we received positive responses and generous help in these cases and many more. We particularly thank Ben Bensaou, Richard Harroch, Bob Langer, and Erica van de Waal for their patience and enthusiasm.

Writing a first book is like one's first camping trip. You don't know what to expect in the wilderness, so you'd better have a guide. Our guide was Chris Parris-Lamb, our agent at the Gernert Company. We treasure his very first feedback to us: "The sample chapter you shared with me is excellent, but . . ." That "but" was an understatement. We could not even imagine how much hard work was ahead. *But*. But Chris has always been there with us. He treats writers like his own children. He expressed joy as we found our voice, and he always encouraged us to keep trying when he knew the highest possible bar had not yet been surpassed. Thank you, Chris!

If Chris was our guide, our editor at Portfolio, Lydia Yadi, was our guardian angel. Without her help, this book would have been longer, thicker, heavier, and less readable. The first time we heard her say, "You need to kill your darlings, unless you want your book just to be a shelf book stopper," we panicked. But kill them we did, and the text shined anew. And then Lydia came back: "Can you cut this chapter further?" Of course not! But we did. And again. And again. Writing is hard, but editing turned out to be far harder. Lydia's calm, gentle persistence has paid off enormously.

As neophytes in publishing, we had no idea who Adrian Zackheim was when we first heard about him. Well, now we know, and we are blessed to have Adrian and Portfolio as our publisher. Publishers are actually a lot like venture capitalists: they make many bets every year in the hope that a few of them will become smash hits. *Forbes* publishes the annual Midas List—the list of exceptionally successful, talented, and, well, lucky venture investors. Founders receiving capital and attention from a Midas List VC have already achieved quite a bit. If there was a similar list of the best "investors" in the publishing industry, Adrian would be at the top. Adrian, your advice was priceless. We are grateful for your support and hope you made the right bet.

The academic community, especially at Stanford, has been instrumental in making this book possible. We thank the entire Venture Capital Initiative team and Ilya's Stanford colleagues, coauthors, and PhD students. Special thanks go to the indefatigable Paul Gompers, Steven Kaplan, and Will Gornall.

Writing a book is a collective effort, and many research assistants helped us in so many ways. When was the first year the Slush conference and sauna event was held? Who is the first person this quotation can be attributed to? Is this story a fact or an urban legend? Our favorite research assistants, Anastasia Sochenko and Anna Elyasova, deserve particular praise. No fact left behind!

Many of our friends read various drafts of this book, patiently providing suggestions and pointing out our strong (less often) and weak (far more often) arguments. Thank you to Alex Edmans, Tanya Fedorova, Victor Huang, Kaushik Mani, Michael Menke, Anna Neverova, Victor Osyka, Vijay Parikh, Steve Rogers, Ignacio Vinke, and Jonathan Walker—our wonderful first readers who committed hours of their time to help us make this book better.

Putting words together into smooth sentences and sentences into effective paragraphs is tougher than we imagined. It took us a long time to eradicate academic style and business jargon. Dr. Stephen Wilbers, the author of *Keys to Great Writing*, influenced our approach to crafting our writing and was patient with our queries and generous with his help. Bruce Barron offered another pair of scrupulous, friendly eyes on multiple drafts, to the point that we started asking ourselves, "What would Bruce say to that?" And special gratitude to Lionel Barber, who helped us to find our style of storytelling and encouraged us to address a wider audience.

Our parents instilled in both of us, from early childhood, a love for the beauty of the written word and an appreciation for its power. If we had known what it takes to write this book, we might have surrendered earlier. If our families were aware of the amount of time we would be absent, they might have locked us up at home. Ilya edited drafts in airplanes, secretly at night during his family trips, and in between meetings with his PhD students. Alex reviewed chapters with a newborn on his lap, a cup of strong coffee in one hand and a milk bottle in the other. But we loved it. Every single second of it. For your patience and love, we thank our families—Anya, Daniel, and Elizabeth (Ilya) and Masha and Timosha (Alex) and all our parents—to whom we dedicate this book.

We would also be remiss if we did not thank each other. In this era of blogs, shorts, and TikTok videos, working on a book was a long journey and investment that each of us believed in. This shared journey made our friendship closer, stronger, and a few hundred pages longer. We have accumulated memories to share over a glass of wine for years to come. This journey has been fun. Thanks to all who have made it even more fun for both of us. Thank you for your help, support, patience, feedback, and encouragement!

Appendix
Venture Mindset Playbook

CHAPTER 1. Home Runs Matter, Strikeouts Don't
Business model: How to win big
1. Build the pyramid of bets
2. Don't play it too safe
3. Don't bet the farm
4. Weed your garden of ideas regularly

CHAPTER 2. Get Outside the Four Walls
Idea sourcing: How to find the next big thing
5. Have faith in your intrapreneurs
6. Use innovation scouts
7. Rely on the wisdom of crowds

CHAPTER 3. Prepare Your Mind
Initial screening: How to evaluate opportunities
8. Do your spadework outside the four walls
9. Leverage your industry expertise
10. Pick your battleground

CHAPTER 4. Say No 100 Times
Due diligence: When to say no
11. Don't hide risks; bring them to light early on
12. Don't clutter your funnel
13. Don't get too skeptical too early

CHAPTER 5. Bet on the Jockey
Selection criteria: What matters
14. Charisma and character matter
15. Find misfits that fit
16. Bet on the team, not the individual
17. Build racetracks for your jockeys

CHAPTER 6. Agree to Disagree
Decisions: How and when to reach consensus
18. Keep the team small
19. Encourage dissent: e.g., use devil's advocate
20. Let rebels make the call
21. Don't require unanimity

CHAPTER 7. Double Down or Quit
Follow-on investments: When to pull the plug
22. Don't double down alone
23. Seek the outsiders' perspective
24. Quit often enough

CHAPTER 8. Make the Pie Bigger
Incentives: How to make them work
25. Make everyone an owner
26. Solve the "1000 to 1001" challenge
27. Reward boldness

CHAPTER 9. Great Things Take Time
Exit: How to avoid short-termism
28. Extend the investment horizon
29. Look beyond short-term gains
30. Ignore temporary swings

Notes

Introduction

xiv **The skepticism was buttressed:** Philip Levinson, "3 Reasons Why Almost Every VC Investor Passed on Zoom," *The Next Web*, January 26, 2021.

xv **Qualcomm owned 2 percent:** Qualcomm owned 1.7 percent of Class B shares at the time of the IPO. See "Zoom Video Communications, Amendment No. 2 to Form S-1 Registration Statement," US Securities and Exchange Commission, April 16, 2019, 121. For Zoom's IPO, see Alex Konrad, "Zoom IPO Values It at $9 Billion—and Mints New Cloud Billionaire Eric Yuan," *Forbes*, April 18, 2019.

xvii **Two years later, when Zoom:** Tom Taulli, "Why Emergence Invested in Zoom in . . . 2015," *Forbes*, September 4, 2020; Ron Miller, "Zoom Video Conferencing Service Raises $100 Million from Sequoia on Billion-Dollar Valuation," *TechCrunch*, January 17, 2017, techcrunch.com/2017/01/17/sequoia-invests-100-million-in-zoom-video-conferencing-service.

xviii **When Qualcomm Ventures invested:** "Zoom Video Communications, Amendment No. 2 to Form S-1 Registration Statement," 96.

xxiii **Another early investor in Zoom:** Ben Bergman, "SentinelOne's First Investor Also Wrote Zoom's First Check," *Insider*, July 1, 2021.

xxiv **One of the first decisions:** Ron Miller, "Zoom Launches $100m Zoom Apps Investment Fund," *TechCrunch*, April 19, 2021.

Chapter 1: Home Runs Matter, Strikeouts Don't

2 **The startup's name was Fab.com:** Fab.com's story is based on the following sources: Matthieu Guinebault, "Fab.com's $300 Million Fundraiser,"

Fashion Network, May 22, 2013; Alyson Shontell, "Fab Hits 1 Million Users 5 Months After Launch," *Business Insider*, November 14, 2011; Seth Fiegerman, "Fab Passes 10 Million Members, Sells 5.4 Products Every Minute," *Mashable*, December 31, 2012; Alyson Shontell, "Fab, a Design Site That Raised $156 Million to Compete with Ikea, Now Has 10 Million Members," *Business Insider*, December 31, 2012; Leena Rao, "Design-Focused Flash Sales Site Fab.com Raises $40M from Andreessen Horowitz, Ashton Kutcher," *TechCrunch*, December 8, 2011; Brian Laung Aoaeh, "Case Study: Fab—How Did That Happen?," *Innovation Footprints*, November 27, 2017; Zachary Crockett, "Sh*t, I'm F*cked: Jason Goldberg, Founder of Fab," *The Hustle*, October 17, 2017; Christina Chaey, "Fab Now Offers Made-to-Order Products, a Physical Retail Store," *Fast Company*, April 30, 2013; Steven Millward, "Fab's $150M Backers Include Tencent and Itochu, Plans to Launch in China and Maybe Japan," *Tech in Asia*, June 19, 2013; Ben Rooney, "Put Emotion at the Heart of E-Commerce, Says Fab Founder," *Wall Street Journal*, February 6, 2013. For "emotional commerce," see Sarah Frier, "Chasing Growth, Fab.com Sheds Executives and Misses Targets," *Bloomberg*, July 4, 2013.

4 **And the founder, Jason Goldberg:** Michael Haley, "Jason Goldberg, Best Known for Fab, Has Raised $8 Million in Seed Funding for Virtual Fitness Startup Moxie from Resolute, Bessemer, Greycroft, Others," *Insider*, April 8, 2021.

4 **Starbucks has around 40 percent:** "Market Share of Selected Leading Coffee Chains in the United States in 2020, by Number of Outlets," Statista, statista.com/statistics/250166/market-share-of-major-us-coffee-shops.

5 **when Pete Alonso broke:** Michael Salfino, "You Can't Have Home Runs Without Strikeouts," *FiveThirtyEight*, June 25, 2019.

6 **Apple acquired Shazam:** Ingrid Lunden, "Apple Closes Its $400m Shazam Acquisition and Says the Music Recognition App Will Soon Become Ad Free," *TechCrunch*, September 24, 2018.

7 **If we now go one step further:** Will Gornall and Ilya A. Strebulaev, "Venture Capital Fund Returns," work in progress, Stanford Graduate School of Business.

8 **"If you invest in something":** Wesley Gottesman, "Thinking of Venture in Bets," *Medium*, July 15, 2019.

10 **To put that figure in perspective:** "Post-its," *Quartz*, February 20, 2018; ODP Corporation, "The ODP Corporation Announces Fourth Quarter and Full Year 2022 Results," *Business Wire*, March 1, 2023.

10 **When Fry was singing in his church's choir:** All Things Considered, "My Big Break," *NPR*, July 26, 2014.

11 **"It was a eureka":** Alvin Soon, "Dr. Geoff Nicholson, the 'Father of Post-it Notes,' on 3M & Innovation," *Hardware Zone*, March 22, 2013; Richard Sandomir, "Spencer Silver, an Inventor of Post-it Notes, Is Dead at 80," *The New York Times*, May 13, 2021.

11 **3M director Richard Carlton:** 3M Company, *A Century of Innovation: The 3M Story*, 2002, 17.

11 **The company has paid dividends:** Prakash Kolli, "American Stocks Paying 100+ Years of Dividends," *Dividend Power*, March 23, 2021.

11 **Analysts have even called 3M:** Brian Hindo, "At 3M, a Struggle Between Efficiency and Creativity," *Inside Innovation—in Depth*, June 11, 2007.

11 **3M's employees:** Steve Alexander, "3M, the Corporate Inventor, Surpasses 100,000 Patents Worldwide," *Minneapolis Star-Tribune*, May 9, 2014.

11 **earning 25 to 30 percent:** Shannon Black, "How the 15% Rule Became a Stepping Stone for 3M's Innovation," *Market Realist*, June 22, 2016; Paul D. Kretkowski, "The 15 Percent Solution," *Wired*, January 23, 1998.

12 **James McNerney:** Dale Buss, "Former GE Executives Successful as CEOs Elsewhere," *InvestmentNews*, December 3, 2001.

12 **If you take over a company:** Brian Hindo, "At 3M, A Struggle Between Efficiency And Creativity," *Inside Innovation*, June 11, 2007.

12 **But that's where the second part:** Hindo, "At 3M, a Struggle."

12 **Many stakeholders:** Don Peppers, "How 3M Lost (and Found) Its Innovation Mojo," *Inc.*, May 9, 2016.

13 **Researchers Mary Benner and Michael Tushman:** Mary Benner and Michael

L. Tushman, "Exploitation, Exploration, and Process Management: The Productivity Dilemma Revisited," *Academy of Management Review* (April 2001): 28, 238–256.

13 **Art Fry, who first came up:** Hindo, "At 3M, a Struggle"; Andrew Haeg, "3M at 100—on the Right Path for Growth?," *Minnesota Public Radio*, June 10, 2002.

13 **the list of Fortune 500 companies:** Mark J. Perry, "Only 52 US Companies Have Been on the Fortune 500 Since 1955, Thanks to the Creative Destruction That Fuels Economic Prosperity," American Enterprise Institute, *AEIdeas*, May 22, 2019.

14 **In 1958, the companies:** Michael Sheetz, "Technology Killing Off Corporate America: Average Life Span of Companies Under 20 Years," *CNBC Markets*, August 24, 2017.

14 **One danger inherent in corporate life:** "Why Avoiding Risk Can Be Good for Managers but Bad for Shareholders," *Knowledge at Wharton*, December 9, 2014.

17 **This is exactly the story:** Benny Evangelista, "How 'Amazon Factor' Killed Retailers Like Borders, Circuit City," *SFGate*, July 10, 2015; Valerie Peterson, "Borders Group History—the Creation of a Bookstore Chain," *LiveAbout*, updated February 3, 2020.

18 **When the *New York Times* A/B tests:** *New York Times* Open Team, "How We Rearchitected Mobile A/B Testing at the *New York Times*," *Medium*, March 4, 2021; Alexandria Symonds, "When a Headline Makes Headlines of Its Own," *New York Times*, March 23, 2017.

19 **The airlines that Airbus:** Daniel Thomas, "Why Did the Airbus A380 Fail?," *BBC News*, February 14, 2019.

20 **Lego is now a well-studied:** "Trouble in Legoland: How Too Much Innovation Almost Destroyed the Toy Company," *Knowledge at Wharton* and *Time*, July 12, 2013; Jonathan Ringen, "How Lego Became the Apple of Toys," *Fast Company*, January 8, 2015.

21 **Rather, it's the beginning:** Lisa Kay Solomon, "Conversation with Storyteller Dan Klein: How to Unlock Creative Collaboration with Presence and Play," LisaKaySolomon.com, February 13, 2018.

22 **Released in 1993:** Mat Honan, "Remembering the Apple Newton's Prophetic Failure and Lasting Impact," *Wired*, August 5, 2013.

22 **One such dramatic example:** Ryan Mac, "Live Blog: Amazon Launches First Phone in Seattle," *Forbes*, June 18, 2014; Taylor Soper, "Ouch: Amazon Takes $170M Write-Down on Fire Phone," *GeekWire*, October 23, 2014; Tricia Duryee, "Amazon Fire Phone Sales Estimated at 35,000—Equal to Just 25% of Employee Base," *GeekWire*, August 26, 2014; Tom Warren, "Apple Sold a Record 4 Million iPhones in 24 Hours," *The Verge*, September 15, 2014; Jeb Su, "4 Reasons the Amazon Fire Phone Will Fail," *Forbes*, June 19, 2014.

23 **"We're working on much bigger failures":** Monica Nickelsburg, "Amazon's Jeff Bezos on the Fire Phone: 'We're Working on Much Bigger Failures Right Now,'" *GeekWire*, May 19, 2016.

23 **successes like the Echo:** Charles Duhigg, "Is Amazon Unstoppable?," *The New Yorker*, October 10, 2019.

23 **"You can't, for one minute":** Catherine Clifford, "Jeff Bezos to Exec After Product Totally Flopped: 'You Can't, for One Minute, Feel Bad,'" *CNBC*, May 22, 2020.

25 **When Alphabet, Google's parent company:** Larry Page, "G Is for Google," *Alphabet, The Keyword*, August 10, 2015, blog.google/alphabet/google-alphabet.

25 **Some of those seeds have become big trees:** Oliver Franklin-Wallis, "Inside X, Google's Top-Secret Moonshot Factory," *Wired*, February 17, 2020.

26 **Google X employees are *rewarded*:** David Grossman, "Secret Google Lab 'Rewards Staff for Failure,'" *BBC News*, January 24, 2014.

26 **These companies know:** Henry Stewart, "8 Companies That Celebrate Mistakes," *Happy*, June 8, 2015, happy.co.uk/blogs/8-companies-that-celebrate-mistakes.

26 **Movies also have a high failure rate:** Stephen Follows, "Is the Number of Box Office Flops Increasing?," *StephenFollows.com*, December 3, 2018.

26 **Hits like *Game of Thrones*:** Arthur De Vany, *Hollywood Economics: How Extreme Uncertainty Shapes the Film Industry* (London: Routledge, 2004), 39.

26 **And they take a long time to produce:** Matthew Jackson, "12 Amazing Facts About Sam Raimi's *Spider-Man*," *Mental Floss*, May 3, 2017.

26 **That is an extraordinarily long:** Lizette Chapman, "Palantir Goes Public After 17-Year Wait," *Los Angeles Times*, September 30, 2020.

26 **The then CEO of Netflix:** "A Guide to All the Netflix Shows That Have Been Canceled (and Why)," *Hollywood Reporter*, July 7, 2017.

27 **The then-president of Pixar:** Ed Catmull, "How Pixar Fosters Collective Creativity", *Harvard Business Review*, September 2008.

Chapter 2: Get Outside the Four Walls

31 **They managed to turn a small:** Lizette Chapman, "Sequoia Capital's Early Dropbox Bet Pays Off with $2 Billion Stake," *Bloomberg*, March 23, 2018.

31 **The investment deal was agreed on:** Arash Ferdowsi dropped out of MIT to pursue the Dropbox dream. Houston completed his MIT undergraduate degree in 2006. Drew Houston, "Thank You, Arash," Dropbox, *Work in Progress*, March 20, 2020, blog.dropbox.com/topics/company/-thank-you--arash.

32 **Nozad had met them:** Jessica Livingston, "Congrats Dropbox!," Y Combinator, Founder Stories, March 23, 2018, ycombinator.com/blog/congrats dropbox.

32 **Nozad traveled a circuitous route:** Anne Gherini, "Pejman Nozad: From Rugs to Riches," Affinity, affinity.co/blog/pejman-nozad.

33 **the technology blog *Mashable*:** Sean Aune, "Online Storage: 80+ File Hosting and Sharing Sites," *Mashable*, July 28, 2007.

33 **Two days later, Sequoia's:** Zoe Bernard, "The Rise of Dropbox CEO Drew Houston, Who Just Made the Forbes 400 After Taking His Company Public," *Insider*, October 4, 2018.

34 **in over 300 large companies:** Neil Thompson, Didier Bonnet, and Sarah Jaballah, "Lifting the Lid on Corporate Innovation in the Digital Age," Capgemini Invent and MIT, 2020, 12.

34 **Mark Siegel:** Sophia Kunthara, "A Peek at Trendy Eyewear Retailer Warby Parker's Funding History," *Crunchbase News*, September 29, 2021.

34 **Steve Anderson:** Somini Sengupta, Nicole Perlroth, and Jenna Wortham, "Behind Instagram's Success, Networking the Old Way," *New York Times*, April 15, 2012.

34 **Jeremy Liew:** Maya Kosoff, "How Snapchat's First Investor Hunted Down Evan Spiegel," *Vanity Fair*, March 14, 2017.

35 **"Success in VC is probably only 10%":** Ramana Nanda, Sampsa Samila, and Olav Sorenson, "The Persistent Effect of Initial Success: Evidence from Venture Capital," *Journal of Financial Economics* 137, no. 1 (July 2020): 231–48.

36 **when Hoffman was raising money:** Reid Hoffman, "Allies and Acquaintances: Two Key Types of Professional Relationships," LinkedIn Pulse, November 27, 2012, linkedin.com/pulse/20121126205355-1213-allies-and-acquaintances-two-key-types-of-professional-relationships; "Reid Hoffman: Founder of LinkedIn," Yo! Success, Success Stories, January 25, 2016, yosuccess.com/success-stories/reid-hoffman-linkedin.

36 **Parker learned about Facebook:** David Kirkpatrick, "With a Little Help from His Friends," *Vanity Fair*, September 6, 2010; Steven Bertoni, "Sean Parker: Agent of Disruption," *Forbes*, September 28, 2011. Reid Hoffman and Mark Pincus invested $40,000 each; Peter Thiel shelled out $500,000. See the site Who Owns Facebook?, whoownsfacebook.com.

37 **About half of all deals come:** Paul Gompers, William Gornall, Steven N. Kaplan, and Ilya A. Strebulaev, "How Do Venture Capitalists Make Decisions?," *Journal of Financial Economics* 135, no. 1 (January 2020): 169–90.

38 **Another one of Ilya's studies:** Ilya A. Strebulaev and Amanda Wang, "Organizational Structure and Decision-Making in Corporate Venture Capital," working paper, Stanford Graduate School of Business, November 16, 2021, accessible at papers.ssrn.com/sol3/papers.cfm?abstract_id=3963514.

39 **Apparently, this is exactly what happened:** "Amazon: Reimagining Commerce," Kleiner Perkins, kleinerperkins.com/case-study/amazon.

39 **Or take David Cheriton:** Laurie J. Flynn, "The Google I.P.O.: The Founders: 2 Wild and Crazy Guys (Soon To Be Billionaires), and Hoping To Keep It That Way," *New York Times*, April 30, 2004.

39 **Winter had just invented:** Mark Gurman, "Why Apple CEO Tim Cook Invested in a Shower Head," *Bloomberg*, January 21, 2020.

40 **When Don Valentine, an investor:** "The Seeds of Success," *Time*, February 15, 1982; interviews by Sally Smith Hughes, "Early Bay Area Venture Capitalists: Shaping the Economic and Business Landscape," Regional Oral History Office, University of California, 2010.

42 **Only 7 percent of all US adults:** Social Media Fact Sheet, Pew Research Center, April 7, 2021.

42 **One undisputed leader:** David Capece, "What Can We Learn from MySpace?," *Fast Company*, January 5, 2010.

42 **Madera was staring with envy:** Nicholas Jackson and Alexis C. Madrigal, "The Rise and Fall of Myspace," *The Atlantic*, January 12, 2011.

43 **Obviously Meritech's partners:** "MySpace Hit #1 US Destination Last Week, Hitwise," *TechCrunch*, July 11, 2006, techcrunch.com/2006/07/11/myspace-hit-1-us-destination-last-week-hitwise.

43 **Soon it became the first social network:** Florian Zandt, "The Rise and Fall of MySpace," Statista, November 12, 2021, statista.com/chart/26176/estimated-number-of-myspace-users-at-key-milestones.

43 ***Stanford Daily* news article:** Shirin Sharif, "All the Cool Kids Are Doing It: Thousands of Stanford Students Join Facebook Web Site," *Stanford Daily*, April 30, 2004, A4.

43 **From when it first appeared on campus:** Abigail Keefe, "New College Craze: TheFacebook.com," *The Loquitur* (Cabrini University), October 7, 2005, theloquitur.com/newcollegecrazethefacebookcom.

43 **Madera sat down with TheFacebook:** Ann Grimes, "Powerful Connections: Social-Networking Web Sites," *Wall Street Journal*, October 30, 2003.

44 **Sequoia decided to invest:** Parmy Olson, "Exclusive: The Rags-to-Riches Tale of How Jan Koum Built WhatsApp into Facebook's New $19 Billion Baby," *Forbes*, February 19, 2014.

45 **In Finland, innovation and promising technology:** Carita Harju, "Slush 2018: World's Leading Start-Up Event Builds the Sauna Village Again,"

Sauna from Finland, June 12, 2018, saunafromfinland.com/news/slush-2018-worlds-leading-start-up-event-builds-the-sauna-village-again.

45 **the Burning Man festival:** Nellie Bowles, "Burning Man Becomes a Hot Spot for Tech Titans," *SFGate*, August 25, 2014, sfgate.com/style/article/Burning-Man-becomes-a-hot-spot-for-tech-titans-4756482.php.

48 **We found that angels and VCs:** Note that this finding refers only to the very first part of the deal funnel and does not mean that female or Asian founders are more likely to receive funding eventually.

49 **David Cowan of Bessemer Ventures:** The story is taken almost word for word from "The Anti-Portfolio: Honoring the Companies We Missed," Bessemer Venture Partners, bvp.com/anti-portfolio.

50 **Ask Garry Tan:** Trung T. Phan, "Garry Tan on Coinbase: 'We're Still in the Early Innings,'" *The Hustle*, April 14, 2021, thehustle.co/garry-tan-q-and-a-coinbase-trung-phan.

50 **Tan invested $300K in Bitbank:** Tan's stake was 0.66 percent at the time of the IPO. Alex Konrad, "How Initialized Investor Garry Tan Turned a $300,000 Bet on Coinbase into a $680 Million 'Golden Ticket,'" *Forbes*, April 14, 2021. Pre-money valuation at IPO was $85.8 billion (PitchBook).

50 **Cuban soon led the seed round:** Anna Mazarakis and Alyson Shontell, "How Box's Founders Got Mark Cuban to Invest in Their Startup While They Were Still in College—Without Ever Meeting Him," *Business Insider India*, July 17, 2017, businessinsider.in/How-Boxs-founders-got-Mark-Cuban-to-invest-in-their-startup-while-they-was-still-in-college-without-ever-meeting-him/articleshow/59635769.cms.

51 **Adam Lyons:** An impossible (?) story of this founder is told in Catherine Clifford, "How a 25-Year-Old High-School Dropout Cold-Emailed Mark Cuban and Got an Investment," CNBC, March 22, 2017, cnbc.com/2017/03/22/25-year-old-high-school-dropout-emailed-mark-cuban-and-got-investment.html. If you think that this is the most unusual step in Adam's life, then hold your breath. He formerly bagged groceries, packed boxes, washed dishes, and sold insurance earlier in his career, only to be fired from each of these jobs. He started the company from a friend's basement while

living off his unemployment checks, until his life took a U-turn that led to winning the Ernst & Young Entrepreneur of the Year Award.

51 **an impoverished office clerk:** Ellen Embleton, "Revisiting Ramanujan," Royal Society, October 2, 2018, royalsociety.org/blog/2018/10/revisiting-ramanujan.

51 **VCs don't want to miss:** As a professor at Stanford, I (Ilya) receives many emails, sometimes a dozen or more per week, from prospective doctoral students. Writing from around the globe, a passionate dream of these young men and women is to come to California and pursue a PhD degree at Stanford. Most of these emails request me to become their thesis adviser and contain an offer to come work for me. The emails are overly long, cumbersomely written, and usually miss the point of what faculty are looking for in selecting PhD students. In a nutshell, these prospective applicants do not know how to write cold pitches. I politely decline most of these offers. Yet in the back of my mind, I am always asking myself whether I have just missed meeting another Ramanujan.

52 **Chester Carlson:** The story of Chester Carlson and xerography is based on the following sources: "October 22, 1938: Invention of Xerography," *APS-News* 12, no. 10 (October 2003), aps.org/publications/apsnews/200310/history.cfm; Antony Anderson, "Review: How We All Became Copycats—*The Anatomy of Xerography: Its Invention and Evolution* by J. Mort," *New Scientist*, May 5, 1990.

52 **When he finally became a manager:** The company was a producer of dry cell batteries (mercury and alkaline Duracell), electronic components including electrolytic capacitors and timer switches, and audible warning devices. "P. R. Mallory and Company," *Encyclopedia of Indianapolis*, revised July 2021, indyencyclopedia.org/p-r-mallory-and-company.

52 **This casual observation:** For an alternative view, see Anderson, "Review: How We All Became Copycats." Carlson was inspired by a brief article written by Hungarian physicist Pál Selényi. But he worked on this invention alone. "Entrepreneurs, Inventors and Innovators: Chester Carlson, Class of 1938, Inventor of Xerography," New York Law School, Digital Commons,

digitalcommons.nyls.edu/entrepreneurs_inventors_innovators/4. "Selényi's pioneering work in electrostatic picture transmission and recording made him the father of xerography, though the business potential of his innovation was not recognized at Tungsram [his employer]. He was the first to record pictures on selenium as well. In 1939, due to the second Jewish law [in Hungary], he was forced to retire," in "Pál Selényi, Physicist: The Father of Xerography," Tungsram, lighting.tungsram.com/en/tungsram-heritage/pal-selenyi-physicist-the-father-of-xerography, accessed July 2023.

52 **The resulting company, Xerox:** Brian Taylor, "GFD Complete Histories—Xerox," Global Financial Data, June 2, 2013, globalfinancialdata.com/gfd-complete-histories-xerox.

52 **Its copy machine 914:** Edward Tenner, "The Mother of All Invention: How the Xerox 914 Gave Rise to the Information Age," *The Atlantic*, July–August 2010. *Fortune* described Xerox in this way due to its high gross margin.

52 **Carlson's invention was roundly rejected:** Katrina C. Arabe, "Chester's Dream: The Genesis of the Modern Photocopier," Thomas, April 9, 2001, thomasnet.com/insights/imt/2001/04/09/chesters_dream/; Joseph J. Ermenc, "Interview of Chester F. Carlson, the Inventor," *NYLS Law Review* 44, no. 2 (January 2001): 265–66.

53 **Bushnell rejected the offer:** Tim Biggs, "The Man Who Refused a Third of Apple for $50K," *Stuff*, March 24, 2015, stuff.co.nz/technology/gadgets/67491648/the-man-who-refused-a-third-of-apple-for-50k. Interestingly, Apple's cofounder Wozniak suggests in an interview that Bushnell and his team did not check carefully because they were distracted by another product at the time: "You guys had the first Pong handle coming out and that was millions of dollars for you so your mind was so focused. You said 'we don't have time to make a computer also' and that came about later"; Husain Sumra, "Steve Wozniak and Atari Founder Nolan Bushnell Recall Steve Jobs and Early Apple Memories Together," *MacRumors*, September 27, 2013, macrumors.com/2013/09/28/steve-wozniak-and-atari-founder-nolan-bushnell-recall-steve-jobs-and-early-apple-memories-together.

53 **"It's kind of fun":** Walter Isaacson, *Steve Jobs* (New York: Simon and

Schuster, 2011), 75; "How Atari's Nolan Bushnell Turned Down Steve Jobs' Offer of a Third of Apple at $50,000," Fairfax Media, video accessible at youtube.com/watch?v=GSHdQVhYqok.

53 **Apple cofounder Steve Wozniak:** Urvaksh Karkaria, "Wozniak: 'I Begged HP to Make the Apple I. Five Times They Turned Me Down,'" *Atlanta Business Chronicle*, January 31, 2013, bizjournals.com/atlanta/blog/atlantech /2013/01/woz-i-begged-h-p-to-make-the-apple-1.html.

53 **the new owner of Atari Corporation:** "Atari's New Owner Orders Layoffs," *New York Times*, July 7, 1984.

54 **In a study of almost one million patents:** Ajay K. Agrawal, Iain M. Cockburn, and Carlos Rosell, "Not Invented Here? Innovation in Company Towns," Working Paper 15437, National Bureau of Economic Research, October 2009, nber.org/papers/w15437.

54 **Markus Reitzig from the University of Vienna:** Markus G. Reitzig and Olav Sorenson, "Intra-Organizational Provincialism," February 12, 2010, papers.ssrn.com/sol3/papers.cfm?abstract_id=1552059.

55 **The effect of "flat earth" thinking:** There are now even books about echo chamber phenomena among flat-earthers connecting it to social media algorithms. But could human nature be to blame? See Kelly Weill, *Off the Edge: Flat Earthers, Conspiracy Culture, and Why People Will Believe Anything* (Chapel Hill, NC: Algonquin Books, 2022).

55 **Nortel was another company:** Douglas Hunter, "Nortel," *The Canadian Encyclopedia*, January 5, 2018, thecanadianencyclopedia.ca/en/article/nortel; "Nortel and the TSE 299," CBC News, August 18, 2000, cbc.ca/news/business /nortel-and-the-tse-299-1.230333.

56 **Nortel is a case study:** This is based, among other sources, on Peter MacKinnon, Peter Chapman, and Hussein Mouftah, "Nortel Technology Lens: Analysis and Observations," Faculty of Engineering, University of Ottawa, March 25, 2015, sites.telfer.uottawa.ca/nortelstudy/files/2014/02/nortel -technology-lens-report-release-version.pdf.

57 **At least ten went public:** Henry W. Chesbrough, *Open Innovation: The*

New Imperative for Creating and Profiting from Technology (Boston: Harvard Business School Press, 2003).

57 **Steve Jobs said that the company behind Alto:** Gil Press, "Apple and Steve Jobs Steal from Xerox to Battle Big Brother IBM," *Forbes*, January 15, 2017.

58 **Xerox invented but failed to benefit:** Chesbrough, *Open Innovation*, 5; "Triumph of the Nerds," PBS television transcript, pbs.org/nerds/part3.html; Daniel P. Gross, "Xerox PARC and Yesterday's Office of Tomorrow," October 29, 2021, dgross.ca/blog/xerox-parc.

58 **Xerox headquarters in Rochester, New York:** Xerox's headquarters were in Rochester until 1973 and then moved to Stamford, Connecticut, an even greater distance from Palo Alto. See "Xerox: Online Fact Book," web.archive.org/web/20100423184011/http://www.xerox.com/go/xrx/template/019d.jsp?id=Historical&view=Factbook.

58 **PARC was so revolutionary:** Dan Tynan, "Tech Meccas: The 12 Holy Sites of IT," *InfoWorld*, August 3, 2009, infoworld.com/article/2631062/tech-meccas--the-12-holy-sites-of-it.html?page=4.

59 **Eric tried to tease out secrets:** Evgenia Pukhaeva, "Slow Coffee in Rome: Sant'Eustachio," *Surreal Generation*, October 24, 2020, surrealgeneration.com/2020/10/24/slow-coffee-in-rome-santeustachio.

60 **Favre explained the simple rule:** "Eric Favre—the Swiss Inventor Who Put Coffee into Capsules," House of Switzerland, Swiss Stories, June 7, 2017, houseofswitzerland.org/swissstories/economics/eric-favre-swiss-inventor-who-put-coffee-capsules.

60 **When Eric returned to his Nestlé office:** The official story of Nespresso is found at "Nespresso: How One Man's Passion Created a Coffee Icon," Nestlé, nestleusa.com/media/nespresso-history-eric-favre-coffee-vacation. An interview with Eric Favre can be found in "Eric Favre: From Nespresso to Monodor, the Story of an Inventor," Lift Conference, Geneva, 2008, accessible at youtube.com/watch?v=JJkRPn3zVsM.

61 **a salesman working for the German chemical:** Ben Bensaou and Karl Weber, *Build to Innovate* (New York: McGraw Hill, 2021). We thank Professor

Bensaou for providing us with additional details based on his interviews at BASF.

61 **What was once just an insulation material:** Kevin J. Delaney, "'Build to Innovate' by Ben M. Bensaou: The Approaches Behind the Magic Eraser, Marvel Studios, and Other Breakthroughs," *Charter*, October 29, 2021, charterworks.com/built-to-innovate-ben-bensaou.

61 **Olay Regenerist, Swiffer Dusters:** Ed Getty, "Open Innovation Model Helps P&G 'Connect and Develop,'" *Tech Briefs*, December 1, 2007, techbriefs.com/component/content/article/tb/pub/features/articles/2482.

61 **After his appointment in 2000:** In corporate innovation workshops, we often share the statistic that P&G has more PhDs among their employees than the top five US universities combined.

62 **Former P&G executives later admitted:** Neil Buckley, "The Power of Original Thinking," *Financial Times*, January 13, 2005.

62 **"key elements that were discovered externally":** Larry Huston and Nabil Sakkab, "Connect and Develop: Inside Procter & Gamble's New Model for Innovation," *Harvard Business Review*, March 2006.

62 **chief scientific officer at . . . Johnson & Johnson:** Michael Ringel, Andrew Taylor, and Hadi Zablit, "Bringing Outside Innovation Inside: The Most Innovative Companies 2016," BCG, January 25, 2017, bcg.com/publications/2017/growth-bringing-outside-innovation-inside.

62 **Their innovative products:** "J&J's Incubator Makes Health Equity High Priority for Selecting New Partners," *S&P Global Market Intelligence*, March 9, 2022, spglobal.com/marketintelligence/en/news-insights/latest-news-headlines/j-j-s-incubator-makes-health-equity-high-priority-for-selecting-new-partners-69184687.

63 **ideas that led to the creation:** "JLabs Navigator," Johnson & Johnson Innovation, jnjinnovation.com/JLABSNavigator.

63 **Netflix started a competition:** Matthew Salganik, "5.3.1 Netflix Prize," *Bit by Bit: Social Research in the Digital Age* (Princeton: Princeton University Press, 2017), open review edition, bitbybitbook.com/en/mass-collaboration/open-calls/netflix-prize; Xavier Amatriain, "On the 'Usefulness' of the Net-

flix Prize," *Medium*, June 23, 2021, xamat.medium.com/on-the-usefulness-of-the-netflix-prize-403d360aaf2.

64 **Researchers from Stanford:** Anna Brown, "A Profile of Single Americans," Pew Research Center, August 20, 2020, pewresearch.org/social-trends/2020/08/20/a-profile-of-single-americans; Michael Rosenfeld, Reuben J. Thomas, and Sonia Hausen, "Disintermediating Your Friends: How Online Dating in the United States Displaces Other Ways of Meeting," *Proceedings of the National Academy of Sciences* 116, no. 36 (2019): 17753–58.

65 **Eighty-five percent of all jobs:** Lou Adler, "New Survey Reveals 85% of All Jobs Are Filled via Networking," LinkedIn Pulse, February 29, 2016, linkedin.com/pulse/new-survey-reveals-85-all-jobs-filled-via-networking-lou-adler.

65 **Two-thirds of people:** "Eighty Percent of Professionals Consider Networking Important to Career Success," LinkedIn, June 22, 2017, news.linkedin.com/2017/6/eighty-percent-of-professionals-consider-networking-important-to-career-success.

65 **In contrast, just one of every ten jobs:** Susan Adams, "Networking Is Still the Best Way to Find a Job, Survey Says," *Forbes*, June 7, 2011.

66 **"Be at your office Monday morning, 7 a.m.":** Annie Riley, "Pejman Nozad: Use Your Differences," *Who Got Me Here* podcast, episode 7, whogotmehere.com/episodes/pejman-nozad, beginning at 12:38.

Chapter 3: **Prepare Your Mind**

70 **To add a realistic twist:** For the purpose of this discussion, we chose startups that pitched to students from across several different years.

70 **Her company, BabyQuip:** "BabyQuip: Rent Baby Gear on Your Next Vacation. Serving 1000+ Locations," BabyQuip, December 13, 2022, accessible at youtube.com/watch?v=u-1ZqAtFZfg.

70 **just a few of the dozens of startups:** Sensate, getsensate.com/pages/meet-sensate; Ashlee Marie Preston, "Finally, a Social Media Platform That Cares About LGBTQ Safety: The Spaces App Is Worth 'Following,'" *Forbes*, August 24, 2022; Blotout, blotout.io; Cleary, gocleary.com; BabyQuip, babyquip.com.

74 **The last remaining shark:** You can view this episode of *Shark Tank* on Hulu (season 11, episode 14) and decide what questions you would ask and whether you would invest and on what terms; see also "BabyQuip Shark Tank Tale," *Shark Tank Tales* (season 11, episode 14), sharktanktales.com/babyquip-shark-tank-update.

74 **We randomly picked dozens of pitches:** The episodes are edited before they appear on TV. Thus, an average pitch lasts longer than what viewers experience.

74 **Canadian researchers:** Andrew L. Maxwell, Scott A. Jeffrey, and Moren Lévesque, "Business Angel Early Stage Decision Making," *Journal of Business Venturing* 26, no. 2 (March 2011): 212–25.

76 **Gandhi described his quest:** Jaclyn Foroughi, Theresia Gouw, and Ilya A. Strebulaev, "Dropbox: Series B Financing," Case F309, Stanford Graduate School of Business, November 11, 2013, 4.

77 **As Thomas Jefferson is reputed:** In fact, this is such a great quotation that it has been attributed to many! According to the Thomas Jefferson Foundation (Monticello), the quote appears nowhere in his writings; see "I am a great believer in luck . . . (Spurious Quotation)," *Thomas Jefferson Encyclopedia*, monticello.org/research-education/thomas-jefferson-encyclopedia/i-am-great-believer-luckspurious-quotation.

77 **Airbnb's exponential growth:** Berber Jin, "The Inside Story of Youniversity Ventures, Keith Rabois's Investing Group That Turned a £380,000 Airbnb Seed Investment into $600 Million," *Insider*, December 11, 2020, businessinsider.com/how-keith-rabois-youniversity-ventures-got-into-airbnbs-seed-round-2020-12.

77 **David Rosenthal:** "The Complete History and Strategy of Airbnb," *Acquired* podcast, season 7, episode 8, December 10, 2020, acquired.fm/episodes/airbnb.

77 **According to Paul Graham:** Paul Graham, Twitter post, December 8, 2020, twitter.com/paulg/status/1336387068633747463?lang=en.

78 **Alexander Fleming's miraculous discovery:** "Discovery and Development of Penicillin," ACS Chemistry for Life, acs.org/education/whatischemistry/landmarks/flemingpenicillin.html#alexander-fleming-penicillin.

78 **"But for the previous experience":** Morton A. Meyers, *Happy Accidents: Serendipity in Major Medical Breakthroughs in the Twentieth Century* (New York: Arcade, 2011).

78 **X-rays, microwaves, and pacemakers:** "X-Rays and Other Accidental Discoveries," BBC Bitesize, bbc.co.uk/bitesize/articles/zg9q8hv; Heather Brown, "5 Best Accidental Inventions," *Famous Scientists*, famousscientists.org/5-best-accidental-inventions.

78 **Louis Pasteur:** "Serendipity and the Prepared Mind: An NHLBI Intramural Researcher's Breakthrough Observations," National Heart, Lung, and Blood Institute, December 24, 2013, nhlbi.nih.gov/directors-messages/serendipity-and-the-prepared-mind.

79 **Its executives agreed to show Apple:** Walter Isaacson, *Steve Jobs* (New York: Simon and Schuster, 2011), 94, chapter 8; Ali Montag, "Here's Why Your Computer Has a Mouse, According to Steve Jobs in 1985," CNBC, May 21, 2018, cnbc.com/2018/05/21/why-your-computer-has-a-mouse-according-to-steve-jobs.html; "The Xerox PARC Visit," Making the Macintosh: Technology and Culture in Silicon Valley, web.stanford.edu/dept/SUL/sites/mac/parc.html.

79 **Jobs himself immediately recognized the potential:** Steve Jobs: The Journey Is the Reward (Scott Foresman, 1987).

79 **"It was so obvious once you saw it":** "Steve Jobs Interview: One-on-One in 1995," *NetworkWorld*, October 6, 2011, networkworld.com/article/2181879/steve-jobs-interview--one-on-one-in-1995.html; video accessible at youtube.com/watch?v=cBk4a_uOi7Q, quote starting at 59:00.

79 **But why Jobs and not PARC?:** Facts for this paragraph are taken from Douglas K. Smith and Robert C. Alexander, *Fumbling the Future: How Xerox Invented, Then Ignored, the First Personal Computer* (Lincoln, NE: iUniverse, 1999).

80 **Consider the computer mouse:** Paul Atkinson, "The Best Laid Plans of Mice and Men: The Computer Mouse in the History of Computing," *Design Issues* 23, no. 3 (Summer 2007): 46–61.

81 **Marc Andreessen:** Bill Snyder, "Marc Andreessen: 'We Are Biased Toward

People Who Never Give Up,'" Stanford Graduate School of Business, *Insights*, June 23, 2014, gsb.stanford.edu/insights/marc-andreessen-we-are-biased-toward-people-who-never-give; video accessible at youtube.com/watch?v=JYYsXzt1VDc.

82 **What made Milner different:** Dan Primack, "Marc Andreessen Talks About That Time Facebook Almost Lost 80% of Its Value," *Fortune*, June 18, 2015.

82 **This approach prepared Milner:** Samidha Sharma, "Yurika! The Billionaire with the Secret Spreadsheet," *Times of India*, August 6, 2015.

83 **Zuckerberg later said of DST:** Richard Wray, "Digital Sky Technologies Takes $200m Stake in Facebook," *The Guardian*, May 26, 2009, theguardian.com/business/2009/may/26/dst-facebook-zuckerberg-microsoft-milner.

83 **"I spend lots of time":** Milner's interview with *The Bell*, in Russian, accessible at youtube.com/watch?v=x0fxbdoMTgg, 1:23:51.

83 **before April 2000 the luxury:** Patrick J. Kiger, "How Do Airplanes Get Inflight WiFi and Live TV?," *HowStuffWorks*, January 31, 2019, science.howstuffworks.com/transport/flight/modern/do-airplanes-get-wifi-and-live-tv.htm; Jane L. Levere, "Business Travel: Passengers on JetBlue Will Be Able to Watch Live Satellite-Television Programming from Their Seats," *New York Times*, July 21, 1999.

84 **One challenge that JetBlue faced:** Bonny Simi was the protagonist of a Stanford GSB business case study. Some facts are taken from that case: Robert A. Burgelman, Joseph N. Golden, and Amit Sridharan, "JetBlue Technology Ventures: Bringing External Innovation In House," Case E660, *Stanford Graduate School of Business*, 2019.

84 **In just a couple years:** "3Victors: Providing Data Science as a Service," JetBlue Ventures, jetblueventures.com/portfolio/3victors.

87 **Each year, somewhere between 50,000:** Scott Meslow, "How Hollywood Chooses Scripts: The Insider List That Led to 'Abduction,'" *The Atlantic*, September 23, 2011.

87 **research conducted by Kimberly Elsbach:** Kimberly D. Elsbach and Roderick M. Kramer, "Assessing Creativity in Hollywood Pitch Meetings: Evidence for a Dual-Process Model of Creativity Judgments," *Academy of Management Journal* 46, no. 3 (June 2003): 283–301.

87 **producers often make a decision:** Carmine Gallo, "The Art of the Elevator Pitch," *Harvard Business Review*, October 3, 2018.

87 **When *Time Out* magazine:** Chris Bourn, "The World of Dating in 2015," *Time Out*, February 4, 2015, web.archive.org/web/20150317003851/http://www.timeout.com/dating-2015/.

87 **Producers also network actively:** Frédéric C. Godart and Ashley Mears, "How Do Cultural Producers Make Creative Decisions? Lessons from the Catwalk," *Social Forces* 88, no. 2 (December 2009): 671–92.

88 **Thanks to a complex eye-tracking study:** "Eye Tracking Study," Ladders, 2018, theladders.com/static/images/basicSite/pdfs/TheLadders-EyeTracking-StudyC2.pdf. Another study found that employers view resumes for less than eleven seconds; "Employers View Resumes for Fewer Than 11 Seconds," Workopolis, April 21, 2014, careers.workopolis.com/advice/employers-view-resumes-for-fewer-than-11-seconds/.

Chapter 4: Say No 100 Times

93 **What you have just witnessed:** The "winner's curse" was coined by three Atlantic Richfield engineers: E. C. Capen, R. V. Clapp, and W. M. Campbell, "Competitive Bidding in High-Risk Situations," *Journal of Petroleum Technology* 23, no. 6 (1971): 641–53. It is interesting that such an important concept was first discussed by industry practitioners, not academic economists. They showed that the low rates of return in offshore oil exploration could be explained by the bidders paying more for the property (oil leases) than it was ultimately worth.

94 **Consider the sudden rise:** Harish Sridharan, "Rise and Fall of Crypto Exchange FTX," Reuters, November 17, 2022, reuters.com/markets/currencies/rise-fall-crypto-exchange-ftx-2022-11-10; Cory Weinberg, "Inside the Venture FOMO Machine That Powered SBF's Meteoric Rise," *The Information*, November 11, 2022, theinformation.com/articles/inside-the-venture-fomo-machine-that-powered-sbfs-meteoric-rise; Karen Kwok, "Review: WeWork's Debacle Had Many Enablers," Reuters, August 6, 2021, reuters.com/article/us-companies-wework-breakingviews-idDEKBN2F71UY.

94 **Ofo, a bicycle-sharing company:** Masha Borak, "Troubled Bike-Sharing

Company Ofo Is Now a Shopping App," *South China Morning Post*, February 5, 2020.

95 **Bill Maris of Google Ventures:** Richard Waters, "Founder of Google's Venture Capital Arm Stepping Down," *Financial Times*, November 8, 2016.

95 **The last two were acquired:** Matthew Herper, "Flatiron Health, Purchased by Roche, Signs Three-Year Deal with Bristol-Myers," *Forbes*, May 2, 2018; "Roche and Foundation Medicine Reach Definitive Merger Agreement to Accelerate Broad Availability of Comprehensive Genomic Profiling in Oncology," Foundation Medicine, press release, June 19, 2018, foundationmedicine.com/press-releases/24c62ccb-a2c4-47cf-b2d5-c7e6378c08fe.

96 **In 2013, another opportunity:** Jillian D'Onfro, "Bill Maris: Here's Why Google Ventures Didn't Invest in Theranos," *Business Insider*, October 21, 2015.

96 **But oddly enough:** Jennifer Reingold, "Theranos' Board: Plenty of Connections, Little Relevant Expertise," *Fortune*, October 15, 2015.

97 **"one of the most egregious white-collar crimes":** Michael Liedtke, "Elizabeth Holmes Gets More Than 11 Years for Theranos Scam," Associated Press, November 18, 2022, accessible at usnews.com/news/business/articles/2022-11-18/elizabeth-holmes-faces-judgment-day-for-her-theranos-crimes.

97 **As he was drilling down:** Erin Griffith, "Silicon Valley Can't Escape Elizabeth Holmes," *New York Times*, January 4, 2022.

97 **A similar result unfolded:** In fact, many VC investors turned down the Theranos opportunity. Almost all the money the company eventually raised came from technology outsiders. Sebastian Mallaby, "What Elizabeth Holmes and Theranos Reveal about Venture Capitalism," *New York Times*, January 26, 2022.

98 **Marc Andreessen surprised:** "Marc Andreessen on Big Breakthrough Ideas and Courageous Entrepreneurs," View from the Top interview, Stanford Graduate School of Business, March 4, 2014, gsb.stanford.edu/insights/marc-andreessen-people-courage-are-determined-succeed.

98 **For every one investment:** Paul Gompers, William Gornall, Steven N. Ka-

plan, and Ilya A. Strebulaev, "How Do Venture Capitalists Make Decisions?," *Journal of Financial Economics* 135, no. 1 (January 2020): 169–90.

101 **Netflix users spend less than twenty minutes:** Angela Moscaritolo, "Netflix Users Waste Ton of Time Searching for Something to Watch," *PCMag*, July 21, 2016, pcmag.com/news/netflix-users-waste-ton-of-time-searching-for-something-to-watch.

101 **three to six hours to buy a car:** Jerrel P. et al., "I Would Like to Know What Is the Average Length of Time a Consumer Spends Buying a Car," Wonder, June 5, 2017, askwonder.com/research/know-average-length-time-consumer-spends-buying-car-vd5g8tr8c#:.

101 **the VC due diligence process:** Gompers, Gornall, Kaplan, and Strebulaev, "How Do Venture Capitalists."

102 **the investment memo written by Bessemer:** Bessemer Venture Partners memos are available at bvp.com/memos.

102 **VCs are disciplined about understanding:** Alice Singer, "Risk Management When Investing in Venture Capital: How to Avoid Debt," CBNation, December 25, 2020, rescue.ceoblognation.com/2020/12/25/risk-management-when-investing-in-venture-capital-how-to-avoid-debt.

103 **"PR FAQ":** An example could be found at "Amazon's Prime Pantry Phenomenon," productstrategy.co/content/files/2022/05/Amazon-PrimePantry-PR-FAQ.pdf.

103 **The first page is a fake:** Colin Bryar, "Working Backwards: How PR/FAQs Help Launch Successful Products like AWS, Kindle and Prime Video," Coda.io, 2023, coda.io/@colin-bryar/working-backwards-how-write-an-amazon-pr-faq.

105 **operation called Fireworks Partners:** "Company News: I.B.M. Forming Unit for Multimedia Developments," *New York Times*, January 21, 1993; Josh Lerner, "Corporate Venturing," *Harvard Business Review*, October 2013.

105 **Ilya and his Stanford research fellow:** Ilya A. Strebulaev and Amanda Wang, "Organizational Structure and Decision-Making in Corporate Venture Capital," working paper, Stanford Graduate School of Business, November 16, 2021, accessible at papers.ssrn.com/sol3/papers.cfm?abstract_id=3963514.

106 **When IBM released information:** "The Reason for All the Fireworks!," *Tech Monitor,* January 24, 1993, techmonitor.ai/technology/the_reason_for _all_the_fireworks.

108 **Consider the case of R. H. Donnelley:** R. H. Donnelley Investor Day presentation, March 22, 2006, media.corporate-ir.net/media_files/irol/74/74700 /presentations/rhdinvestorday.pdf; Jon Harari, "Death of the Yellow Page Directories," LinkedIn Pulse, May 29, 2019, linkedin.com/pulse/death-yellow -page-directories-jon-harari; Andrew Bary, "Flashing Yellow, with Lots of Green," *Barron's,* August 18, 2008, barrons.com/articles/SB121884884595 646323; "Yellow Pages Offer Walk Through Time," Associated Press, February 22, 2005, accessible at deseret.com/2005/2/22/19878504/yellow-pages -offer-walk-through-time.

110 **The Pulitzer Prize, one of the most prestigious:** Jeevan Sivasubramaniam, "How You (or Anyone) Can Be a Pulitzer Prize Nominee," Berrett-Koehler Publishers, bkconnection.com/bkblog/jeevan-sivasubramaniam/how-you-or -anyone-can-be-a-pulitzer-prize-nominee; "Deconstructing the Pulitzer Fiction Snub," *New York Times,* April 18, 2012, nytimes.com/2012/04/19/opinion /deconstructing-the-pulitzer-fiction-snub.html; Michael Moats, "The Story of the Pulitzer That Never Was," Fiction Advocate, July 11, 2012, fictionad vocate.com/2012/07/11/the-story-of-the-pulitzer-that-never-was.

110 **At Google, where the chances:** It was not always the case. Google limited the number of interviewers after a detailed review. "What's the Optimum Number of Interviews According to Google?," Cowen Partners Executive Search, cowenpartners.com/whats-the-optimum-number-of-interviews-according -to-google. Sources vary on the chances of getting a Google job, all reporting a figure less than 1 percent. This source, citing a former Google HR director, reports 0.2 percent: Max Nisen, "Here's Why You Only Have a 0.2% Chance of Getting Hired at Google," *Quartz,* October 22, 2014, qz.com/285001/heres -why-you-only-have-a-0-2-chance-of-getting-hired-at-google.

110 **Zillow reports:** Sangdi Lin, "Predicting Sparse Down-Funnel Events in Home Shopping with Transfer and Multi-Target Learning," Zillow, April 16, 2020, zillow.com/tech/predicting-sparse-down-funnel-events.

110 **Emmy Award–winner Michaela Coel:** Erica Gonzales, "Michaela Coel

Turned Down Netflix's $1 Million Offer for *I May Destroy You*," *Harper's Bazaar*, July 7, 2020, harpersbazaar.com/culture/film-tv/a33234332/michaela-coel-turned-down-netflix-deal.

Chapter 5: **Bet on the Jockey**

115 **Ali's book:** Ali Tamaseb, *Super Founders: What Data Reveals About Billion-Dollar Startups* (New York: PublicAffairs, 2021). In case you were wondering what Ali's first book was—it doesn't compete with *Super Founders* in popularity, but over 20,000 readers appreciated his effort to describe how competitors prepare for the Iranian Physics Olympiads.

116 **Swedish enthusiast Markus Persson:** Alex Cox, "The History of Minecraft—the Best Selling PC Game Ever," *Tech Radar*, September 4, 2020, techradar.com/news/the-history-of-minecraft.

116 **Supercell, founded in Helsinki:** "Hay Day Success Story," *Success Story*, successstory.com/products/hay-day; "Supercell: About Us," supercell.com/en/about-us.

116 **Supercell was overwhelmed with investors:** Mike Butcher, "Supercell Raises $12m from Accel Partners to Power Social Web Games," *TechCrunch*, May 27, 2011, techcrunch.com/2011/05/26/supercell-raises-12m-from-accel-partners-to-power-social-web-games; Supercell profile, PitchBook, pitchbook.com/profiles/company/52225-57#overview; "SoftBank Buys $1.5 Billion Stake in Finnish Mobile Games Maker Supercell," CNBC, October 15, 2013, cnbc.com/2013/10/15/softbank-buys-15-billion-stake-in-finnish-mobile-games-maker-supercell.html. The valuations mentioned here and in connection to other startups in the book are in fact "post-money valuations," equal to the product of the total number of diluted shares and the price per share paid by investors in the latest round. As Gornall and Strebulaev found, post-money valuations for highly valued VC-backed companies are on average 50 percent above fair valuations. Still, a $3 billion post-money valuation made Supercell a high-valued unicorn; see Will Gornall and Ilya A. Strebulaev, "Squaring Venture Valuations with Reality," *Journal of Financial Economics* 135, no. 1 (January 2020): 120–43.

116 **A storied VC investor, Accel Partners:** Rachel Weber, "Accel Sells Supercell

Shares, SoftBank Ups Stake," GamesIndustry.biz, June 1, 2015, gamesindustry.biz/accel-sells-supercell-shares-softbank-ups-stake; Om Malik, "Tiny Speck," OM.co, om.co/gigaom/glitch-5-million-vc-funding.

117 **Butterfield described the new game:** Matthew Ingram, "Q&A: Stewart Butterfield on the Launch of Glitch," GigaOM, February 9, 2010, web.archive.org/web/20100215221349/https://gigaom.com/2010/02/09/qa-stewart-butterfield-on-the-launch-of-glitch. See also "The Startups Team, Slacking Off: Interview with Stewart Butterfield," Startups.com, June 4, 2018, startups.com/library/founder-stories/stewart-butterfield; Nick Douglas, "I'm Slack CTO Cal Henderson, and This Is How I Work," *Lifehacker*, September 13, 2017, lifehacker.com/im-slack-cto-cal-henderson-and-this-is-how-i-work-1803819796.

117 **Four years of development:** Daniel Terdiman, "Glitch Launches; *CNET* Offers an Instant-Entry Pass," *CNET*, September 27, 2011; Dean Takahas, "Online Game Startup Tiny Speck Raises $10.7M from Andreessen Horowitz and Accel," *GamesBeat*, April 12, 2011, venturebeat.com/games/online-game-startup-tiny-speck-raises-10-7m-from-andreessen-horowitz-and-accel; "The Big Pivot: Slack's Stewart Butterfield," *Masters of Scale* podcast, episode 13, mastersofscale.com/stewart-butterfield-the-big-pivot/.

117 **reviews were lukewarm:** Emily St. James, "Glitch," *AV Club*, October 17, 2011, avclub.com/glitch-1798227936.

117 **Butterfield and Henderson had decided:** "Why Did Glitch Shut Down?," Startup Cemetery, *Failory*, failory.com/cemetery/glitch.

117 **One employee at Tiny Speck:** Johnny Rodgers, "The Death of Glitch, the Birth of Slack," November 2012, johnnyrodgers.is/The-death-of-Glitch-the-birth-of-Slack.

117 **The forty-two-person team:** Christian Nutt, "The Story of Glitch: Why This Odd MMO Is Shutting Down," *Informa Tech*, November 30, 2012, gamedeveloper.com/business/the-story-of-i-glitch-i-why-this-odd-mmo-is-shutting-down#.ULkcf4P-EsQ.

117 **In November 2012, two years:** Justin Olivetti, "Glitch Closing Down, Cites Limited Audience," *Engadget*, November 14, 2012.

NOTES • *299*

118 **Tiny Speck still had a nice pile of money:** Lizette Chapman, "How One VC Firm Amassed a 24% Stake in Slack Worth $4.6 Billion," *Bloomberg*, June 21, 2019, bloomberg.com/news/articles/2019-06-21/investing-in-slack-work-made-billions-for-vc-firm-accel?sref=PF9CBsza. Some other sources report an even higher number of $6 million.

118 **You could still have recovered:** Tiny Speck received angel funding of $1.5 million in 2009, followed by Series A funding of $5 million in 2010 and a Series B round of $10.7 million in 2011. If they had $5 million left in the bank, that would be 29 cents per dollar invested. If they desired, VC investors could have clawed back even more, if angel investors had fewer rights.

118 **the Accel investors refused:** Chapman, "How One VC Firm."

118 **The original investment memo:** Andrew Braccia, "Slack: It's Always Been About the People," Accel, June 20, 2019, accel.com/noteworthy/slack-its-always-been-about-the-people.

118 **Ben Horowitz, a cofounder:** Caroline Fairchild, "How Ben Horowitz Accidentally Invested in Slack," LinkedIn Pulse, April 28, 2015, linkedin.com/pulse/how-ben-horowitz-accidentally-invested-slack-caroline-fairchild.

120 **This is how YouTube was born:** Paige Leskin, "YouTube Is 15 Years Old. Here's a Timeline of How YouTube Was Founded, Its Rise to Video Behemoth, and Its Biggest Controversies Along the Way," *Insider*, May 30, 2020.

120 **This is how Instagram was born:** Eric Markowitz, "How Instagram Grew from Foursquare Knock-Off to $1 Billion Photo Empire," *Inc.*, April 10, 2012, inc.com/eric-markowitz/life-and-times-of-instagram-the-complete-original-story.html; Sriram Krishnan, "How We Took Instagram to a Billion Users: Instagram Co-Founder Mike Krieger," YouTube, January 24, 2021, youtube.com/watch?v=sfqTlk4vDJw.

120 **This is how Twitter was born:** Adam L. Penenberg, "An Insider's History of How a Podcasting Startup Pivoted to Become Twitter," *Fast Company*, August 9, 2012; Nicholas Carlson, "The Real History of Twitter," *Business Insider*, April 12, 2011.

121 **Jimmy Jemail:** Jimmy Jemail, "The Question: How Important Is a Jockey to

a Horse?," *Sports Illustrated Vault*, October 8, 1956, vault.si.com/vault/1956/10/08/the-question-how-important-is-a-jockey-to-a-horse.

122 **More recent evidence from horse racing:** Christopher Beam, "Do Jockeys Matter in Horse Races?," *Slate*, May 12, 2009, slate.com/news-and-politics/2009/05/do-jockeys-matter-at-all-in-horse-racing.html.

122 **Jerry Bailey, the Hall of Fame jockey:** Joe Drape, "Faster Horses? Study Credits Jockeys," *New York Times*, July 16, 2009.

122 **Len Ragozin's *Sheets* . . . And Bill Benter's algorithm:** Kit Chellel, "The Gambler Who Cracked the Horse-Racing Code," *Bloomberg*, May 3, 2018, bloomberg.com/news/features/2018-05-03/the-gambler-who-cracked-the-horse-racing-code?sref=PF9CBsza.

122 **Ilya and his colleagues looked:** Gompers, Gornall, Kaplan, and Strebulaev, "How Do Venture Capitalists."

123 **the jockey factor still came out on top:** One exception was in the healthcare space, especially in the late-stage rounds. A possible explanation is that in many biotech investments, much of the initial uncertainty has been resolved before investors put in their money; for example, scientific research on a drug's effectiveness may already have occurred.

123 **General Georges Doriot:** William D. Bygrave and Jeffry Timmons, *Venture Capital at the Crossroads* (Cambridge, MA: Harvard Business School Press, 1992), 104.

123 **One of the founders of Greylock Partners:** Henry F. McCance, interview conducted by Carole Kolker, October 14, 2010, Computer History Museum, archive.computerhistory.org/resources/access/text/2019/03/102781068-05-01-acc.pdf. The quotation has been slightly modified for clarity.

125 **Gmail's story:** The story of Gmail ideation and development, and Paul Buchheit's role in it, is vividly described by Jessica Livingston in *Founders at Work: Stories of Startups' Early Days* (Berkeley, CA: Apress, 2007), see page 162 for quotes. See also Harry McCracken, "How Gmail Happened: The Inside Story of Its Launch 10 Years Ago," *Time*, April 1, 2014.

127 **Gmail is not the only product:** On Google News, see Harry McCracken, "An Exclusive Look Inside Google In-House Incubator Area 120," *Fast

Company, December 3, 2018; on Google Talk, Gary Price, "Where Did Google Talk Come From?," *Search Engine Watch*, August 30, 2005, searchenginewatch.com/2005/08/30/where-did-google-talk-come-from; on Google Scholar, Richard Van Noorden, "Google Scholar Pioneer Reflects on the Academic Search Engine's Future," *Scientific American*, November 10, 2014.

127 **The word "intrapreneurship":** Meredith Somers, "Intrapreneurship, Explained," MIT Management Sloan School, June 21, 2018, mitsloan.mit.edu/ideas-made-to-matter/intrapreneurship-explained; Norman Macrae, "Intrapreneurial Now: Big Goes Bust," *The Economist*, April 17, 1982, 47–48; Gerald C. Lubenow, "Jobs Talks About His Rise and Fall," *Newsweek*, September 29, 1985.

128 **Consider the Happy Meal:** Oriana González, "Hispanic Heritage: Happy Meals Migrated from Guatemala," *Axios*, October 7, 2021, axios.com/2021/10/07/guatemala-mcdonalds-happy-meal-hispanic-heritage.

129 **Paul Buchheit did not stop:** Livingston, *Founders at Work*.

129 **Bodexpress:** Zach Brook, "How Bodexpress Ran the 2019 Preakness Without a Jockey," NBC Sports, May 18, 2019, nbcsports.com/betting/horse-racing/news/how-bodexpress-ran-the-2019-preakness-without-a-jockey.

132 **Tony Xu had no experience:** Kelsey Doyle, "DoorDash CEO Tony Xu on Why Obsession with Detail Matters," View from the Top interview, Stanford Graduate School of Business, June 16, 2021, gsb.stanford.edu/insights/doordash-ceo-tony-xu-why-obsession-detail-matters.

132 **Brian Chesky and Joe Gebbia:** "Airbnb Founders: Brian Chesky, Nathan Blecharcyzk, and Joe Gebbia," Hostaway, hostaway.com/airbnb-founders.

132 **The founders of Flatiron Health:** Matthew Herper, "At 24, Two Entrepreneurs Took On Cancer. At 32, They're Worth Hundreds of Millions," *Forbes*, November 14, 2018.

132 **Investor Paul Graham agreed:** Morgan Brown, "AirBnb: The Growth Story You Didn't Know," GrowthHackers, growthhackers.com/growth-studies/airbnb.

133 **By the time Poulsen's tenure ended:** Myles McCormick and Anjli Raval, "Orsted Chief Henrik Poulsen Resigns," *Financial Times*, June 15, 2020.

133 **Poulsen's example fits well with the research:** Abu M. Jalal and Alexandros P. Prezas, "Outsider CEO Succession and Firm Performance," *Journal of Economics and Business* 64, no. 6 (November–December 2012): 399–426.

133 **Tristan Botelho and Melody Chang:** Tristan L. Botelho and Melody Chang, "The Evaluation of Founder Failure and Success by Hiring First: A Field Experiment," *Organization Science* 34, no. 1 (2022): 484–508.

134 **The Slack cofounders met:** Mat Honan, "Remembering the Apple Newton's Prophetic Failure and Lasting Impact," *Wired*, August 5, 2013.

134 **Together, Henderson and Butterfield:** "Talking Leadership, Failure, Side-Projects and Success with Cal Henderson," *The Orbit Shift* podcast, season 1, episode 10, November 10, 2020, theorbitshift.com/2020/11/10/talking-leadership-failure-side-projects-and-success-with-cal-henderson.

135 **Andy Rachleff:** Parsa Saljoughian, "7 Lessons from Andy Rachleff on Product-Market Fit," *Medium*, May 11, 2017, medium.com/parsa-vc/7-lessons-from-andy-rachleff-on-product-market-fit-9fc5eceb4432.

136 **Steven Kaplan from the University of Chicago:** Steven N. Kaplan, Berk A. Sensoy, and Per Strömberg, "Should Investors Bet on the Jockey or the Horse? Evidence from the Evolution of Firms from Early Business Plans to Public Companies," *Journal of Finance* 64, no. 1 (2009): 75–115.

137 **Today it takes McDonald's:** "How Long Does It Take to Cook a Burger on the Grill?," McDonald's, May 21, 2018, mcdonalds.com/gb/en-gb/help/faq/how-long-does-it-take-to-cook-a-burger-on-the-grill.html.

138 **Think of Toyota's legendary:** "Toyota Production System," Toyota Company Information, Vision and Philosophy, global.toyota/en/company/vision-and-philosophy/production-system.

138 **And consider Amazon:** Justinas Baltrusaitis, "Amazon Hires 50,000 More Workers for 2021 Holiday Season Than in 2020," *Finbold*, November 23, 2021.

138 **Frederick Taylor:** For the history of Taylor's principles, see, for example, David A. Hounshell, "The Same Old Principles in the New Manufacturing," *Harvard Business Review*, November 1988. Taylor's own book is still quite readable: Frederick Winslow Taylor, *The Principles of Scientific Management* (New York/London: Harper & Brothers, 1913).

139 **DVD format was quickly approaching:** After hitting a high of $16.3 billion in DVD sales in 2005, there was a 3 percent drop in 2006. In 2007, DVD sales actually rose by about half a percent. From 2007 to 2008, DVD sales slumped by 26 percent. Sarah Whitten, "The Death of the DVD: Why Sales Dropped More than 86% in 13 Years," CNBC, November 8, 2019. And see "Hollywood Video Owner Files for Bankruptcy," NBC News, February 3, 2010, nbcnews.com/id/wbna35222092; Eric Savitz, "Chicken Soup Completes Redbox Acquisition, Ending a Weird Meme-Stock Tale," *Barron's*, August 11, 2022; Robert Channick, "Redbox Rolls Out Streaming Video Service," *Chicago Tribune*, December 13, 2017.

139 **Netflix is a rare example:** "How Netflix Became the Leader in Original Content," *Socialnomics*, December 5, 2018, socialnomics.net/2018/12/05/how-netflix-became-the-leader-in-original-content/.

140 **At the core, his idea:** Bill Snyder, "Netflix Founder Reed Hastings: Make as Few Decisions as Possible," Stanford Graduate School of Business, November 3, 2014, gsb.stanford.edu/insights/netflix-founder-reed-hastings-make-few-decisions-possible.

140 **"The horse was good":** John Hecht, "Netflix Chief Downplays Nielsen Plans to Measure Streaming Service Viewership," *Hollywood Reporter*, November 24, 2014, hollywoodreporter.com/tv/tv-news/netflix-chief-downplays-nielsen-plans-751931.

140 **three winemakers from the US West Coast:** James Laube, "Technique vs. Terroir," *Wine Spectator*, October 2, 2013; Eric Stern, "The Cube Project: Challenging Assumptions About Terroir and Technique," *Wine Business*, May 13, 2013; Dwight Furrow, "The Cube Project Demonstrates the Fragility of Terroir," *Edible Arts*, October 3, 2013.

142 **Led by Robert Langer:** Profile of Robert Langer, *Forbes*, forbes.com/profile/robert-langer/; "Professor Robert S. Langer," MIT Langer Lab, langerlab.mit.edu/langer-bio; "Highly Cited Researchers 2023," AD Scientific Index 2023, adscientificindex.com/scientist/robert-langer/1343674; "Case Study: Robert Langer," History Associates Incorporated, February 10, 2021, lemelson.mit.edu/sites/default/files/2021-02/%20LMIT_Langer_CaseStudy.pdf; Lucas Tan, "Prof Who Went on to Co-Found Moderna Was Told to 'Find

Another Job' After Pitching Drug Delivery Idea," *The Straits Times* (Singapore), February 4, 2023, straitstimes.com/singapore/moderna-co-founder-told-to-find-another-job-after-pitching-vaccine-delivery-idea.

142 **Judah Folkman of Boston Children's:** Varun Saxena, "Robert Langer Talks Science, Business and How They Intersect," *Fierce Pharma*, October 15, 2014, fiercepharma.com/partnering/robert-langer-talks-science-business-and-how-they-intersect.

143 **Most of his patents and businesses:** Langer's drug delivery method was instrumental to the foundation of mRNA vaccines. Laura Hood, "How Robert Langer, a Pioneer in Delivering mRNA into the Body, Failed Repeatedly but Kept Going: 'They Said I Should Give Up, but I Don't Like to Give Up,'" *The Conversation*, April 26, 2022, theconversation.com/how-robert-langer-a-pioneer-in-delivering-mrna-into-the-body-failed-repeatedly-but-kept-going-they-said-i-should-give-up-but-i-dont-like-to-give-up-181417.

143 **Langer believed in Moderna's potential:** Zoe Corbyn, "Moderna Co-Founder Robert Langer: 'I Wanted to Use My Chemical Engineering to Help People,'" *The Guardian*, March 12, 2022.

Chapter 6: Agree to Disagree

148 **An even more eye-opening result:** Erica van de Waal, Christèle Borgeaud, and Andrew Whiten, "Potent Social Learning and Conformity Shape a Wild Primate's Foraging Decisions," *Science* 340, no. 6131 (2013): 483–85, science.org/doi/10.1126/science.1232769; it includes videos with monkeys.

148 **A classic experiment, conducted back in the 1960s:** B. Latané and J. Darley, "Group Inhibition of Bystander Intervention in Emergencies," *Journal of Personality and Social Psychology* 10, no. 3 (November 1968): 215–21; see also "The Smoky Room Experiment: Trust Your Instincts," Academy 4SC, academy4sc.org/video/the-smoky-room-experiment-trust-your-instincts.

152 **From our vantage point:** We had a chance to observe only four teams out of ten in their rooms that day, glued to our screens and quickly taking notes. Fifteen minutes later, when we switched to the other six rooms—as you can guess by now—the decision was already made and the teams had either left

the room or were discussing how they would present their proposal. We wish we had recorded all the teams' discussions!

154 **a reaction to Hoffman's:** "David Sze Disagreed with Reid Hoffman's Airbnb Investment," *The Pitch* podcast, episode 8, December 7, 2020, 02:06, pod clips.com/c/mRrrjC; see also "Reid Hoffman—Surprising Entrepreneurial Truths," *The Jordan Harbinger Show*, episode 611, jordanharbinger.com /reid-hoffman-surprising-entrepreneurial-truths.

155 **We found that High IPO VC firms:** Of every 100 High IPO VC firms, only 40 reported that they followed the unanimity rule, whereas 52 of 100 Low IPO VC firms followed this rule; Paul Gompers, William Gornall, Steven N. Kaplan, and Ilya A. Strebulaev, "How Do Venture Capitalists Make Decisions?," *Journal of Financial Economics* 135, no. 1 (January 2020): 169–90.

156 **Consider the British broadcaster:** Urmee Khan, "BBC 'Meeting Culture' Stopping People Doing Jobs, Says Boss," *The Telegraph*, April 1, 2010.

156 **At the Mattel toy company:** Paul Ziobro, "Floundering Mattel Tries to Make Things Fun Again," *Wall Street Journal*, December 22, 2014.

156 **The famous undefeated boxer Mike Tyson:** It was Tyson's first defeat after thirty-seven victories, thirty-three of them by knockout. James Sterngold, "Tyson Loses World Title in a Stunning Upset," *New York Times*, February 11, 1990; Betswapgg, "Against the Grain: How Contrarian Betting Can Boost Your Sports Betting Payouts," *Medium*, March 8, 2023, medium.com/@Betswapgg /against-the-grain-how-contrarian-betting-can-boost-your-sports-betting -payouts-8780bf748cbc; Lee Cleveland, "Tyson vs Douglas Odds: Some Lost a Fortune," *FightSaga*, July 3, 2022, fightsaga.com/fightsaga/news/tyson-vs -douglas-odds-some-lost-big-money.

157 **The consensus is built:** Business Insider, "RAY DIALO: You Have to Bet Against the Consensus and Be Right to Be Successful in the Markets," YouTube video, 3:27, September 22, 2017, youtube.com/watch?v=NovJFwpJSCI.

158 **John Maynard Keynes:** David Chambers, "Keynes' Asset Management: King's College, 1921–1946: The British Origins of the US Endowment Model," Centre for Economic Policy Research, *Vox EU*, October 20, 2014, cepr.org /voxeu/columns/keynes-asset-management-kings-college-1921-1946-british

-origins-us-endowment-model; Mark Johnston, "Keynes the Investor," *Econfix*, August 1, 2012, econfix.wordpress.com/2012/08/01/keynes-the-investor.

158 **Andy Rachleff, a cofounder:** Clara Lindh Bergendorff, "On VC Non-Consensus, Outsized Returns, and Why I Won't Wear a Patagonia Vest," *Forbes*, March 8, 2020. The original idea is attributed to Howard Marks from Oaktree, who described this fact in a very similar matrix. Howard Marks, "I Beg to Differ," Oaktree, July 26, 2022, oaktreecapital.com/insights/memo/i-beg-to-differ.

159 **One revealing example from a corporate:** "Enron's PRC: A Walk Down Memory Lane of a Symbol of Poor Governance," *People Matters*, April 29, 2018, peoplematters.in/article/performance-management/enrons-prc-a-walk-down-memory-lane-of-a-symbol-of-poor-governance-18115.

159 **Clinton Free and Norman Macintosh:** Clinton Free and Norman B. Macintosh, "Management Control Practice and Culture at Enron: The Untold Story," CAAA 2006 Annual Conference Paper, August 6, 2006, ssrn.com/abstract=873636.

160 **Ray Dalio insists:** Cat Clifford, "Billionaire Ray Dalio: Here Are 'the Most Valuable 3 Minutes of Thoughts That I Could Possibly Share,'" CNBC, June 22, 2018, cnbc.com/2018/06/22/ray-dalios-top-success-tip-listen-to-people-who-disagree-with-you.html.

160 **General John Monash:** John Monash, "War Letters of General Monash: Volume 1, 24 December 1914–4 March 1917," Australian War Memorial, awm.gov.au/collection/C2077750?image=1.

161 **Investors review deals in small groups:** Gompers, Gornall, Kaplan, and Strebulaev, "How Do Venture Capitalists."

161 **Many companies have followed:** "Two-Pizza Teams," Amazon Web Services, docs.aws.amazon.com/whitepapers/latest/introduction-devops-aws/two-pizza-teams.html; Charles Wilkin, "Robert Sutton: 'Do Your Team Meetings Pass the Two-Pizza Test?,'" *Wired*, April 2014, wired.co.uk/article/team-meetings-two-pizza-test.

161 **When the leadership at Mattel changed:** Ziobro, "Floundering Mattel."

161 **Richard Hackman and Neil Vidmar:** J. Richard Hackman and Neil Vidmar, "Effects of Size and Task Type on Group Performance and Member Reactions," *Sociometry* 33, no. 1 (March 1970): 37–54.

162 **nine out of ten nurses confided:** David Maxfield, Joseph Grenny, Ron McMillan, Kerry Patterson, and Al Switzler, "Silence Kills: The Seven Crucial Conversations in Healthcare," *Vital Smarts*, 2011, hks.harvard.edu/sites /default/files/Academic%20Dean's%20Office/communications_program /workshop-materials/Moss_Article%20ref%20in%20Workshop%20Si lence%20Kills.pdf.

162 **Kennedy took this principle:** Robert F. Kennedy, *Thirteen Days: A Memoir of the Cuban Missile Crisis* (New York: W. W. Norton, 1969).

162 **Reading the transcripts of heated exchanges:** Irving L. Janis, "Groupthink," in *Readings in Managerial Psychology*, ed. Harold J. Leavitt, Louis R. Pondy, and David M. Boje (Chicago: University of Chicago Press, 1971). A more detailed discussion can be found in Morten Hansen, *Collaboration: How Leaders Avoid the Traps, Build Common Ground, and Reap Big Results* (Boston: Harvard Business Press, 2009).

163 **Pitted against the candidate's advocate:** Tim Brinkhof, "Devil's Advocate Used to Be an Actual Job Within the Catholic Church," *Big Think*, July 11, 2022, bigthink.com/high-culture/devil-advocate-catholic-church.

163 **venture firm a16z often designates:** "Marc Andreessen," *Tim Ferriss Show* podcast, episode 163, January 1, 2018, tim.blog/2018/01/01/the-tim-ferriss -show-transcripts-marc-andreessen/.

163 **When Warren Buffett contemplates:** Aaron De Smet, Tim Koller, and Dan Lovallo, "Bias Busters: Getting Both Sides of the Story," *McKinsey Quarterly*, September 4, 2019.

163 **That person's role:** For a detailed discussion of how the system works, see William Kaplan, *Why Dissent Matters: Because Some People See Things the Rest of Us Miss* (Montreal/Kingston: McGill-Queen's University Press, 2017); an excerpt is available in "How Israeli Intelligence Failures Led to a 'Devil's Advocate' Role," *Toronto Star*, May 21, 2017, thestar.com/news/insight/how -israeli-intelligence-failures-led-to-a-devils-advocate-role/article_2189cca3 -c059-5608-a666-40656f907534.html.

164 **popularized by Adam Grant:** Adam Grant, *Originals: How Non-Conformists Move the World* (New York: Viking, 2016).

169 **Dollar Shave Club:** "Shaving Start-Up Firm Bought by Unilever," BBC Business, July 20, 2016, bbc.com/news/business-36791928.

169 **The now ubiquitous PowerPoint:** Ian Parker, "Absolute PowerPoint," *The New Yorker*, May 28, 2001; "Oral History of C. Richard 'Dick' Kramlich, Part 1," interview by David C. Brock, March 31, 2015, Computer History Museum, archive.computerhistory.org/resources/access/text/2016/03/102740064-05-01-acc.pdf; Daniel Geller and Dayna Goldfine (dirs.), *Something Ventured*, Zeitgeist Films, 2011, video accessible at vimeo.com/105745528; Robert Gaskins, *Sweating Bullets: Notes About Inventing PowerPoint* (San Francisco/London: Vinland Books, 2012).

169 **Professor Andy Wu:** Andy Wu, "Organizational Decision-Making and Information: Angel Investments by Venture Capital Partners," working paper, November 10, 2015, accessible at dx.doi.org/10.2139/ssrn.2656896.

169 **At Founders Fund, partners:** Dan Primack, "Peter Thiel's Founders Fund Isn't Really Peter Thiel's Founders Fund," *Axios*, February 19, 2020, axios.com/2020/02/19/peter-thiel-founders-fund.

170 **Some partnerships resist this tendency:** Brandon Wales, "Getting to 'Yes': The Black Box of Venture Capital Decision Making," Headline, May 6, 2020, headline.com/asia/en-us/post/getting-to-yes-the-black-box-of-venture-capital.

Chapter 7: Double Down or Quit

175 **"Venture capital is high-risk poker":** "Sequoia's Michael Moritz: Venture Capital Is 'High-Risk Poker,'" Bloomberg Originals, October 19, 2015, accessible at youtube.com/watch?v=k8Qxk5p2xnE. The earliest reference to poker and VC we could find is in Fred Wilson, "The Poker Analogy," AVC, November 17, 2004, avc.com/2004/11/the_poker_analo.

176 **Chess and Go:** Although in both of these games luck may determine who makes the first move, it does not matter overall, as the players alternate black and white positions between games.

176 **"Real life is not like that":** "6 Psychological Gains Playing Poker Can Give You," *American Post*, March 7, 2023, americanpost.news/psychological-gains-playing-poker.

176 **His own poker skills:** John von Neumann and Oskar Morgenstern, *Theory of Games and Economic Behavior* (1944; Princeton, NJ: Princeton University Press, 2007).

177 **A round of Texas Hold 'em:** Until somebody calls, players also can "check" by passing the action but retaining the option to fold, raise, or bet again later in the same betting round.

177 **The players now possess:** For a discussion, see Richard D. Harroch and Lou Krieger, *Poker for Dummies* (Hoboken, NJ: John Wiley & Sons, 2000).

177 **Many fascinating books:** For example, see Maria Konnikova, *The Biggest Bluff: How I Learned to Pay Attention, Master Myself, and Win* (New York: Penguin Press, 2020); Annie Duke, *Thinking in Bets: Making Smarter Decisions When You Don't Have All the Facts* (New York: Portfolio/Penguin, 2018). For a well-known blog post describing the analogy between poker and early-stage VC dating to 2004, Fred Wilson, November 17, 2004, "The Poker Analogy," avc.com/2004/11/the_poker_analo.

178 **poker players, who fold:** Patrick Harvey, "When to Fold in Poker (Before and After the Flop)," Upswing Poker, July 7, 2021, upswingpoker.com/when-to-fold-in-poker-before-after-flop.

178 **Airbnb had already gained momentum:** Eric Rosenbaum and Ellen Sheng, "Marriott Built Its Own 'Airbnb' Before Coronavirus Crashed Business Travel. Did It Help?," CNBC, September 13, 2020, cnbc.com/2020/09/13/marriott-built-its-airbnb-before-coronavirus-crash-did-it-help.html.

179 **Its bet earned Sequoia a seat:** Cory Weinberg, "Airbnb's Biggest IPO Winners," *The Information*, December 7, 2020, theinformation.com/articles/airbnbs-biggest-ipo-winners.

179 **The first time the Airbnb founders:** Brian Chesky, "How Much Money Did Airbnb Raise? What Is the Company's Financing History?," Quora, 2015, quora.com/How-much-money-did-Airbnb-raise-What-is-the-companys-financing-history/answer/Brian-Chesky; Rebecca Aydin, "How 3 Guys Turned

Renting Air Mattresses in Their Apartment into a $31 Billion Company, Airbnb," *Insider*, September 20, 2019.

179 **The valuation of the company:** "AirBnB IPO: All You Need to Know," Eqvista, January 6, 2021, eqvista.com/airbnb-ipo-all-you-need-to-know. Here and elsewhere, when we refer to the valuation of privately owned VC-backed companies, we are speaking of post-money valuation.

179 **In 2010, what started:** Jenna Wortham, "Airbnb Raises Cash to Expand Budget-Travel Service," *New York Times*, November 10, 2010.

180 **Series C. In February 2013:** Jessica E. Lessin, "Thiel in Talks to Invest in Airbnb at $2.5 Billion Valuation," *Wall Street Journal*, October 19, 2012; Robert Lavine, "The Big Deal: Airbnb Checks in to $10bn Club," *Global Corporate Venturing*, August 10, 2014, globalventuring.com/corporate/the-big-deal-airbnb-checks-in-to-10bn-club. All the valuations mentioned here are post-money valuations reported in PitchBook and other sources.

180 **An average unicorn raises:** Ilya Strebulaev, "How Many Rounds Do Start-ups Raise by the Time They Become a Unicorn?," LinkedIn, June 2023, linkedin.com/posts/ilyavcandpe_stanford-stanfordgsb-venturecapital-activity-7067499237495762945-RraZ.

183 **"If you're not embarrassed":** Reid Hoffman, Twitter post, March 29, 2017, twitter.com/reidhoffman/status/847142924240379904.

183 **"minimum lovable product":** Danny Sheridan, "June 16: Minimum Lovable Product," Fact of the Day 1 (*Substack*), June 16, 2021, factoftheday1.com/p/june-16-minimum-loveable-product.

184 **"Option" refers to the idea:** If you take a finance class, you will note the similarity with financial options, such as stock options. However, although options are all about rights and not obligations, the technical way in which options are usually taught does not convey the sense of flexibility on the part of the decision maker.

184 **Consider a16z's investment:** Riley McDermid, "Picplz 1, Instagram 0 as VC Firm Andreessen Horowitz Chooses Photo App Rival," *VentureBeat*, November 11, 2010, venturebeat.com/entrepreneur/picplz-1-instagram-0-as-vc-firm-andreessen-horowitz-defects-to-photo-app-rival.

184 **Most drug candidates fail:** Piet H. van der Graaf, "Probability of Success in Drug Development," *Clinical Pharmacology & Therapeutics* 111, no. 5 (April 19, 2022): 983–85.

185 **Consider iron ore mining:** Phoebe Sedgman and Jasmine Ng, "Iron Ore Seen Stabilizing by Biggest Shipper as Mines Shut Down," *Bloomberg*, September 17, 2014, bloomberg.com/news/articles/2014-09-17/iron-ore-seen-stabilizing-by-australia-as-mine-closures-spread#xj4y7vzkg; Daniel Fitzgerald, "Iron Ore Mining Comeback in NT Sparks Environmental, Fishing and Cultural Concerns," ABC News (Australia), September 17, 2018, abc.net.au/news/rural/2018-09-18/nt-iron-ore-mine-comeback-spark-environmental-fishing-concerns/10060256.

185 **Or consider Hollywood:** James Jianxin Gong, S. Mark Young, and Wim A. Van der Stede, "Real Options in the Motion Picture Industry: Evidence from Film Marketing and Sequels," *Contemporary Accounting Research* 28, no. 5 (Winter 2011): 1438–66.

185 **movie *My Big Fat Greek Wedding*:** Kira Deshler, "The Untold Truth of *My Big Fat Greek Wedding*," *Looper*, April 27, 2022, looper.com/845207/the-untold-truth-of-my-big-fat-greek-wedding.

186 **Rob Hall:** Jon Krakauer, *Into Thin Air* (New York: Villard, 1997).

186 **They began fixing the ropes:** Juan Felipe Aegerter Alvarez, Aferdita Pustina, and Markus Hällgren, "Escalating Commitment in the Death Zone: New Insights from the 1996 Mount Everest Disaster," *International Journal of Project Management* 29, no. 8 (December 2011): 971–85; Katie Serena, "Rob Hall Is Proof That It Doesn't Matter How Experienced You Are—Everest Is Still a Deadly Climb," *All That's Interesting*, April 6, 2018, allthatsinteresting.com/rob-hall.

187 **"escalation of commitment":** Dustin J. Sleesman, Anna C. Lennard, Gerry McNamara, and Donald E. Conlon, "Putting Escalation of Commitment in Context: A Multilevel Review and Analysis," *Academy of Management Annals* 12, no. 1 (2017).

187 **In poker, if a player:** See, for example, Jan Simpson, "The Sunk Cost Fallacy in Poker," 888 Poker, November 6, 2022, 888poker.com/magazine/strategy

/sunk-cost-fallacy-poker; Techienerd, "Typical Beginner Mistakes," Pokerology, July 4, 2023, pokerology.me/beginner-mistakes.

187 **Nick Leeson:** Jason Rodrigues, "Barings Collapse at 20: How Rogue Trader Nick Leeson Broke the Bank," *The Guardian*, February 24, 2015; Richard W. Stevenson, "Breaking the Bank: Big Gambles, Lost Bets Sank a Venerable Firm," *The New York Times*, March 3, 1995.

189 **Personalization is key to this escalation:** B. M. Staw, "Knee-Deep in the Big Muddy: A Study of Escalating Commitment to a Chosen Course of Action," *Organizational Behavior and Human Performance* 16 (1976): 27–44; M. A. Davis and P. Bobko, "Contextual Effects on Escalation Processes in Public Sector Decision Making," *Organizational Behavior and Human Decision Processes* 37, no. 1 (1986): 121–38.

191 **The first person to win:** Another "millionaire" in 2001, known as "Coughing Major" Charles Ingram, turned out to be a fraud. That is a separate and intriguing story in itself.

193 **"Everyone's baby is beautiful":** Jessica Mathews, "Lightspeed Formed a Re-Investment Team to Help the VC Prepare for a Downturn," *Fortune*, July 20, 2022.

193 **James Ephrati:** Gené Teare, "How Lightspeed Venture Partners Doubles Down," *Crunchbase News*, September 26, 2022, news.crunchbase.com/venture/lightspeed-investment-strategy-alloy-tost-brze-ampl.

193 **Pixar developed the concept:** "Lessons in Candour from Pixar's Braintrust," Destination Innovation, shortform.com/blog/pixar-braintrust.

194 **the wisdom of crowds:** James Surowiecki, *The Wisdom of Crowds* (New York: Doubleday, 2004), chapter 1.

195 **Versatile Venture Capital:** "Criteria," Versatile VC, versatilevc.com/criteria.

195 **Ilya's research has shown:** Michael Ewens, Matthew Rhodes-Kropf, and Ilya A. Strebulaev, "Insider Financing and Venture Capital Returns," Stanford University Graduate School of Business Research Paper No. 16-45, October 9, 2016, accessible at papers.ssrn.com/sol3/papers.cfm?abstract_id=2849681.

195 **a large German electric utility, RWE:** "A Case Study in Combating Bias," *McKinsey Quarterly*, May 11, 2017.

196 **Be like Walmart:** Arnab Shome, "Walmart to Launch New Fintech with Ribbit Capital Partnership," *Finance Magnates*, December 1, 2021, finance magnates.com/fintech/news/walmart-to-launch-new-fintech-with-ribbit-capital-partnership.

196 **Be like Alphabet:** "Google's Self-Driving Sister, Waymo, Gets First Outside Investors," Reuters, March 3, 2020, accessible at auto.economictimes.indiatimes.com/news/aftermarket/googles-self-driving-sister-waymo-gets-first-outside-investors/74450729?redirect=1.

196 **At each stage, only about half:** Will Gornall and Ilya A. Strebulaev, "A Valuation Model of Venture Capital–Backed Companies with Multiple Financing Rounds," working paper, February 12, 2021, accessible at papers.ssrn.com/sol3/papers.cfm?abstract_id=3725240.

196 **Only about one of every sixty:** Ilya Strebulaev, LinkedIn post, January 15, 2023, linkedin.com/posts/ilyavcandpe_stanford-stanfordgsb-venturecapital-activity-7021853740760539136-jpgu.

197 **As Marc Andreessen put it:** Tren Griffin and Chris Dixon, "12 Things I Learned from Chris Dixon About Startups," Andreessen Horowitz, January 18, 2015, a16z.com/2015/01/18/12-things-learned-from-chris-dixon-about-startups.

197 **when it introduced its McPlant burger:** Felix Behr, "The Reason McDonald's Has Stopped Serving Its Plant-Based Burger," *Tasting Table*, August 3, 2022.

197 **Smith met with David Liddiment:** Brian Viner, "Three Wise Men, a Star and a Miracle," *Independent*, December 23, 1999.

198 **the launch of Prime Now:** "Amazon Prime Experiences Another Record-Breaking Holiday Season," Amazon press release, *Business Wire*, December 26, 2014, businesswire.com/news/home/20141226005033/en/Amazon-Prime-Experiences-Another-Record-Breaking-Holiday-Season.

199 **Prime Now was initially launched:** Ben Fox Rubin, "Why Amazon Built a

Warehouse Inside a Midtown Manhattan Office Tower," *CNET*, December 21, 2015, cnet.com/tech/services-and-software/why-amazon-built-a-warehouse-inside-a-midtown-manhattan-office-tower; Ángel González, "For Amazon Exec Stephenie Landry, the Future Is Now," *Seattle Times*, May 21, 2016.

201 **Not surprisingly, according to a recent report:** Brian Solis, Jerome Buvat, Subrahmanyam KVJ, and Rishi Raj Singh, "The Innovation Game: Why and How Businesses Are Investing in Innovation Centers," Capgemini Consulting and Altimeter, 2015, capgemini.com/consulting/wp-content/uploads/sites/30/2017/07/innovation_center_v14.pdf.

201 **The Google X moonshot factory:** Astro Teller, "The Unexpected Benefit of Celebrating Failure," TED Talk, February 2016, ted.com/talks/astro_teller_the_unexpected_benefit_of_celebrating_failure/transcript; Astro Teller, "The Secret to Moonshots? Killing Our Projects" (adapted from 2016 TED Talk), *Wired*, February 16, 2016, wired.com/2016/02/the-secret-to-moonshots-killing-our-projects/; "Watch How Google X Employees Deal with Failure: An Inside Look at the Inner-Workings of Google's Top-Secret Research Lab," *Fast Company*, April 15, 2014.

201 **First, ideas are investigated:** Astro Teller, "A Peek Inside the Moonshot Factory Operating Manual," *Medium*, July 23, 2016, blog.x.company/a-peek-inside-the-moonshot-factory-operating-manual-f5c33c9ab4d7.

202 **Foundry leader Obi Felten:** Obi Felten, "How to Kill Good Things to Make Room for Truly Great Ones," *Medium*, March 9, 2016, blog.x.company/how-to-kill-good-things-to-make-room-for-truly-great-ones-867fb6ef026.

Chapter 8: Make the Pie Bigger

207 **Zaccaria Stagnario:** Diego Puga and Daniel Trefler, "International Trade and Institutional Change: Medieval Venice's Response to Globalization," *Quarterly Journal of Economics* (2014): 753–821; Ellen Kittell and Thomas Madden eds., *Medieval and Renaissance Venice* (Urbana/Chicago: University of Illinois Press, 1999), chapter 1; Clayton M. Christensen, Efosa Ojomo, and Karen Dillon, "How We Build National Institutions Plays a Crucial Role in Ensuring Prosperity for Developing Nations," *Quartz*, January 15, 2019,

qz.com/africa/1523669/clayton-christiensen-develop-national-institutions-for-prosperity.

209 **The sperm whale-hunting business:** Lance E. Davis, Robert E. Gallman, and Karin Gleiter, *In Pursuit of Leviathan: Technology, Institutions, Productivity, and Profits in American Whaling, 1816-1906* (Chicago: University of Chicago Press, 1997), chapter 10; "How Much Did Things Cost in 1850's USA?," Another Androsphere Blog, March 14, 2013, anotherandrosphereblog.blogspot.com/2013/03/how-much-did-things-cost-in-1850s-usa.html.

209 **An estimated one-third:** Lance Davis, Robert E. Gallman, and Teresa Hutchins, "Productivity in American Whaling: The New Bedford Fleet in the Nineteenth Century," Working Paper 2477, *National Bureau of Economic Research*, December 1987, nber.org/papers/w2477.

209 **owners of capital and "all hands":** Tom Nicholas, *VC: An American History* (Cambridge, MA: Harvard University Press, 2019); see also Tom Nicholas and Jonas Peter Atkins, "Whaling Ventures," Harvard Business School Case 813-086, October 2012, revised February 2019, hbs.edu/faculty/Pages/item.aspx?num=43322.

210 **Whales were divided up:** Davis, Gallman, and Gleiter, *In Pursuit of Leviathan*; "Whales and Hunting," New Bedford Whaling Museum, whalingmuseum.org/learn/research-topics/whaling-history/whales-and-hunting.

210 **This management fee does not depend:** This is a simplification, as in later years of VC funds the fee is often the percentage of the assets under management. Also, the fee may deviate from 2 percent or could change over the VC fund horizon.

211 **The term "carried interest":** Paul Solman, "Is Carried Interest Simply a Tax Break for the Ultra Rich?," *PBS News Hour*, October 29, 2015, pbs.org/newshour/economy/carried-interest-simply-tax-break-ultra-rich; Vladimir V. Korobov, "Carried Interest: What It Represents and How to Value It and Why," Marcum Accountants and Advisors, November 7, 2019, marcumllp.com/insights/carried-interest-what-it-represents-and-how-to-value-it-and-why.

211 **Australian researchers invited participants:** C. Bram Cadsby, Fei Song, and Francis Tapon, "Sorting and Incentive Effects of Pay for Performance:

An Experimental Investigation," *Academy of Management Journal* 50, no. 2 (April 2007): 387–405.

212 **Sue Fernie and David Metcalf:** Sue Fernie and David Metcalf, "It's Not What You Pay, It's the Way That You Pay It and That's What Gets Results: Jockeys' Pay and Performance," *Labour* 13, no. 2 (June 1999): 385–411.

212 **Twitter's IPO:** Peter Delevett, "2013: Twitter's IPO Means 1,600 New Millionaires—and More Good News for Silicon Valley," *Mercury News*, November 8, 2013.

214 **Arthur Rock, son of a Russian immigrant:** Owen Edwards, "Legends: Arthur Rock," *Forbes*, June 1, 1998; Sally Smith Hughes, interview with Arthur Rock, "Early Bay Area Venture Capitalists: Shaping the Economic and Business Landscape," Regional Oral History Office, University of California, 2009, digitalassets.lib.berkeley.edu/roho/ucb/text/rock_arthur.pdf.

214 **Fairchild was a big shot:** Fairchild, "The 50th Year Photo Album," accessible at web.archive.org/web/20160303174538/http://corphist.computerhistory.org /corphist/documents/doc-473a252347d41.pdf?PHPSESSID=ccd241; "Fairchild Lunar Mapping Camera System Scrapbook Hutchins," NASM.2015 .0048, National Air and Space Museum, Smithsonian Institution, airand space.si.edu/collection-archive/fairchild-lunar-mapping-camera-system -scrapbook-hutchins/sova-nasm-2015-0048; "Sherman Mills Fairchild," accessible at web.archive.org/web/20191118003924/http://www.bcwarbirds.com /sherman_fairchild_bio.htm.

214 **Fairchild sensed that big ideas:** Leslie Berlin, *The Man Behind the Microchip: Robert Noyce and the Invention of Silicon Valley* (New York: Oxford University Press, 2005), 89; Joseph Blasi, Douglas Kruse, and Aaron Bernstein, *In the Company of Owners: The Truth About Stock Options (and Why Every Employee Should Have Them)* (New York: Basic Books, 2003).

214 **His and Rock's intuitions:** Legally, Fairchild Semiconductor was a division of Fairchild Camera; the strong results of Fairchild Camera are attributed to a semiconductor's growth divisions. See Leslie R. Berlin, "Robert Noyce and Fairchild Semiconductor, 1957-1968," *Business History Review* 75, no. 1 (2001): 63–101.

214 **These eight founders:** David Laws, "Fairchild, Fairchildren, and the Fam-

ily Tree of Silicon Valley," Computer History Museum, December 20, 2016, computerhistory.org/blog/fairchild-and-the-fairchildren; Berlin, *The Man Behind the Microchip*, 134.

215 **Intel, founded by two:** Hughes, interview with Arthur Rock.

215 **Today, Intel still grants stock:** To be precise, Intel grants RSUs (restricted stock units). "Intel Corporation Restricted Stock Unit Agreement Under the 2021 Inducement Plan (For Relative TSR Performance-Based RSUs)," JUSTIA, accessed July 2023, contracts.justia.com/companies/intel-694/contract/174133.

216 **A group of McKinsey researchers:** "A Bias Against Investment?," *McKinsey Quarterly*, September 1, 2011; see also Dan Lovallo, Tim Koller, Robert Uhlaner, and Daniel Kahneman, "Your Company Is Too Risk-Averse," *Harvard Business Review Magazine*, March–April 2020.

216 **Of the twenty-eight academic studies:** Sari Pekkala Kerr, William R. Kerr, and Tina Xu, "Personality Traits of Entrepreneurs: A Review of Recent Literature," Working Paper 24097, National Bureau of Economic Research, December 2017: "In a meta-analysis of 14 studies, Stewart and Roth (2001) find that the risk propensity of entrepreneurs is greater than that of managers. This conclusion is challenged, for example, by Miner and Raju (2004), who present data from 14 other studies that used projective techniques to measure risk preferences rather than self-report measures."

218 **Consider the $5 million outcome:** The reality is a bit more complicated, as VC contracts are less trivial than the example suggests, but the intuition portrayed here holds generally.

219 **The contracts between venture investors and founders:** Technically, such a payoff structure is called a long position in a call option.

221 **a study of more than 1,800 managers:** Oriana Bandiera, Luigi Guiso, Andrea Prat, and Raffaella Sadun, "Matching Firms, Managers, and Incentives," 2010, www0.gsb.columbia.edu/faculty/aprat/papers/managers.pdf.

221 **the city of Hanoi:** Michael G. Vann, "Of Rats, Rice, and Race: The Great Hanoi Rat Massacre, an Episode in French Colonial History," *French Colonial History* 4 (2003): 191–204.

222 **Singapore:** Yahoo Lifestyle Singapore, "Singapore Is Voted the Cleanest and Greenest City in the World, According to *Time Out* Survey," *Yahoo News*, September 13, 2021, news.yahoo.com/singapore-is-voted-the-cleanest-and-greenest-city-in-the-world-according-to-time-out-survey-073032402.html; Kiki Streets, "Is Chewing Gum Against the Law in Singapore?," World Atlas, April 25, 2017, worldatlas.com/articles/singapore-laws-to-know-before-you-get-there.html.

222 **Or consider AT&T:** Canice Prendergast, "The Provision of Incentives in Firms," *Journal of Economic Literature* 37, no. 1 (March 1999): 7–63; "A Fair Day's Pay," *The Economist*, May 6, 1999.

223 **the home mortgage originator Countrywide:** "Manhattan U.S. Attorney Sues Bank of America for over $1 billion for Multi-Year Mortgage Fraud Against Government Sponsored Entities Fannie Mae and Freddie Mac," US Attorney's Office, Southern District of New York, press release, October 24, 2012, justice.gov/archive/usao/nys/pressreleases/October12/BankofAmericanSuit.php.

223 **As Sears found out:** Lawrence M. Fisher, "Sears Auto Centers Halt Commissions After Flap," *New York Times*, June 23, 1992.

223 **Wells Fargo learned this lesson:** Elizabeth C. Tippett, "How Wells Fargo Encouraged Employees to Commit Fraud," *The Conversation*, October 7, 2016, theconversation.com/how-wells-fargo-encouraged-employees-to-commit-fraud-66615.

223 **the "single large prize":** Joshua Graff Zivin and Elizabeth Lyons, "The Effects of Prize Structures on Innovative Performance," Working Paper 26737, National Bureau of Economic Research, February 2020, nber.org/system/files/working_papers/w26737/w26737.pdf.

225 **As Professor Alex Edmans has shown:** Alex Edmans, *Grow the Pie: How Great Companies Deliver Both Purpose and Profit* (Cambridge: Cambridge University Press, 2020).

226 **Franklin founded the first franchisee system:** "Franchise and Retirement from Printing," Benjamin Franklin Historical Society, web.archive.org/web/20170224211649/http://www.benjamin-franklin-history.org/franchise-and-retirement-from-printing/.

226 **interesting study of the real estate industry:** Ronald Rutherford, Thomas Springer, and Abdullah Yavas, "Conflicts Between Principals and Agents: Evidence from Residential Brokerage," *Journal of Financial Economics* 76, no. 3 (2005): 627–65.

226 **Starbucks introduced "bean stocks":** Samantha Sharf, "Why Starbucks Pays Its Baristas with Stock: A Beginners' Guide to Company Stock," *Forbes*, March 18, 2015.

226 **KKR bought C.H.I.:** "Case Study: C.H.I. Overhead Doors," Ownership Works, ownershipworks.org/chi-overhead-doors; Kirk Falconer, "Deal of the Year: KKR's Exit of CHI Overhead Doors," *Buyouts*, April 2, 2023, buyoutsinsider.com/deal-of-the-year-kkrs-exit-of-chi-overhead-doors.

227 **Since introducing the new incentive:** Pete M. Stavros, "Incentivizing Employees and Creating Value," KKR Investor Day, 2018, accessible at youtube.com/watch?v=et8T5s-To0Q.

227 **In 2022, KKR:** "CHI Overhead Doors Employees Reap Cash Reward Following Nucor Deal," CNBC, May 17, 2022, accessible at youtube.com/watch?v=0zeExiZ4Bb4.

227 **Hourly employees received on average:** Miriam Gottried, "KKR to Sell CHI Overhead Doors to Nucor, Generating Windfall for Itself and Employees," *Wall Street Journal*, May 16, 2022.

228 **a "1000 to 1001" challenge:** Peter Thiel with Blake Masters, *Zero to One: Notes on Startups, or How to Build the Future* (New York: Crown Business, 2014).

228 **Waymo, a driverless car subsidiary:** Alistair Barr and Mark Bergen, "One Reason Staffers Quit Google's Car Project? The Company Paid Them So Much," *Bloomberg*, February 13, 2017, bloomberg.com/news/articles/2017-02-13/one-reason-staffers-quit-google-s-car-project-the-company-paid-them-so-much?sref=PF9CBsza. The Waymo example also shows how phantom shares can backfire due to too big a success. Waymo employees were paid bonuses based on their equity stake in Waymo, before the "exit." For some of them, the bonuses were so large that they quit their jobs.

228 **Charlie Ayers:** Jillian D'Onfro, "Here's the Decadent Meal That Won Over

Google's Early Employees and Persuaded Them to Hire Their First Chef," *Business Insider India*, October 9, 2014.

229 **David Choe:** Nick Bilton and Evelyn M. Rusli, "From Founders to Decorators, Facebook Riches," *New York Times*, February 1, 2012.

229 **"McDonald's has made more millionaires":** George F. Will, "Lovin' It All," *Washington Post*, December 27, 2007.

229 **Only 15 to 20 percent of the shares:** Ilya Levtov, "How Much Equity Do Founders Have When Their Company IPOs?," *Priceonomics*, December 8, 2016, priceonomics.com/how-much-equity-do-founders-have-when-their.

229 **Lyft, Box, and Pandora:** Lyft: Paul R. La Monica, "Here's Who Will Get Rich from the Lyft IPO," CNN Business, March 29, 2019, edition.cnn.com/2019/03/29/tech/lyft-investors-ipo/index.html; Box: Ben Kepes, "Box's IPO, Revenue/Expenditure Mismatches and the Cult of 'Growth at All Costs,'" *Forbes*, March 24, 2014; Pandora: Nicole Perlroth, "Pandora Files for IPO, Reveals Founder Owns Less Than 3%," *Forbes*, February 11, 2011.

Chapter 9: Great Things Take Time

233 **Toddie Lee Wynne:** Pam Stranahan, "When Were Towns on Matagorda Island? Part II: Barrier Islands," History Center for Aransas County, theachistorycenter.com/history-mystery-1/when-were-towns-on-matagorda-island%3F.

233 **After multiple delays, in the late afternoon:** Alan Peppard, "Islands of the Oil Kings, Part 3: Reach for the Stars," *Dallas Morning News*, December 18, 2014, res.dallasnews.com/interactives/oilkings/part3/.

234 **"We're not sure what happened":** "'Welcome to the Rocket Business': Private Rocket Destroyed in Test-Firing Explosion," UPI, August 5, 1981, upi.com/Archives/1981/08/05/Welcome-to-the-rocket-business-Private-rocket-destroyed-in-test-firing-explosion/7158365832000.

234 **It was the year 1981:** "The Launch of Conestoga 1, Space Services Inc. of America, September 9, 1982," Celestis, celestis.com/about/conestoga-1/; Dan Balz, "Commercial Rocket Explodes on Pad During Test in Texas," *Washington Post*, August 6, 1981; Stephen Harrigan, "Mr. Hannah's Rocket,"

Texas Monthly, November 1982; Michael A. G. Michaud, *Reaching for the High Frontier* (New York: Praeger, 1986), chapter 12; Tom Richman, "The Wrong Stuff," *Inc.*, July 1, 1982; UPI, "Welcome to the Rocket Business."

234 **Twenty-five years later:** Braddock Gaskill, "Elon Musk/SpaceX Interview, Part 1," *NSF*, July 28, 2006, nasaspaceflight.com/2006/07/elon-muskspacex-interview-part-1; Brian Berger, "Falcon 1 Failure Traced to a Busted Nut," Space.com, July 19, 2006, space.com/2643-falcon-1-failure-traced-busted-nut.html.

235 **SpaceX's third attempt:** Stephen Clark, "Falcon 1 to Launch Today," *Spaceflight Now*, August 2, 2008, spaceflightnow.com/falcon/003/preview.html; Jeremy Hsu, "Strike Three for SpaceX's Falcon 1 Rocket," NBC News, August 3, 2008, nbcnews.com/id/wbna25990806.

235 **The day after the third failed attempt:** Anthony Ha, "Private Rocket Company SpaceX Gets $20m from the Founders Fund," *VentureBeat*, August 6, 2009, venturebeat.com/business/private-rocket-company-spacex-gets-20m-from-the-founders-fund/.

235 **"The fourth launch . . . was the last money":** Catherine Clifford, "9 Years Ago SpaceX Nearly Failed Itself Out of Existence: 'It Is a Pretty Emotional Day,' Says Elon Musk," CNBC, September 29, 2017, cnbc.com/2017/09/29/elon-musk-9-years-ago-spacex-nearly-failed-itself-out-of-existence.html.

235 **SpaceX opened the whole new era:** Patrick Kariuki, "SpaceX vs. Virgin Galactic vs. Blue Origin: What Are the Differences?," *Make Use Of*, November 30, 2021, makeuseof.com/spacex-virgin-galactic-blue-origin-differences.

235 **Among the remnants of 320 people:** John Zarella and Tom Cohen, "Ashes of 'Star Trek' Actor on Private Rocket," CNN, May 25, 2012, edition.cnn.com/2012/05/24/showbiz/spacex-scottys-ashes/index.html.

236 **"Everybody pooh-poohed SpaceX":** Ed Browne, "Bill Nelson: Everybody Pooh-Poohed SpaceX. Look at Them Now," *Newsweek*, September 12, 2022.

236 **Musk admitted how extremely risky:** Elon Musk, Twitter post, September 19, 2020, twitter.com/elonmusk/status/1307356512411672578.

238 **its founder, Don Valentine:** Connie Loizos, "Don Valentine, Who Founded

Sequoia Capital, Has Died at Age 87," *TechCrunch*, October 26, 2019; "Our History," Sequoia, sequoiacap.com/our-history.

238 **the largest, oldest, and tallest trees:** Soumya Karlamangla, "California Is Home to the Tallest, Largest and Oldest Trees in the World," *New York Times*, October 21, 2022; Ivana Simic, "Hyperion—the World's Tallest Tree," Tales by Trees, December 22, 2017, talesbytrees.com/hyperion-the-worlds-tallest-tree; "Measurement of Hyperion, the Tallest Tree in the World," Monumental Trees, monumentaltrees.com/en/trees/coastredwood/video.

238 **Wildfires can be devastating:** "Why the Giant Sequoia Needs Fire to Grow," *Nature* on PBS, March 14, 2017, accessible at youtube.com/watch?v=lmNZGr9Udx8.

239 **"The little fellow is the best customer":** "Bank of America: The Humble Beginnings of a Large Bank," available at occ.treas.gov/about/who-we-are/history/1866-1913/1866-1913-bank-of-america.html

239 **Some of Giannini's bets:** Felice Bonadio, "A. P. Giannini and the Bank of Italy: California's Mixed Multitudes," *International Migration Review* 27, no. 2 supplement (1993): 107–123, onlinelibrary.wiley.com/doi/pdf/10.1111/j.2050-411X.1993.tb00085.x.

240 **Giannini even financed William Hewlett:** Steve Forbes, "What Can We Learn from America's Greatest Banker?," *Forbes*, November 2, 2016.

241 **Bill Gurley of Benchmark:** Bill Gurley, Twitter post, June 21, 2022, twitter.com/bgurley/status/1539024219010240512?lang=en.

241 **investor Fabrice Grinda:** Fabrice Grinda, "Winter Is Coming!," November 18, 2022, fabricegrinda.com/winter-is-coming.

241 **As Sheryl Sandberg said:** Sandberg's Harvard Business School Speech to the Class of 2012, accessible at youtube.com/watch?v=2Db0_RafutM, 5:28.

241 **Unicorns:** Bart Eshwar, "The Crazy Story Behind the Creation of the Term 'Unicorn,'" *OfficeChai*, October 18, 2016, officechai.com/startups/origin-of-the-term-unicorn; Aileen Lee, "Welcome to the Unicorn Club: Learning from Billion-Dollar Startups," *TechCrunch*, November 2, 2013, techcrunch.com/2013/11/02/welcome-to-the-unicorn-club. In defining a unicorn, a post-money valuation is used.

242 **Or more informally, they are stuck:** VCs do not generally participate in the sporadic secondary trading that has arisen in the past several years, because the amounts exchanged on these secondary platforms tend to be very small. Sometimes, VC funds do partially sell their stakes to their peers in secondary transactions. Some smaller VC funds and angel investors tend to do it more often.

243 **Among all the unicorns that have gone public:** Will Gornall and Ilya A. Strebulaev, "Squaring Venture Valuations with Reality," *Journal of Financial Economics* 135, no. 1 (January 2020): 120–43.

244 **The silver lining is the average unicorn valuation:** Gornall and Strebulaev, "Squaring Venture Valuations with Reality."

245 **Amazon founder Jeff Bezos:** Jeffrey P. Bezos, "Amazon.com 1997 Letter to Shareholders", media.corporate-ir.net/media_files/irol/97/97664/reports/Shareholderletter97.pdf.

246 **It took more than sixty-five years for electricity:** Max Roser, Hannah Ritchie, and Edouard Mathieu, "Technological Change," Our World in Data, ourworldindata.org/technology-adoption; Diego Comin and Bart Hobijn, "An Exploration of Technology Diffusion," *American Economic Review* 100 (December 2010): 2031–59.

246 **The telephone was a luxury:** K.N.C., G.S., and P.K., "Happy Birthday World Wide Web," *The Economist*, March 12, 2014.

246 **And only half a dozen years later:** Jake Chapman, "Driving the New American Century," *TechCrunch*, March 12, 2016, techcrunch.com/2016/03/12/driving-the-new-american-century.

247 **skepticism is better than hubris:** Michigan Savings Bank president quote via the Quote Investigator, July 17, 2021, quoteinvestigator.com/2021/07/17/auto-fad; Riggio quote from Warren St. John, "Barnes & Noble's Epiphany," *Wired*, June 1, 1999; Ballmer quote from Ina Fried, "These People Thought the iPhone Was a Dud When It Was Announced 10 Years Ago," *Vox*, January 9, 2017; Smith quote from "Logistics Needs a Shake-up: Surging Demand Requires New Distribution Methods," *The Economist*, October 26, 2017.

248 **Davide Oldani, the chef-owner:** Gary P. Pisano, Alessandro Di Fiore, Elena Corsi, and Elisa Farri, "Chef Davide Oldani and Ristorante D'O," Harvard Business Review Case 613-080, January 2013, hbs.edu/faculty/Pages/item.aspx?num=44165.

249 **Then the tide turned:** Stuart Dredge, "MySpace—What Went Wrong: 'The Site Was a Massive Spaghetti-Ball Mess,'" *The Guardian*, March 6, 2015.

249 **"Delete Your Account":** Jay Babcock, "January 30 Is International Delete Your MySpace Account Day," *Arthur*, January 22, 2008, arthurmag.com/2008/01/22/january-30th-is-international-delete-your-myspace-account-day.

249 **The CEO who said he would be surprised:** Matthew Garrahan, "Fox Interactive to miss revenue target," *Financial Times*, April 4, 2008.

249 **Soon enough, MySpace failed:** Jennifer Saba, "News Corp Sells MySpace, Ending Six-Year Saga," Reuters, June 29, 2011, reuters.com/article/us-newscorp-myspace/news-corp-sells-myspace-ending-six-year-saga-idUSTRE75S6D720110629.

249 **"The boss said we have to make":** Dredge, "MySpace—What Went Wrong."

250 **The deal with Google required:** Yinka Adegoke, "How MySpace Went from the Future to a Failure," NBC News, April 8, 2011, nbcnews.com/id/wbna42475503.

250 **Geoff Yang, a Redpoint partner:** Dan Primack, "The VC Who Wanted MySpace Back," *Fortune*, July 1, 2011.

251 **The average tenure of large US companies' CEOs:** James M. Citrin, Claudius A. Hildebrand, and Robert J. Stark, "The CEO Life Cycle," *Harvard Business Review*, November–December 2019, hbr.org/2019/11/the-ceo-life-cycle; Matteo Tonello and Jason Schoetzer, "CEO Succession Practices in the Russell 3000 and S&P 500," Harvard Law School Forum on Corporate Governance, January 15, 2021, corpgov.law.harvard.edu/2021/01/15/ceo-succession-practices-in-the-russell-3000-and-sp-500.

251 **Almost four out of five:** Mark J. Roe, "The Imaginary Problem of Corporate Short-Termism," *Wall Street Journal*, August 17, 2015.

251 **Shai Bernstein:** Shai Bernstein, "Does Going Public Affect Innovation?," *The Journal of Finance*, 70, no. 4 (August 2015): 1365–1403.

252 **"We like things to work in five to seven years":** Eric Jackson, "6 Things Jeff Bezos Knew Back in 1997 That Made Amazon a Gorilla," *Forbes*, November 16, 2011; Julia Kirby and Thomas A. Stewart, "The Institutional Yes," *Harvard Business Review*, October 2007.

252 **John Deere:** Jim Mertens, "John Deere Chairman Says Global Markets Are Key to Company's Future," WQAD News 8 (Moline, IL), August 15, 2016, wqad.com/article/news/agriculture/ag-in-the-classroom/deere-chairman-says-global-markets-are-key-to-company-future/526-8008aa6f-ab3b-4654-acbe-d277e1e91649.

253 **Kaspi.kz made a dramatic transition:** Mario Gabriele, "Kaspi: The Shape-shifter," *The Generalist*, August 22, 2021, generalist.com/briefing/kaspi.

253 **Adobe, the software giant:** Rob Walker, "How Adobe Got Its Customers Hooked on Subscriptions," *Bloomberg*, June 8, 2017, bloomberg.com/news/articles/2017-06-08/how-adobe-got-its-customers-hooked-on-subscriptions.

254 **the famous marshmallow experiment:** W. Mischel, E. B. Ebbesen, and A. Raskoff Zeiss, "Cognitive and Attentional Mechanisms in Delay of Gratification," *Journal of Personality and Social Psychology* 21, no. 2 (1972): 204–18. Their first study is described in W. Mischel and E. B. Ebbesen, "Attention in Delay of Gratification," *Journal of Personality and Social Psychology* 16, no. 2 (1970): 328–37, but it does not involve the famed marshmallows.

255 **What really made this experiment famous:** Jonah Lehrer, "Don't! The Secret of Self-Control," *The New Yorker*, May 11, 2009.

255 **Half a century of subsequent research:** Jennifer Ouellette, "New Twist on Marshmallow Test: Kids Depend on Each Other for Self Control," *Ars Technica*, January 21, 2020, arstechnica.com/science/2020/01/new-twist-on-marshmallow-test-kids-depend-on-each-other-for-self-control.

256 **John Warner and Saul Pleeter:** John T. Warner and Saul Pleeter, "The Personal Discount Rate: Evidence from Military Downsizing Programs," *American Economic Review* 91, no. 1 (March 2001): 33–53.

256 **Impatient workers afflicted:** Stefano DellaVigna and M. Danielle Paserman, "Job Search and Impatience," Working Paper 10837, *National Bureau of Economic Research*, October 2004, nber.org/papers/w10837.

256 **A higher extent of impatient hyperbolism:** Timothy J. Richards and Stephen F. Hamilton, "Obesity and Hyperbolic Discounting: An Experimental Analysis," *Journal of Agricultural and Resource Economics* 37, no. 2 (August 2012): 181–98.

256 **"The stock market is a device":** Annalyn Kurtz, "5 Lessons Ordinary Investors Can Learn from Warren Buffett," *U.S. News & World Report*, May 4, 2018, money.usnews.com/investing/buy-and-hold-strategy/articles/2018-05-04/5-lessons-ordinary-investors-can-learn-from-warren-buffett.

258 **Jared Diamond's stories:** Jared Diamond, *Collapse: How Societies Choose to Fail or Succeed,* 2nd ed. (New York: Penguin, 2011).

259 **red wine ages faster in space:** Hanneke Weitering, "Red Wine in Space May Age Faster Than on Earth, Study Finds," Space.com, May 5, 2021, space.com/red-wine-in-space-aged-faster.

Conclusion

261 **Żabka, the leading Polish retailer:** Dayeeta Das, "Żabka Launches Cashierless Store Format, Żappka," *ESM Magazine,* June 16, 2021, esmmagazine.com/technology/zabka-launches-cashierless-store-format-zappka-136704; Kevin Rozario, "Poland's Biggest Convenience Chain Overtakes Amazon in European Race for Autonomous Stores," *Forbes,* January 18, 2022.

262 **Today an average visit:** Bill Briggs, "A Grocer That Sells Smoothies, Snacks and 'Easier Lives'? Welcome to Żabka's Autonomous Stores," Microsoft Source, January 10, 2023, news.microsoft.com/source/features/digital-transformation/a-grocer-that-sells-smoothies-snacks-and-easier-lives-welcome-to-zabkas-autonomous-stores.

264 **Steve Jobs was not even aware:** Zameena Mejia, "Steve Jobs Almost Prevented the Apple iPhone from Being Invented," CNBC, September 12, 2017, cnbc.com/2017/09/12/why-steve-jobs-almost-prevented-the-apple-iphone-from-being-invented.html.

264 **Howard Schultz:** Sheila Farr, "Starbucks: The Early Years," HistoryLink.org, February 15, 2017, historylink.org/file/20292.

265 **Nintendo:** Tegan Jones, "The Surprisingly Long History of Nintendo," *Gizmodo*, September 20, 2013, gizmodo.com/the-surprisingly-long-history-of-nintendo-1354286257; "The Industry's Finest—Gunpei Yokoi," VGChartz, September 10, 2009, vgchartz.com/article/5145/the-industrys-finest-gunpei-yokoi/.

Index

a16z (Andreessen Horowitz), 1, 4, 98, 163, 170, 179–80, 181, 184
Accel Partners, 85–86, 116–18
adjacent innovation, 25
Adobe, 253–54
advance provision of feedback, 164–65
Agadi, Giovanni, 207–8
Agrawal, Ajay, 54
agree to disagree principle, xxiv, 147–73
   advance provision of feedback, 164–65
   anti-veto power, empowering leaders with, 167
   consensus versus contrarian approach, 154–60
   devil's advocate role, assigning, 163–64
   group-induced bias and, 147–54
   juniors first rule, 162–63
   Lekkerism and, 165–70
   mindset checks for, 173
   path dependence and, 152–54
   small teams, 161
   unanimity in decision-making process and, 155, 171–73
   Zoom investment and, xxiv
Airbnb, 77–78, 132, 178–80
Airbus, 18–19
Alexander, Robert, 80
Allen, Sam, 253
all-or-nothing behavior, 18–19

"all for one and one for all" paradigm, 170
Alphabet. *See* Google
Alto, 56–57
Amazon, xxviii, 17, 22–24, 103, 161, 171–72, 198–99
Amazon Web Services, 22
analysis paralysis, 82
Anderson, Steve, 34
Andreessen, Marc, 81, 98, 197
antiportfolio, 8–9
"anti-veto" power, empowering leaders with, 167
Apple, xxviii, 22, 23–24, 53
Arnold, Paul, 43–44
Atari Corporation, 53
AT&T, 222
authentic dissent, 164
Ayers, Charlie, 228–29
Azure, xxvii

BabyQuip, 73–74
Bailey, Jerry, 122
Ballmer, Steve, 247
Bank of Italy (Bank of America), 239–40
Barings Bank, 187–88
BBC, 156
Bechtolsheim, Andy, 39
Benner, Mary, 13
Bent, Mercedes, 132
Benter, Bill, 122
Bernstein, Shai, 251

Bessemer Venture Partners, 8–9
"best and the rest" principle, 4–5, 7
bet on the jockey principle, xxiv, 115–44
  business model and, 135–40
  charisma and character of founders, 130–31
  founding team, betting on, 134–35
  hiring CEOs from unrelated industries and, 133
  intrapreneurial culture, building, 124–29
  management team, importance of, 121–24
  market size and, 135
  mindset checks for, 143–44
  misfits that fit character of founders, 132–34
  "people over process" mindset and, 139–43
  super founders and, 115–21
  Zoom investment and, xxiv
Beyond Meat, 197
Bezos, Jeff, 22, 23, 245, 252
Bitbank (Coinbase), 50
Blicharski, Tomasz, 261–62, 266
Blue River Technology, 252–53, 266
Borders, 17
Botelho, Tristan, 133
Box, 50–51
Braccia, Andrew, 118, 119
Brin, Sergey, 25, 50
Brooks, Andrew, 140–41
Brydges, Robert, 191, 196
Buchheit, Paul, 125, 126, 129
Buffett, Warren, 163, 256
Building Robotics, 41–42
Burbn. *See* Instagram
Burning Man festival, 45
Bushnell, Nolan, 53
business model, 135–40

Butterfield, Stewart, 117, 119, 134–35
bystander effect, 149

Caissie, Rene, 130–31
Campbell, Bill, 39
Careem, 4
Carlson, Chester, 52–53
Carlton, Richard, 11
carried interest, 211
Catmull, Ed, 27
Celestis, 235–36
Chafer, Charles, 234, 236
Chang, Melody, 133
charisma and character of founders, 130–31
Cheriton, David, 39
Chesky, Brian, 132, 179
C.H.I. Overhead Doors, 226–27, 266
Choe, David, 229
Cockburn, Iain, 54
Coel, Michaela, 110–11
Coin, 3
Coinbase, 50
cold pitches, 46–51
colleganza contract, 207–9
Connect and Develop (C&D) strategy, 61–62
consensus-seeking culture, dangers of, 154–60
Cook, James, 257
Cook, Tim, 39–40
core products, 24–25
corporate unicorns, 242
Countrywide, 223
Cowan, David, 9, 49–50
"critical flaw approach," 71–76
Cuban, Mark, 50–51, 73–74

Dalio, Ray, 157, 160
Darley, John, 148–49

David, Ned, 39
deal funnel strategy, 98–100
decision trees, 181
Deshpande, Sachin, xi, xii–xiv, xiii, xviii, xxiv
devil's advocate role, assigning, 163–64
DFJ, 235, 236
DiDi, 4
Disagree and Commit principle, 171–72
discounting future rewards, 255–56
disruptive innovation, 25
diversification, 9
Dixon, Chris, 35
DocuSign, 243
Doerr, John, 39
Dollar Shave Club, 168–69
DoorDash, 132
Doriot, Georges, 123
Dorsey, Jack, 212
double down or quit principle, xxiv–xxv, 175–204
  Airbnb investment and, 178–80
  escalation of commitment and, 182–86
  50-50 principle and, 196–98
  flexibility, importance of, 202–4
  funding rounds and, 177–82
  kill rates for projects and, 198–202
  mindset checks for, 204
  outsiders' perspectives, 194–96
  poker strategies and, 175–82
  real optionality and, 182–86
  unbiased / external perspectives and, 192–94
  unbiased perspective, seeking, 192–94
  Zoom investment and, xxiv–xxv
Dragons' Den (TV show), 74–75
Dropbox, 31–33, 65–66
due diligence, 98, 101–4

Easter Island, 257–58
Echo, 23
echo chamber effect, 55–56
Edmans, Alex, 225
Edwards, David, 191, 194
Eggen, Patrick, xi, xiii–xiv, xiv, xxiii, xxv
Elsbach, Kimberly, 87
Emergence Capital, xvii, 41–42, 101
employee bonus programs, 248
employees, as owners / stockholders, 225–27
employee's contribution to company's valuation, rewarding, 227–28
Enron, 159
Ephrati, James, 193
errors of commission, 8, 14
errors of omission, 8, 14
escalation of commitment, 186–91
Etsy, 243
Eventbrite, 243
exits, 243

Fab.com, 1–2
Facebook, 43, 82–83, 180, 229
Fairchild, Sherman, 214
Fairchild Semiconductor, 213–15
Fan Munce, Claudia, 54
fast-rejection mindset, 71–76
Favre, Eric, 59–60
Felten, Obi, 202
Ferdowsi, Arash, 31, 32, 33
Fernández de Cofiño, Yolanda, 128, 129
Fernie, Sue, 212
Fever, 3
"50-50" principle, 196–98
financing mechanisms, for startups, xvi–xvii
Fire Phone, 22–23
Fireworks Partners, 105, 106

Flatiron Health, 132
Fleming, Alexander, 78
flexibility, 182–86
Folkman, Judah, 142
FOMO (fear of missing out), 93–95
Ford, William Clay, 137
founders
  charisma and character of, 130–31
  misfits that fit character of, 132–34
  super founders, 115–21
Founders Fund, 169–70, 180, 235, 236
founding team, 134–35
franchise system, 225–26
Franklin, Benjamin, 224, 225–26
Free, Clinton, 159
Freed, Ian, 23
Fry, Art, 10–11, 13
FTX, 94
Fumbling the Future (Smith and Alexander), 80

Game of Thrones (TV show), 26
Gandhi, Sameer, 31, 35, 76–77, 81
Gebbia, Joe, 132, 179
get outside the four walls principle, xxiii, 31–66
  cold pitches, responding to, 46–51
  Dropbox investment and, 31–33
  echo chamber effect and, 55
  innovation scouts, using, 61–62
  internal and external innovation, balancing, 60–63
  internal innovation, 52–54, 59–63
  mindset checks for, 66
  networking and, 36–41, 65–66
  Not Invented Here (NIH) syndrome, 54–58
  opportunities, creating, 41–46
  picking and, 34–35
  public as source for new ideas, 63–64

sourcing and, 34–36
Zoom investment and, xxiii
Giannini, Amadeo Peter, 239–40
Glitch (video game), 117–18
Gmail, 124–27
Goetz, Jim, 44
Goldberg, Jason, 2
Google, xxviii, 17, 23–24, 39, 50, 110, 125–27, 165, 196, 229
Google Glass, 26
Google Ventures, 95–96
Google X, 25–26, 201–2
Gouw, Theresia, 85–86
Graham, Paul, 77–78, 132
Grant, Adam, 164
great things take time principle, xxv, 233–59
  growth from adversity and economic downturns, 238–41
  illiquidity of investments in startups and, 241–45
  long-term thinking and, 245–46, 247–54
  long-term trends, danger of ignoring, 237–38
  mindset checks for, 259
  patience requirement, 241–47
  short-term versus long-term thinking, 247–54
  SpaceX investment and, 234–37
Grinda, Fabrice, 241
group-induced bias, 147–54
Grow the Pie (Edmans), 225
Gurley, Bill, 8, 241

Hackman, Richard, 161
Hall, Rob, 186–87
Happy Meal, 128
Hardy, G. H., 51
Harroch, Richard, 175, 184, 190

Hastings, Reed, 26-27, 140
Hemingway, Ernest, 237-38
Henderson, Cal, 117, 134-35
Heraud, Jorge, 253, 266
Hoffman, Reid, 36-37, 154, 179, 183
Holmes, Elizabeth, 97
home runs matter, strikeouts don't
  principle, xxiii, 1-28
  all-or-nothing behavior, avoiding, 18-19
  "best and the rest" principle, 4-5, 7
  budgeting process and, 15-16
  diversification and, 9
  errors of omission versus errors of commission, 8, 14
  fear of missing upside success, 7-10
  frequent failures, expectation of, 3-4
  hunting home runs, 20-23
  initial small bets, placing, 9
  innovation and, 10-15
  mindset checks for, 28
  playing it too safe and, 18
  risky and traditional investments, blending, 23-27
  success-to-failure ratio, 5-7
  unsuccessful ideas, killing, 19-20
  Zoom investment and, xxiii
Horowitz, Ben, 118-19
Houseman, Thomas, 140-41
House of Cards (TV show), 26, 140
Houston, Drew, 31, 32, 33
Hummer Winblad, 195
Hurley, Chad, 120
hyperbolic discounting, 256

IBM, 105, 106
illiquidity, of investments in startups, 241-45
I May Destroy You (TV show), 110-11
Impossible Burger, 263

incentives. *See making the pie bigger* principle
industry expertise, 83-84
innovation, 10-15
innovation scouts, 61-62
Instagram, 34, 120, 184
Intel, 16, 215
internal innovation, 52-54, 59-63
intrapreneurship, 124-29
Intuit, 26
investment memorandum, 101-2, 103-4
iPhone, 22, 23
IPO rate, 155

Jacobs, Brian, 41-42, 65, 101
Jalal, Abu, 133
Jawbone, 181
J-curve, of typical VC-backed company, 243-44
Jemail, Jimmy, 121
JetBlue Airways, 83-84
JetBlue Technology Ventures (JTV), 83-84, 266
JLABS, 62-63
Jobs, Steve, 40, 53, 57, 79-80, 81, 127, 264
Joby Aviation, 243
John Deere, 252-53, 266
Johnson & Johnson, 62-63
Juicero, 3
"juniors first" rule, 162-63

Kahoot, 167
Kaplan, Steven, 136-37
Kashyap, Nagraj, xi, xiii-xiv, 167
Kaspi.kz, 253
Kennedy, John F, 162-63
Keppel, Judith, 191, 192
Keynes, John Maynard, 158
kill rates for projects, 198-202

KKR, 226–27
Klein, Dan, 21
Koch, Leslie, 39
Kramer, Roderick, 87
Kramlich, Dick, 169

Lafley, A. G., 61–62, 266
Lake, Karina, 73–74
Landry, Stephanie, 198
Langer, Robert, 142–43, 266
Langer Lab, 142–43
Latané, Bibb, 148–49
Laube, James, 141
Leach, Robert, 97
Lee, Aileen, 241
Leeson, Nick, 187–88
Lego, 20
Lekkerism, 165–70
  dangers of, 170
  minority rules, 169–70
  right to make own decision and, 168–69
Leone, Doug, 33, 65–66
Lerner, Josh, 105
Levie, Aaron, 50–51
Levine, Jeremy, 102
Liddiment, David, 197–98
Liew, Jeremy, 34
Lightspeed Capital, 192–93
limited partnership agreements, 210
LinkedIn, 102
liquidity event, 243
long-term thinking, 245–46, 247–54
Lumo, 84
Lyft, 4, 246
Lyons, Adam, 51

Macintosh, Norman, 159
McAdoo, Greg, 77–78, 81
McCance, Henry, 123–24

McDonald's, 128, 137–38, 197, 229
McNerney, James, 12–13
Madera, Paul, 42–43, 134, 249
Maier, Fran, 73–74
making the pie bigger principle, xxv, 207–30
  aligning incentives and contributions, 224–29
  compensation revolution and, 213–15
  employee contribution to company's valuation, rewarding, 227–28
  employees made owners / stockholders and, 225–27
  marshmallow experiment and, 254–55
  mindset checks for, 230
  number of partners and, 224–25
  1000 to 1001 challenge and, 227–28
  poorly set incentives, examples of, 221–24
  principal-agent problem and, 226–27
  profit-sharing incentives and, 207–10
  risk preferences, and incentives, 215–21
  start-up team, incentives for, 211–13
  stock options as element of compensation and, 215
  "2 and 20" contracts, 210–11
  vesting and, 227
management team, 121–24
Maples, Mike, 8, 120, 130, 132–33, 158–59, 246
Maris, Bill, 95–97
maritime ventures, 207–10
market size, 135
Marks, Howard, 158
marshmallow experiment, 254–55
Mashable (blog), 33
Mattel, 156, 161
Mendeleev, Dmitri, 77
Menlo Ventures, 1, 4

Meritech, 42–43
Metcalf, David, 212
Milner, Yuri, 82–83
Minecraft (video game), 116
minimum lovable product (MLP), 183
minimum viable product (MVP), 183
mining industry, 185
Mischel, Walter, 254
Mitchell, Kate, 131
Miura-Ko, Ann, 246
Monash, John, 160
MongoDB, 243
Moore, Gordon, 215
Moritz, Michael, 33, 175–76
Movie Gallery, 139
movie industry, 26, 185
MoviePass, 3
Mr. Clean Magic Eraser, 61
Munger, Charlie, 256
Murdoch, Rupert, 249
Museum of Failure, 3
Musk, Elon, 80, 234, 236
My Big Fat Greek Wedding (film), 185
MySpace, 42–43, 249–50

Nebia, 39–40
Nelson, Bill, 236
Nespresso, 60
Nestlé, 60
Netflix, 17, 26–27, 63–64, 139–40
networking, 36–41, 65–66
Newton, 22
Nicholson, Geoff, 10
Nintendo, 265
Nortel, 55–56
No Rules Rules (Hastings), 140
Not Invented Here (NIH) syndrome, 54–58
Noyce, Robert, 215
Nozad, Pejman, 31–33, 65–66

Odeo, 120
Ofo, 94
Ola, 4
Oldani, Davide, 248
O'Leary, Kevin, 74
"1000 to 1001" challenge, 227–28
OpenAI, 263
O'Reilly, Charles, 12
Originals (Grant), 164
Ørsted (Dong Energy), 133
outsiders' perspectives, and follow-on decisions, 194–96

Page, Larry, 25, 50
Palantir Technologies, 243
Palo Alto Research Center (PARC), 57–58, 79–80
Parker, Sean, 36–37
Pasteur, Louis, 78–79
path dependence, 152–54
pay-for-performance, 212
PayPal, 3
penicillin, 78
"people over process" mindset, 139–43
Percival, Sean, 249
Persil Power, 3
Persson, Markus, 116
pharmaceutical industry, 27, 184–85
picking, 34–35
Piggy Bank Auction game, 91–93
Pincus, Mark, 36–37
Pixar, 193
playing it too safe, 18
Pleeter, Saul, 256
poker, 175–82
Post-it notes, 10–11
Poulsen, Henrik, 133
PowerPoint, 169

preparing your mind principle,
  xxiii–xxiv, 69–89
  "critical flaw approach," 71–76
  examples of prepared mind in action,
    76–81
  fast-rejection mindset, 71–76
  focusing on specific domain and,
    85–86
  industry expertise and, 83–84
  mindset checks for, 89
  speed of decision making and, 86–88
  "tap, build, and prepare" approach,
    82–83
  Zoom investment and, xxiii
Prezas, Alexandros, 133
PR FAQ (Press Release and Frequently
  Asked Questions), 103–4
Prime Now, 198–99, 200
principal-agent problem, 226–27
Procter & Gamble (P&G), 16,
  61–62, 266
profit-sharing, 207–9
Project Caribou (Gmail), 124–27
Puga, Diego, 208
Pulitzer Prize, 110

Qualcomm Ventures, xi, xiii–xiv

Rachleff, Andy, 135, 158
Ragozin, Len, 122
Ramanujan, Srinivasa, 51
Rampell, Alex, 8, 130, 136, 159
real optionality, 182–86
Redbox, 139
"red flag approach," 71–76
Redpoint Ventures, 250
Reitzig, Markus, 54
rejection rate, 98–100
Renaud, Leslie Mead, 140–41
R. H. Donnelly (RHD), 108–9

Ribbn, 44
ride-sharing apps, 4
Riggio, Steve, 247
risk preferences, 215–21
risk-reduction engineers, 102–3
Roberts, Bryan, 159, 168–69
Rock, Arthur, 214
rocket launches, 233–34
Romano, Michael, 193
Rosell, Carlos, 54
Rosenthal, David, 77
RWE, 195

Saasbee. *See* Zoom
Salehizadeh, Bijan, 97
Salesforce, 42
Samuels, Cami, 38–39, 135–36
Sandberg, Sheryl, 241
Saper, Jake, 41–42
Sauvage, Nicolas, 168, 266
say no 100 times principle, xxiv, 91–112
  bureaucratic clutter, getting rid of,
    105–9
  deal funnel strategy and, 98–100
  due diligence, conducting, 98, 101–4
  excessive skepticism, avoiding,
    111–12
  FOMO (fear of missing out) and,
    93–95
  investment memorandum and, 101–2,
    103–4
  mindset checks for, 112
  Piggy Bank Auction game and, 91–93
  risk-reduction engineers and, 102–3
  small ideas and incremental changes,
    cluttering deal funnel with, 107–9
  winner's curse and, 93–95
Schmidt, Eric, 25
Schmitz, Rolf Martin, 195
Schultz, Howard, 264–65

scientific management, 138
Sears, 223
Sensoy, Berk, 136–37
Sequoia Capital, xvii, 31, 33, 44–45, 65–66, 77, 178–79, 180, 181
Shark Tank (TV show), 73–74
Shazam, 6
Shopee, xxvii
short-term versus long-term thinking, 247–54
Siegel, Mark, 34
Simi, Bonny, 83–84, 154–55, 266
Singer, David, 77, 97
Six Sigma, 12, 14
Skype, 17
Slack, 118–19, 134–35
Slush, 45
Smith, Douglas, 80
Smith, Fred, 247
Smith, Paul, 197–98
Snapchat, 34
Solyndra, 182
Sorenson, Olav, 54
sourcing, 34–36
Space Services Inc., 234
SpaceX, 234–37, 243
Spider-Man (film), 26
Spiegel, Evan, 34
Stagnario, Zaccaria, 207–8
Starbucks, 4, 264–65
Stavros, Pete, 227, 266
stock options, as element of compensation, 215
Stoffels, Paul, 62
Strömberg, Per, 136–37
Subotovsky, Santi, xviii
success-to-failure ratio, 5–7
The Sun Also Rises (Hemingway), 237–38
Supercell, 116

super founders, 115–21
Super Founders (Tamaseb), 115
Systrom, Kevin, 34
Sze, David, 154

Tai, Bill, xi
Tamaseb, Ali, 115
Tan, Garry, 50
"tap, build, and prepare" approach, 82–83
Tata, Ratan, 26
Taylor, Frederick, 138
Teller, Astro, 201, 266
Theory of Games and Economic Behavior (von Neumann), 176
Theranos, 96–98
Thermo Fisher Scientific, 223–24
Thiel, Peter, 36–37, 228
3M company, 10–14
Tiny Speck, 116–19
Toyota, 138
Toy Story 2 (film), 193
Trefler, Daniel, 208
Trulia, 85–86
Tushman, Michael, 13
Twitter, 120, 212–13
"2 and 20" contracts, 210–11

Uber, 3, 4, 180, 243, 246
unanimity in decision-making process, 155, 171–73
unbiased / external perspectives, and follow-on decisions, 192–94
unicorns, xxvii, 241–42, 263–64
unpredictability, 64–66
unsuccessful ideas, killing, 19–20

Valentine, Don, 40
van de Waal, Erica, 147
VantagePoint Capital Partners, 250

Vassalo, Steve, 256–57
Venrock, 168
venture capital funds, xvii–xx. *See also* Venture Mindset
Venture Mindset, xx–xxviii, 261–67
   agree to disagree principle (*See agree to disagree* principle)
   bet on the jockey principle (*See bet on the jockey* principle)
   corporate innovators and venture investors, commonalities between, xxv–xxvi
   decision-making approach of, xx–xxi
   defined, ix–x
   double down or quit principle (*See double down or quit* principle)
   get outside the four walls principle (*See get outside the four walls* principle)
   great things take time principle (*See great things take time* principle)
   home runs matter, strikeouts don't principle (*See home runs matter, strikeouts don't* principle)
   making the pie bigger principle (*See making the pie bigger* principle)
   preparing your mind principle (*See preparing your mind* principle)
   say no 100 times principle (*See say no 100 times* principle)
Versatile Venture Capital, 195
vesting, 227
Vidmar, Neil, 161
von Neumann, John, 176

Walmart, 196
Warby Parker, 34
Warner, John, 256
Waymo, 26, 228

Wells Fargo, 223
WeWork, 94
whale hunting, 209–10
WhatsApp, 44–45
white space, 77
Who Wants to Be a Millionaire? (TV show), 191–92, 197–98
Will, George, 229
Williams, Evan, 120, 212
winner's curse, 93–95
Winter, Philip, 39
Wojcicki, Susan, 49–50
Wozniak, Steve, 53
Wu, Andy, 169
Wynne, Toddie Lee, 233

Xerox, 52–53, 58, 79–80
Xu, Tony, 132

Yang, Geoff, 250
Y Combinator, 134
Yellow Pages, 108
Yokoi, Gunpei, 265
YouTube, 120
Yu, Gideon, 82
Yuan, Eric, xv, xvi, xxiv

Żabka, 261–62
Zachary, George, 120
The Zebra, 51
Zelle, xxvii
Zero to One (Thiel), 228
Zillow, 110
Zoom, xi–xvii, xxviii, 17
Zoom Ventures, xxviii
Zuckerberg, Mark, 36–37, 43, 82–83
Zynga, 36